BENGAL

BIHAR AND ORISSA SIKKIM

BENGAL

BIHAR AND ORISSA
SIKKIM

L. S. S. O' MALLEY

GYAN

Published by

GYAN

Gyan Publishing House
5, Ansari Road
Daryaganj, New Delhi-110002
Phone: 011-47034999, 9811692060
E-mail: books@gyanbooks.com

Distribution Network
gyanbooks.com
India, USA, Canada, UK, Australia, France

ISBN: 978-81-212-8915-3 (PB)
First Published, 1917

2nd Impression 2023

Printed at: Gyan Press, Delhi.

BENGAL BIHAR AND ORISSA SIKKIM

AUTHOR: L. S. S. O' MALLEY

Provincial Geographies of India

General Editor
Sir T. H. HOLLAND, K.C.I.E., D.Sc., F.R.S.

BENGAL
BIHAR AND ORISSA
SIKKIM

BENGAL
BIHAR AND ORISSA
SIKKIM

BY

L. S. S. O'MALLEY

OF THE INDIAN CIVIL SERVICE

FELLOW OF THE ROYAL STATISTICAL SOCIETY AND OF THE ROYAL ANTHROPOLOGICAL INSTITUTE

Cambridge:
at the University Press
1917

EDITOR'S PREFACE

IN 1910, when I was asked by the Cambridge University Press to suggest a suitable sub-division of the Indian Empire into natural geographical units for treatment in separate volumes, I was embarrassed by the fact that the Province of Bengal, as it had been known for many years before 1905, was then restricted, for administrative convenience, to the western three-quarters of the old province, the eastern districts having been lumped with Assam to form the Lieut.-Governorship of Eastern Bengal and Assam. To find an author who could give, in true perspective and as the result of personal intimacy, an outline sketch of two such dissimilar units as old Bengal and Assam seemed to be impossible; and thus it was decided, in spite of the obvious disadvantages, especially in nomenclature, to cut off Assam, which differed so greatly from the rest of the new province of Eastern Bengal, leaving to the ingenuity of the author the problem of designing for the residual area a geographical name that was sufficiently expressive without clashing with the new official nomenclature.

Faithfulness, however, to the principles of classification on physical and ethnographical grounds brought its own reward; for, before Mr O'Malley's manuscript got into type, a re-shuffling of boundary lines in 1912 resulted in the obliteration of the artificial partition that was set up in 1905: Assam became again a separate administration under a Chief Commissioner; Eastern and Western Bengal were reunited as a Governorship, while the districts, still further west, in Bihar and Orissa, formed a new province under a Lieut.-Governor.

In many respects the Gangetic portion of Bihar might be conveniently grouped with Bengal, while the divisions of Chota Nagpur and Orissa differ in certain features both from Bengal and, in other respects, from one another, being still imperfectly connected with natural lines of communication.

One hopes now that, for the sake of administrative stability, no further changes in the boundary lines will be made before this edition is out of print. Accordingly, in spite of overlapping interests—the perpetual enemy of all forms of natural classification—it is decided to treat together in one volume the newly constituted province of Bengal, the closely related districts in Bihar, and the two less advanced divisions of Chota Nagpur and Orissa. This decision was mainly influenced by the fortunate discovery of an author who was personally acquainted with both provinces, with a recent, precise and evenly distributed stock of information gained as Census officer and editor of the new district gazetteers.

The success of Mr Thurston's sketch of the Madras Presidency and associated States justifies Mr O'Malley's adoption of the same model for this second volume of the provincial series. But it is through chance, not artificially designed symmetry, that the next area taken up after Madras follows the order in which British influence has spread in India.

T. H. H.

February 1916.

CONTENTS

CONTENTS

LIST OF ILLUSTRATIONS AND MAPS

Figs. 7 and 95 are reproduced from photographs by Messrs Burlington Smith, photographers, Darjeeling, and Figs. 55, 56 and 94 from photographs by Messrs Johnston and Hoffmann, photographers, Calcutta. The majority of the other illustrations are reproduced from photographs kindly lent by friends, among whom may be gratefully mentioned Mr J. H. E. Garrett, who has recently retired from the Indian Civil Service (Figs. 2, 3, 13, 20, 30, 32, 34, 65, 66, 70, 71, 73, 76, 77, 78, 84, 85 and 86); Mr C. E. A. W. Oldham, I.C.S. (Figs. 14, 31, 53, 61, 67, 68, 72, 79, 92, 93, 96 and 98); Mr Charles Russell (Figs. 8, 10, 11, 15, 37, 45, 46, 47, 48, 49, 50, 54, 64 and 74); Lieut.-Col. W. J. Buchanan, C.I.E., I.M.S. (Figs. 38 and 51); Mr F. Palmer, C.I.E. (Fig. 36); the Rev. J. Graham, D.D., C.I.E. (Fig. 63), and Mr F. W. Martin (Figs. 9 and 59).

CHAPTER I

PHYSICAL ASPECTS

THE country dealt with in this volume, though only one-ninth of the total area of India, is nearly as extensive as the German Empire, while its population is considerably more than a quarter of that of the whole Indian Empire. It includes: (*a*) The Presidency of Bengal, with an area of 84,092 square miles and a population of 46,305,642 persons. It is somewhat smaller than Great Britain, but contains nearly a million more inhabitants than the whole of the British Isles. (*b*) The Province of Bihar and Orissa, which extends over 111,829 square miles and has 38,435,293 inhabitants. Its area is a little greater than that of Italy, while it is only a little less populous than France. (*c*) The State of Sikkim, a small and sparsely populated country, with an area of 2818 square miles and a population of 87,920 persons.

The name Bengal has at different periods borne very different meanings. Under the Muhammadan rule it designated the Bengali-speaking area in the alluvial basins of the Ganges and Brahmaputra, of which the limits roughly corresponded with those of the modern Presidency. Under British dominion its significance was changed. The term "Bengal Establishment" was applied to all the settlements of the East India Company in north-eastern India, from Balasore in Orissa to Patna in the heart of Bihar. These were grouped together in the

Presidency of Bengal, which bore the official title of Fort William in Bengal, Fort William being the name given to the English settlement at Calcutta in honour of William III. As the limits of British authority were extended, the ceded and conquered territories in northern India were added to the Presidency, until it comprised all the British possessions outside the Bombay and Madras Presidencies.

This wide connotation of the name Bengal was perpetuated until recently by the military system of "Presidency Armies" and "Commands." The whole of northern India was allotted to the Bengal army until 1895, while, from 1895 until the reorganization of the Indian army in 1905, the Bengal Command included the United Provinces, Bihar and Orissa, Assam, and parts of the Central Provinces, as well as the present Bengal. The old use of the term has not altogether fallen into desuetude. The term Bengal Civil Service is still occasionally used for members of the Indian Civil Service serving in northern India, while the India Office List shows all members of that service in the Punjab, North-West Frontier Province, United Provinces, Central Provinces, Bengal, Bihar and Orissa, Assam and Burma as members of the Bengal Establishment.

Different administrative areas have also gone by the name of Bengal during the last sixty years. In 1854 a separate province of Bengal was created which included practically the whole of the present provinces of Bengal and Bihar and Orissa, and also Assam, which was detached and placed under a Chief Commissioner in 1874. Thenceforward the name was applied to the territory under the administration of the Lieutenant-Governor of Bengal, i.e., Bihar, Chota Nagpur and Orissa, as well as the present Bengal, which was, and still often is, distinguished by the appellation of Lower Bengal or "Bengal proper." In 1905 the province of Bengal was reduced to a much smaller area, as shown in the map on page 158, but this arrangement did not last long, for in 1912 the Presidency of Bengal was created. The opportunity was taken to revive the old official designation of Fort William in Bengal, but it is usually called Bengal, and in ordinary speech the name of Fort William is only applied to the fort

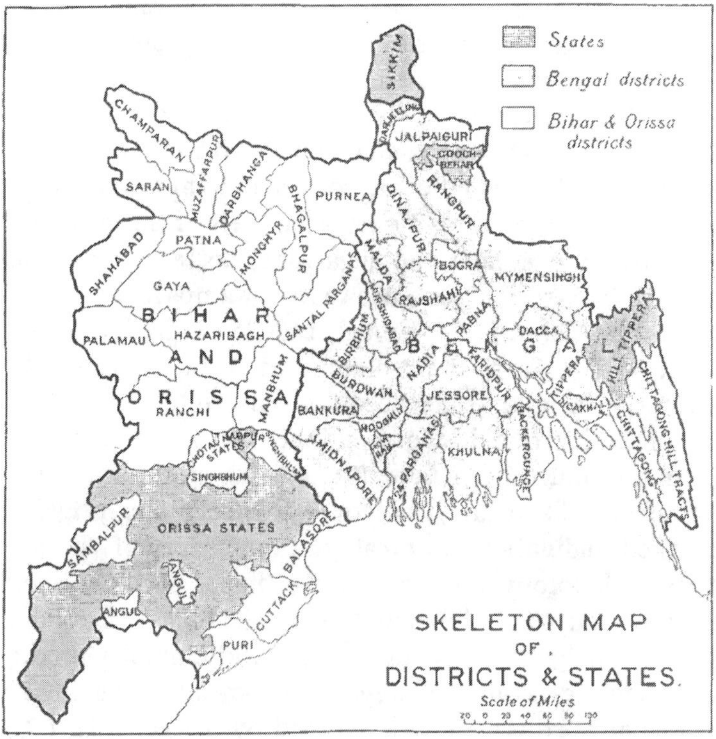

Fig. 1. Skeleton Map of Districts and States

in Calcutta. In this volume the name Bengal refers solely to the newly created Presidency.

Bengal lies between the twenty-second and twenty-seventh parallels of north latitude, while its limits east and west lie between the eighty-seventh and ninety-third degrees of east longitude. It stretches from the Himalayas to the sea, being bounded on the north by the Himalayan countries of Nepal, Bhutān and Tibet, while its southern coast is washed by the waters of the Bay of Bengal. To the east lie Assam and Burma, and on the west it is bounded by Bihar and Orissa. Nearly the whole of it is a fertile alluvial plain watered by the Ganges and Brahmaputra and by their numerous tributaries and effluents. For thousands of square miles neither a hill nor a rock can be seen, nor can even a stone be found in the silt-formed soil. Far different is the appearance of this deltaic country from that of the alluvial river-plains to the north-west. " The air is now languorous and vapour-laden, the vegetation luxuriant and tropical. The firm grey plain of wheat and millets and sugarcane, dotted with clumps of park-like trees, gives place to rice swamps and bamboos, palm and plantain." Though there is a gradual rise of level to the north, it is so small as to be imperceptible. Calcutta, 86 miles from the sea, is only 18 to 21 feet above mean sea level, and Siliguri, at the foot of the Himalayas over 300 miles from Calcutta, has an elevation of only 400 feet. There are, moreover, scarcely any ridges or marked undulations to break the uniformity of the level flats. Monotony therefore is the defect of the scenery. At the same time, the monotony of the scenery is relieved by the prodigality of nature. Heat and humidity produce a prolific vegetation. The eye accustomed to the sunbaked plains of northern India is soothed by perennial turf and the fresh greenness of the countryside ; while scattered homesteads, nestling in thickets of bamboos, palms, plantains and evergreen plants, have a certain quiet charm of their own.

With the exception of some small areas to the extreme north and south-east, which will be described later, the whole country is remarkably homogeneous. Certain natural divisions are, however, recognized, the difference between which depends mainly on the extent to which the process of land-making by the great rivers is in progress, is gradually disappearing or has altogether ceased. The first is **North Bengal**, which lies from west to east, between Purnea and the Brahmaputra and, from north to south, between the lower spurs of the Himalayas and the Ganges. The country slopes gradually southwards in a wide alluvial plain, watered by rivers debouching from the Himalayas, and broken only by the Barind. This is a comparatively high belt of older formation on the confines of Dinājpur, Mālda, Rājshāhi and Bogra ; it is still in many places covered with brushwood jungle, interspersed with large trees, the remains of an extensive forest. North Bengal has been subject to great fluvial changes. The Tīsta river once flowed through its centre to meet the Ganges, but in 1787 it changed its course and broke into another channel by which it found its way to the Brahmaputra. Owing to the vagaries of this torrential river, the country is seamed with silted channels.

West Bengal is the country to the west of the Bhāgirathi and Hooghly rivers, which stretches from the Bay of Bengal to the fringe of the Chota Nagpur plateau. It includes two distinct zones, one a semi-aquatic rice plain, the other a rolling upland country, which lies outside the true delta. The former, which comprises the districts of Hooghly and Howrah and the east of Burdwān, Midnapore and Bānkura, is a low-lying delta formed by the Bhāgirathi, Dāmodar, Ajay and Rupnarayan rivers. Between the rivers the surface sinks into basins, some of which are only a few feet above mean sea level. To the west a hard ferruginous soil takes the place of the deltaic detritus, and wide expanses of scrub jungle are found instead of the closely tilled fields of the eastern lowlands. In the north-western corner the poverty of the soil is compensated by richness of mineral resources, which have made this part of West Bengal a hive of industry. It is here that the Rāniganj coal-field is situated, while the iron-ore and clays found in close proximity to the coal measures partly feed the blast furnaces at Barākar and the pottery works at Rāniganj.

In **Central Bengal,** lying between the Bhāgirathi on the west and the Padma and Madhumati on the north-east and east, we enter on a typical delta, in which the process of land formation has nearly entirely ceased. Nowhere higher than 70 feet above sea level, its elevation sinks in the south to between 10 and 20 feet. The greater portion has now been raised, by the deposit of silt, to a height which ensures it against inundation, but at the same time prevents it from receiving the fertilizing layer that the floods formerly left behind them. It is a land of dead and dying rivers—to use the expressive Indian terms—of low rice plains and swamps (called *bils*), which will never be filled in because the rivers no longer distribute the silt-laden waters of the Ganges, being locked into their channels by the high banks of silt which they have deposited. Engineering skill has, however, shown that even the morasses can be made available for tillage and human habitation. In the 24-Parganas district the Magra Hāt drainage scheme has recently reclaimed a swampy area of 290 square miles, where formerly the inhabitants were said to be "inured to a semi-amphibious life by a long course of preparation resulting in the survival of the fittest." There is one large but shallow lake, called the Salt Water Lake, which extends over 30 square miles in the vicinity of Calcutta.

Eastern Bengal, lying to the east of the Padma and the Madhumati, is the united delta of the Ganges and Brahmaputra, in which the creative energies of those great rivers have full and free play. It is a fertile semi-aquatic plain, rich in crops of rice and jute, and covered by a network of rivers, streams and creeks. Boats take the place of carts, the waterways serve as roads. The land is subject to annual inundation and silt fertilization. The slope of the country is away from and not towards the chief rivers, and the water in the minor channels flows from and not towards the main streams. In the rains a volume of turgid water spreads itself over the country; low-lying areas are inundated to a depth of 8 to 14 feet, the water covering

Fig. 2. A Bengal *Bil*

everything but the river banks and the artificial mounds on which the houses are built. Strange as it may appear, this is the healthiest part of Bengal and the land is thickly populated, the density in some parts being over 1000 per square mile.

The level is only broken by a low tableland in the north-east, called the Madhupur Jungle, which, as its name implies, was formerly covered with forest. Its average height above the plain is only 40 feet, but its ridges have exercised an influence out of all proportion to their height, for the hard clay of which they are composed has resisted the erosion of the great rivers and deflected them to the south-east. These rolling uplands covered with short grass or dark green forest afford a welcome relief to the monotony of the alluvial flats. Away from the great rivers with their moving panorama of boats, from the dug-out canoe to the large cargo boat with its high bow, broad stern, bulged-out belly and spreading square sails, the scenery is generally tame and dull.

"In the lowest parts of all," writes Mr B. C. Allen of the typical district of Dacca, "the depth of the flood is such that the houses have to be perched on hillocks, where there is barely room for a cowshed and none for anything so pleasant as a garden. This dismal country is really least unattractive in the rains. It is then covered with water, which is green with jute, and all the creeks and channels are full. These minor streams flow between banks which are higher than the neighbouring country and are generally fringed with trees, and thus form more attractive waterways than the great rivers, from which little can be seen but a dreary waste of waters, with here and there a few huts rising precariously above the flood which threatens to engulf them. The people who live in these tracts have become almost amphibious in their habits. In the height of the inundation no land is to be seen, and all travelling has to be done by boat. To say that travelling has to be done by boat gives, however, but an inadequate idea of the real condition of affairs. Half a dozen huts are clustered together on a little hillock a few yards square, and the inhabitants cannot proceed beyond that hillock, whether to visit their neighbours or their fields, to go to market or to school, without wading, swimming or travelling in or on something that can float. This expression is used advisedly, for the people by no means confine themselves to boats. For minor excursions rafts made of plantain trees are much in vogue or circular earthenware pipkins, more difficult of navigation than a coracle. A visitor to one of these hamlets in the rains may see a grey-bearded patriarch swimming towards him from the fields and may be asked for alms by an old woman standing in water breast-high amongst the jute plants."

From the preceding pages it will be seen that the greater part of Bengal is a delta in various stages of formation. The process is connected with great changes in the lower course of the Ganges, which have taken place within historic times. Formerly the main body of its waters flowed southwards to the sea through the Bhāgirathi, but as this channel silted up, the main stream made its way into other distributaries, moving further and further eastward until it found an outlet in the Padma, as the present main stream is called. The effect of its movements on the land surface is lucidly described by that eminent geologist, the late Dr Thomas Oldham, whose description throws such light on the physical geography of Bengal, that it may be quoted *in extenso*.

"I suppose no one will hesitate to acknowledge that the whole of the country lying between the Hooghly on the west and the Meghna on the east is only the delta caused by the deposition of the debris carried down by the rivers Ganges and Brahmaputra, and their tributaries. It is also equally well known that in such flats the streams are constantly altering their courses, eating away on one bank and depositing on the other, until the channel in which they formerly flowed becomes choked up, and the water is compelled to seek another course. It is also certain that, in this peculiar delta, the general course of the main waters of the Ganges has gradually tracked from the west towards the east, until, of late years, the larger body of the waters of the Ganges have (*sic*) united with those of the Brahmaputra, and have together proceeded to the sea as the Meghna. Every stream, whether large or small, flowing through such a flat, tends to raise its own bed or channel, by the deposition of the silt and sand it holds suspended in its waters; and by this gradual deposition the channel bed of the stream is raised above the actual level of the adjoining flats. It is impossible to suppose a river continuing to flow along the top of a raised bank, if not compelled to do so by artificial means, and the consequence of this filling in and raising of its bed is that, at the first opportunity, the stream necessarily abandons its original course, and seeks a new channel in the lower ground adjoining, until, after successive changes, it has gradually wandered over the whole flat and raised the entire surface to the same general level. The same process is then repeated, new channels are cut out, and new deposits formed.

"Bearing these admitted principles in mind, look to the delta of the Ganges and Brahmaputra. The Ganges river, emerging from its upper levels round the Rājmahāl Hills, and prevented by their solid rocky barrier from cutting further to the west, sought its channel in the lower ground adjoining, and originally the main body of its waters flowed along the general course now indicated by the Bhāgirathi and Hooghly. But, gradually filling up this channel, it was again compelled to seek a new course in the lower, because as yet comparatively unfilled-in, ground lying to the east. And the same process being repeated, it wandered successively from the rocky western limit of the delta-flat towards the eastern. If this progress eastwards was allowed to be sufficiently slow to admit of the gradual filling in of the country adjoining, the delta was formed continuously up to the same general level, and the larger streams or channels, passing through this flat to the sea, became unavoidably diminished in size and in the quantity and force of the water they carried, the main body passing around further to the east and having its course in the channels successively formed there."

The southernmost portion of the delta goes by the name of the **Sundarbans**, meaning literally the forests of *sundri* trees (*Heritiera littoralis*). The area so designated is 6500 square miles in extent, or about half the size of Holland. It stretches for nearly 200 miles along the Bay of Bengal, and its average breadth inland is from 60 to 80 miles. It is sometimes depicted as a desolate region, half-land half-water, a labyrinth of interminable forest and swamp, devoid of human habitation. This is no longer the case with the northern portion, where the morasses have been converted into fertile rice fields. The jungle is, moreover, being steadily pushed back and the margin of cultivation extending southward. Its spread is conditional on the eradication of jungle, the construction of dams and dykes to keep out salt water, a rainfall sufficient to wash the salt out of the soil, and last, but not least, a supply of drinkable water—that first essential of human settlement It need not be altogether fresh, for the people seem to get inured to brackish water, which they drink regularly, without any apparent evil consequences: in many parts fresh water is more difficult to get than food. The southern portion of the Sundarbans is still a network of tidal waters, sluggish rivers, inosculating creeks and forest-clad islands. No less than 2000 square miles are under forest, the most plentiful and important species being the *sundri*. It is "a sort of drowned land, covered with jungle, smitten by malaria, and infested by wild beasts; broken up by swamps, intersected by a thousand river channels and maritime backwaters, but gradually dotted as the traveller recedes from the sea-board with clearings and patches of rice land."

There are two tracts outside the alluvial area which have still to be described, viz. a hilly region on the south-east frontier and a small Himalayan area to the north. The former consists of a succession of low hill ranges occupying the district of Chittagong, the Chittagong Hill Tracts and Hill Tippera. In the district first named the hills enclose cultivated river valleys of considerable extent; they are separated from the sea by a belt of alluvial land, which near the coast merges into a mangrove swamp with vegetation like that of the Sundarbans. The Chittagong Hill Tracts and Hill Tippera are made up of forest-clad hills and ravines, sparsely inhabited by aboriginal tribes of Mongoloid origin, who are only just beginning to learn the use of the plough.

To the north the frontier district of Darjeeling contains a small portion of the Himalayas. The mountains rise from the plains in a succession of bold spurs and ridges separated by deep valleys and attain a height of 12,000 feet in the Singalīla range. On one of the ridges the hill station of Darjeeling is perched at a height of 7000 feet above sea level. Below that height many of the slopes are laid out with tea-gardens, but above it primeval forest still holds its own. The country at the base of the Himalayas is known as the **Tarai**, i.e., the wet lands. It is a marshy belt of land, notorious for its unhealthiness, which was formerly covered with dense forest. This has been partially cleared away, giving place to trim tea-gardens and ordinary cultivation; but wide stretches are left, in which the *sāl* tree (*Shorea robusta*) predominates. In this forest region gigantic trees tower a hundred feet or more above one's head, and there is a luxuriant undergrowth of matted cane brakes, bamboo thickets, etc. Further into the plains the forest growth is replaced by savannahs, reedy flats and grassy plains with grass growing 20 feet high, through which one can scarcely force one's way unless on an elephant.

In Jalpaiguri this Tarai country is known as the **Duārs,**

Fig. 3. In the Tarai

or more strictly the Western Duārs, as it is the western portion of the Bhutān Duārs, or doors of Bhutān, a tract that was annexed from Bhutān in 1865. This submontane region has an average breadth of 22 miles and a total area of nearly 2000 square miles, of which a quarter is still under forest. In the north a series of wooded plateaux, rising to between 1200 and 1500 feet high, form a connecting link between the hills and the plains. Their soil, climate and rainfall (which reaches 180 inches in the year), are all well adapted to the growth of the tea plant, the cultivation of which is carried on in a chain of tea-gardens. The land at the foot of these plateaux, which fifty years ago was under heavy grass and reed jungle, has now been brought under the plough and yields magnificent crops of rice, jute and tobacco

Sikkim presents the most extraordinary contrasts within its narrow limits. Its mountains tower up far above the snow line, reaching an altitude of 28,146 feet in Kinchinjunga on the western boundary. The valleys between them descend to a minimum level of little more than 700 feet. Every variety of climate and vegetation is found—tropical, temperate and Alpine. On the higher elevations is perennial snow. In the lower valleys a tropical vegetation runs riot in a steamy hot-house atmosphere. The rainfall in the south is heavy, averaging 133 inches in the year at Gangtok, but in some of the valleys to the north it falls to 20 inches or less. It is a land of stupendous heights and depths; but what perhaps most strikes the ordinary traveller, who has to keep below the snow line, is the peculiar V-shaped valleys with steep and often precipitous slopes. The rivers at their base run in deep ravines, the ascent from which is almost precipitous for the first few hundred feet. So narrow and deeply cut are their channels, that though their roar may be heard from afar, the stream itself is often invisible until within a few hundred yards.

The population is practically confined to the ridges, slopes and valleys below 7000 feet, that being the highest level at which maize, the staple food of the people, will ripen. In addition to maize, millets and pulses are extensively cultivated, while rice is raised on the slopes below 4000 feet. Irrigation being essential to rice cultivation, and there being no such thing in the country as

Fig. 4. A Sikkim Valley

large level fields, the hillsides are laboriously carved out into terraces, one above the other, the outer edge of each being banked up so as to retain a supply of water for the rice plants. Some of the terraced fields are so narrow that the use of the plough is impossible, and the soil has to be turned over with a hoe. From 7000 feet to 14,000 feet, which is the level of tree growth, the country is under virgin forest and uninhabited except for occasional settlements of graziers. From 15,000 feet upwards there is a mass of snow-clad peaks and glaciers, which form the source of most of the rivers, but from 12,000 to 15,000 feet the aspect is less bare and rugged, and some grassy plateaux with small lakes are to be found. The ridges at the latter height are clothed with rhododendron and coniferous forests, while the grass lands are carpeted with Alpine flowers, primulas, aconite, iris and the like.

The province of **Bihar and Orissa** extends from the borders of Nepal and Darjeeling to the Bay of Bengal and the northern districts of Madras. It is bounded on the east by the Presidency of Bengal and on the west by the United Provinces and the Central Provinces. It is by no means a homogeneous area, for it is made up of three sub-provinces, viz., Bihar, Chota Nagpur and Orissa, which differ widely in their physical features, the character of their peoples, their languages and land systems.

Bihar, which consists of the Patna, Tirhut and Bhāgalpur Divisions or Commissionerships, has an area of 42,361 square miles and a population of 23¾ millions, which is very nearly equal to that of the Punjab. It consists of the eastern portion of the Gangetic valley that lies between the lower spurs of the Himalayas on the north and the Chota Nagpur plateau on the south. It is an alluvial plain watered and drained by the Ganges and its tributaries, such as the Gandak, Son, Gogri and Kosi, which sometimes sweep down in disastrous floods. The climate is drier than that of Bengal, and the rainfall, which averages 50 inches in the year, is not only lighter but more capricious, its vicissitudes exposing the country to occasional periods of scarcity. Throughout almost its whole extent the general aspect is that of an unbroken level, diversified by clusters of villages, mango orchards, clumps of bamboos and groves of palm trees. In the hot weather it presents a dreary appearance, for as far as the eye can see there is a wide expanse of bare dun-coloured fields enclosed by small embankments which give them a curious chess-board appearance. In the rains, however, it is covered with waving sheets of green rice and maize, and in the cold weather teeming crops of wheat, barley, and other grains and pulses are raised.

Till a few years ago the fields in the vicinity of the villages were white, during the latter season of the year, with the opium-yielding poppy, a plant with white flowers which is better suited to the climate than the red or purple variety that is grown in Mālwa. Its cultivation was abandoned in 1911 in order to give effect to the agreement with China for the gradual diminution and final extinction of the export of Indian opium to that country.

Bihar is so called after the town of Bihar in the Patna district, which was its capital at the time of the Muhammadan invasion. This town, again, derived its name from a great *vihāra*, or Buddhist monastery, which was established there in the tenth century A.D. The Muhammadans, by a playful conceit, which was, however, based on a real admiration for its climate and fertility, declared that the name meant the land of eternal spring (from the Persian *bahār*).

Chota Nagpur, which consists of the Division of the same name and of the two small States of Kharsāwan and Saraikela, extends over 26,769 square miles and has 5¾ million inhabitants. It is thus nearly as large as Scotland

and has a million more inhabitants. The greater part is an upland region with a general elevation of 2000 to 2500 feet. A large part is still covered with forest, in which *sāl* (*Shorea robusta*) predominates, or with low scrubwood jungle. Cultivation is mainly confined to the valleys and depressions between the ridges, which are enriched with detritus washed down from above. The rainfall is fairly heavy, averaging 53 inches in the year, but owing to the broken undulating surface it runs off rapidly, and to admit of rice cultivation, which requires standing water, the slopes have to be carved into terraces, which spread down them in a fan-like formation. On the higher levels maize, millets, oilseeds and pulses are raised, but the crests of the ridges are infertile. Its agricultural resources are limited, and failures of the harvests occur periodically, but scarcity does not press hardly on the hardy aboriginal races, who can supply their needs from the forests and, even in the fat years, make considerable use of edible jungle products, such as the fruit of the *mahua* tree (*Bassia latifolia*). On the other hand, Chota Nagpur possesses great mineral wealth, especially in coal, the principal fields being the Jherria field in Mānbhūm, the Giridih field in Hāzāribāgh (where also there are mica mines) and the Daltonganj field in Palāmau.

The scenery is diversified and often beautiful. Open country and rolling downs alternate with richly wooded hills enclosing peaceful and secluded valleys. Streams of clear spring-fed water may be seen rippling down over rock-strewn beds, and wooded glens with "pools, shaded and rock-bound, in which Diana and her nymphs might have disported themselves." Even in the hot weather, when the whole country seems scorched and parched, the eye can be refreshed by the evergreen verdure of the woods, and there is a welcome touch of colour in the scarlet blossoms of the *palās* tree (*Butea frondosa*).

The name is a corruption of Chutia Nagpur, Chutia being a village on the outskirts of Rānchi which was at one time the seat of the Nāgbansi chiefs, who ruled over the central plateau.

Orissa is the name given to the whole country in which the speakers of the Oriya language form the dominant people. It includes the Orissa Division and the Orissa Feudatory States, the latter of which occupy as large an area as Ireland. Altogether, this sub-province extends over 41,789 square miles and has a population of 9 million persons. Physically, it is a heterogeneous area, for it comprises two very different tracts, viz. the alluvial delta of the Mahānadi and other rivers flowing into the Bay of Bengal and a hilly hinterland made up of the Feudatory States and the districts of Angul and Sambalpur.

The Feudatory States are sometimes called the Garhjāts, a hybrid word meaning forts. The Hindustani word *garh*, meaning a fort, has been Persianized into the plural Garhjat, and the English, in ignorance of this, have added the letter *s*, so as to make a double plural like "fortses." The name is due to the country having been studded with the fortresses of the chiefs; a similar designation is that of Chhattisgarh in the Central Provinces, meaning the land of the thirty-six forts.

The three sub-provinces fall within four natural divisions, viz., North Bihar, South Bihar, Orissa and the Chota Nagpur Plateau, the delimitation of which is determined by physical and ethnological affinities and not by political and linguistic considerations, as is the case with the sub-provinces.

North Bihar is the portion of Bihar lying to the north of the Ganges. To the north-east and north-west there is a submontane strip of prairie land and denuded forest, but the remainder of the country is an alluvial plain nearly entirely under cultivation, which supports a teeming population; the density averages 646 persons to the square mile and in some parts rises to over 1000 per square mile. It is watered by a number of rivers flowing southwards from the Himalayas, which have gradually raised their beds by the deposition of silt and flow on ridges slightly above the general level of the surrounding country. Most of them are apt to overflow their banks after heavy rainfall in the mountains of Nepal, and in past ages they have frequently changed their courses. There are numerous marshes and meres, some of which are large enough to be regarded as fresh-water lakes or lagoons; they are generally shallow sheets of water, expanding in the rains and contracting during the dry season. Some represent the deeper portions of abandoned river beds, e.g., the Kābar Tāl in the Monghyr district and a chain of 43 lakes, with an aggregate area of 139 square miles, in Champāran, which mark a former channel of the Gandak. Others are merely trough-like depressions between present river beds. In the rains they are filled by the overflow of the rivers, but for the remainder of the year they dry up, either entirely or in part, and admit of cultivation or form prairies covered with the rank *pod* grass and the graceful pampas, but with an undergrowth of more succulent herbage, which affords abundant pasture for great herds of cattle.

Four of the districts of North Bihar, viz., Sāran, Champāran, Darbhanga and Muzaffarpur, constitute the Tirhut Division, the creation of which in 1908 brought into official use the old popular designation of this part of the country. **Tirhut** is a corruption of Tīrabhukti, a Sanskrit name meaning the river-side land, which can be traced back to the fourth or fifth century A.D., for it is inscribed on seals of that period which have been excavated at the village of Basārh (the ancient Vaisāli) in the Muzaffarpur district. Tirhut used to be pre-eminently the land of indigo, but the industry has declined very rapidly since synthetic indigo was put on the market in 1897, and the area under the plant is now only a third of what it was before that year.

South Bihar is the portion of Bihar lying south of the Ganges within the districts of Shāhābād, Patna, Gaya, and Monghyr. The greater part of it is an alluvial plain

Fig. 5. Umga Hill in Gaya District

sloping gently northwards to the Ganges, but the south of Shāhābād is occupied by the Kaimur Hills, which form a rocky plateau mainly used for pasturage. Further east, in the south of Patna, Gaya and Monghyr, there are a number of ridges and spurs projecting from the plateau of Chota Nagpur, as well as semi-detached ridges and isolated peaks that rise abruptly from the level plain and appear to form irregular links between the ridges. Much of the southern area is broken country with a fringe of brushwood jungle; the soil is poor, it has little or no irrigation, and it yields precarious crops. The land to the north, on the other hand, is highly cultivated, extensively irrigated and well populated. It was the rice exported from here that first acquired the name of Patna rice, now so well known in the market. As early as the seventh century A.D. the Chinese pilgrim, Hiuen Tsiang, noted that the country grew a rice of a delicious flavour, which was commonly called "rice for the use of the great"; a heretic king was, he solemnly declared, converted to Buddhism by the fragrant scent of this product of the land of Buddhism.

The climate is drier than that of North Bihar, and away from the Ganges there is a marked absence of swamps and water-logged areas. The rivers, moreover, with the exception of the Son, have a smaller catchment area than those north of the Ganges, and are not of any great size. Large demands are made on them for irrigation, and the greater part of their water is diverted into irrigation channels and reservoirs and thence distributed over the fields. They dry up soon after the cessation of the rains, and for the greater part of the year their channels are either waterless or contain only an attenuated stream.

Orissa proper, as the third natural division may be called to distinguish it from the sub-province of the same name, stretches along the sea-board from the Chilka lake to the Subarnarekha river and comprises the three districts of Puri, Cuttack and Balasore. It is a narrow strip, fifteen to seventy miles broad, in which three distinct zones are found, viz., an unproductive maritime belt, a central plain of rich alluvium, and a hilly submontane tract. The land along the coast is largely impregnated with salt. Salt manufacture was formerly an important industry and a century ago yielded the East India Company a yearly revenue of 18 lakhs of rupees. It is a low-lying swampy area traversed by sluggish brackish creeks which creep to the sea through banks of black mud bearing a mangrove vegetation. It has aptly been described as the Sundarbans on a miniature scale. Near the sea this desolate region gives place to sandy ridges, 50 to 80 feet high, and the latter to dunes, which are sometimes covered with creepers and wild convolvulus, and drifts of blown sand. The central zone forms the delta of the Mahānadi, Brāhmani and Baitarani rivers. It is a fertile alluvial plain, intersected by deltaic rivers which throw out a network of branches. In many ways it resembles Bengal. "A warm steamy atmosphere favours the same palm and rice cultivation, and all the conditions of a productive but enervated human existence are present." In the western fringe the land rises in rocky undulations, isolated peaks and long ranges of hills, with wooded slopes and fertile valleys.

Orissa contains the one large lake of the province, the **Chilka Lake.** This is a shallow pear-shaped lake lying mainly in the Puri district, but extending at its southern extremity into the Ganjām district of the Madras Presidency. It is 44 miles long and has an area varying between 344 and 450 square miles, for it expands in the rainy season and contracts in the dry weather. It was originally a bay of the sea, which first began to shoal up owing to deposits of silt brought in by the rivers and carried up the Bay of Bengal by the violent south winds of the monsoon, and was eventually cut off from the sea by a spit formed by the same agency. The sandy bar which now separates it from the Bay of Bengal is pierced by one narrow outlet, through which the tide pours in. This is sufficient to keep the water of the lake salt from December to June, but in the rains the sea water is driven out by the volume poured in by the rivers, and the Chilka becomes a fresh-water lake.

The low mud flats formed by the silt deposit of

the rivers which feed it are encroaching on the lake, and its depth scarcely anywhere exceeds 12 feet and averages only 5 to 6 feet. The sea is also incessantly at work building up the bar; this is steadily growing in width, and in some years the channel through it can only be kept open by artificial means. There are a number of islands in the lake, of which the largest, the Pārikud islands on the east, are partially joined to the bar. One small island in the south, which goes by the characteristically English name of Breakfast Island, is capped by a building and pillar said to have been erected by an early Collector of Ganjam, who bore the Pickwickian name of Snodgrass and is the hero of several good stories.

The term **Chota Nagpur Plateau** is used to designate the elevated country extending from the Gangetic valley to the hilly tableland of the Central Provinces and approaching close to the Bay of Bengal on the south-east. It is not intended to imply that it forms a tableland like the steep-walled precipice behind Cape Town with its long and lofty horizontal top. The word plateau is, in fact, a technical expression for an area of which the lowest levels are at a considerable height above the sea. The plateau as thus defined extends far beyond Chota Nagpur itself, stretching into the inner highlands of Orissa on the south-east and, through the Santāl Parganas, as far as the bank of the Ganges on the north-east. The administrative areas included in it are the whole of the Chota Nagpur Division, all the Orissa States, the Angul and Sambalpur districts of the Orissa Division and the district of the Santāl Parganas.

It is a rugged region of inequalities, consisting of a succession of plateaux, hills and valleys, drained by several large rivers, such as the Dāmodar, Barākar, Subarnarekha, Brāhmani, Baitarani and Mahānadi. The

Fig. 6. A River Valley in Chota Nagpur

land is still largely covered by forest, and is thinly peopled, mainly by primitive tribes, who still use the bow and arrow. One wild race, the Bīrhors, live on the wild animals they net, and chiefly on the *hanumān* or long-tailed monkey, whose flesh they eat, while the skin is used for their drums. In the more remote areas very little change has taken place since 1866, when Sir Alfred Lyall wrote, "I suppose there is no wilder or less known part of India than the interminable forests south-east of Nagpur towards the sea. It is a hilly forest country inhabited by what we call forest tribes, with here and there an oasis of cultivation and civilized settlement by the superior races."

CHAPTER II

MOUNTAINS AND HILLS

THE **Himalayas** (literally the abode of snow, from the Sanskrit *hima*, snow, and *ālaya*, dwelling-place) are, like the ancient Gaul, divided into three parts. The first is a great range of snowy peaks, which form the axis of the chain. The second consists of the Lower or Outer Himalayas, which form a broad belt of mountains of inferior but still very considerable height to the south of the snows. The third is the Sub-Himalayan zone, in which comparatively low hills are found, either as ridges or spurs contiguous to the Outer Himalayas or separated from them by flat-bottomed valleys known as Dūns. All three are represented in the area dealt with in this volume. The first is found in Sikkim, constituting a great dividing wall between it and Tibet; the second in the south of Sikkim and in the Darjeeling district, where the mountains consist of long tortuous ranges, the general direction of which is from north to south. A small portion of the third zone is found in the Sumeswar and Dūn Hills in the extreme north of the Champāran district in Bihar.

Sikkim is enclosed on three sides by Himalayan ranges in a horse-shoe shape. The main chain stretches from west to east along the northern frontier as far as Dongkya (23,184 feet). Its mean elevation is from 18,000

Fig. 7. Kinchinjunga

to 19,000 feet, but several peaks rise to over 20,000 feet, prominent among which is Chomiumo (22,385 feet). To the south it throws out, almost at right angles, an immense spur culminating in Kinchinjunga, which, with an altitude of 28,146 feet, is the third highest mountain in the world, being exceeded in height only by Mount Everest (29,002 feet) and Mount Godwin Austen (28,278 feet). This majestic mountain lies on the frontier between Sikkim and Nepal, considerably to the south of the line of water-parting between the Tibetan plateau and India. The name means "the five treasure-houses of the great snows" and refers to its five peaks. The highest, which is lit up with a golden glow by the rising sun, is the treasury of gold; another, which remains in a silvery shade till the sun is well up, is the treasury of silver; the other three are the treasuries of gems, grain and holy books, a collocation showing the articles to which the Buddhistic Tibetans, living in an inclement climate, attach most value.

From Kinchinjunga the Singalīla range stretches southward in a long ridge, about 60 miles in length, which forms the boundary first between Sikkim and Nepal and then between Darjeeling and Nepal. The trijunction point of Nepal, Sikkim and British India is at Phalūt, 11,811 feet above sea level. This ridge is the watershed of two great river systems. The rain that falls on its western flank makes its way eventually into the Ganges; the streams that rise along its eastern face swell the volume of the Tīsta, an affluent of the Brahmaputra. The range is so named after the Singalīla hill (12,130 feet), from which, as well as from Phalūt, incomparable views of the Himalayas can be obtained. Both command a panorama of snowy peaks in Nepal, Sikkim and Bhutān, some 200 miles long. Forty peaks, each of which exceeds 20,000 feet, stand up north, east and west, and among them is Mount Everest, part of which appears from behind the shoulder of Peak XIII.

From Dongkya a lofty range runs southward under the name of the Chola range, dividing Sikkim from the Chumbi Valley and Bhutān. The trijunction point of Sikkim, Tibet and Bhutān is on the western shoulder of Gipmochi (14,520 feet). Here the range divides into two great spurs, one of which runs to the south-east into Bhutān and the other to the south-west into the

Darjeeling district, enclosing between them the valley of the Di-chu or Jaldhāka river. From a hill above the frontier station of Gnatong (which lies in a small basin at a height of 12,030 feet), this river can be seen winding its way through the lowland country below, while to the west the view extends across the whole breadth of Sikkim to the titanic peaks of Kinchinjunga, the *coup d'œil* thus embracing five miles on end of the earth's surface. Along this range there are a few passes into Tibet, of which the most frequented is the Jelep Lā (14,390 feet) near Gnatong, along which the wool and other produce of Tibet is brought on pack mules. It is rarely blocked by snow for any length of time, and its comparatively easy ascent accounts for its name, which means "the lovely level pass."

From the enclosing ranges on the north, west and south lateral ranges project into both Sikkim and Darjeeling, some of which rise into peaks of great height. On the north-east, not far from Dongkya, is Kinchinjhau (22,720 feet), the crest of which, from a distance, looks like a shelving tableland of snow; the name means "the great bearded peak of snow." On the west of Sikkim, in the neighbourhood of Kinchinjunga, are Kabru (24,015 feet) and Pandim (22,020 feet); the name of the latter means "the king's minister" and has been given to this peak because it stands at the side of Kinchinjunga, that monarch among the mountains of the Sikkim Himalayas. To the east of Kinchinjunga is the graceful, snow-mantled crest of Siniolchu or D2 (22,520 feet), perhaps the most beautiful in form of all the Himalayan mountains.

The Himalayas being exposed to the full force of the monsoon from the Bay of Bengal, have a heavy rainfall, rising in places to 200 inches a year, and a luxuriant vegetation. The wealth of their flora may be realized from the fact that there are no less than 440 recorded species of orchids and 25 different species of rhododendrons. The latter are not the garden shrubs of Europe; some form almost impenetrable thickets, others are great trees with red twisted stems. Another consequence of the heavy rainfall is that leeches abound and are a veritable pest to travellers and cattle. During the rains on a clear day the scenery vividly recalls the Biblical account of "the good land, the land of brooks of water, of fountains and depths that spring out of valleys and hills." Only too often, however, the mountains are shrouded by envious mists. "One wanders through an atmosphere of almost everlasting mist and cloud, amidst a weird array of gaunt moss-covered trees with long beard-like parasites drooping and dripping rain showers as they are gently stirred by the wind." The level of the perpetual snow-line varies from 15,000 to 16,000 feet, and glaciers extend a little lower. There are a few small lakes at high altitudes, such as Changu near the Nathu Lā pass and Bidangcho near the Jelep Lā, which lie between 11,000 and 12,000 feet.

A railway on the 2 feet gauge has been laid along a cart road as far as Darjeeling, 51 miles from the plains; it reaches a height of 7407 feet at Ghoom, four miles from that station. The cart roads can be counted on the fingers of one hand, and the other roads are too steep and narrow for cart traffic. Merchandise away from the railway is borne by human porters, mules and pack ponies, the tracks descending steep valleys and climbing sharp ridges. Distance is measured not by miles but by hours.

The people live for the most part in scattered homesteads, each surrounded by a patch of cultivation. Villages are neither numerous nor large, consisting merely of occasional clusters of such homesteads. There are two considerable towns, Darjeeling and Kurseong, both, like

Mount Zion, "beautiful for situation." They are hill sanitaria and educational centres for European and Eurasian children. Kālimpong, on the east of the Tīsta, is of some importance as an entrepot for wool and other exports from Tibet, and is the site of the St Andrew's Colonial Homes, in which excellent work is being done in educating and training poor European and Eurasian children.

Immediately to the south of the Himalayas, in the district of Jalpaiguri, lie the **Sinchula Hills**, which range in height from 4000 to 6000 feet and form the boundary between British territory and Bhutān. The military station of Buxa is situated on an outlying spur averaging 1800 feet above sea level. It enjoys a rainfall of 209 inches a year and commands one of the principal passes into Bhutān, which is known as the Buxa Duār, i.e., the Buxa door.

On the north-east of the Bay of Bengal there is a succession of low ranges running in a south-easterly direction parallel with each other and with the coast line. The Sītakund Hill in the Chittagong district, which is a place of pilgrimage for Hindus, rises to 1115 feet, but greater altitudes are found in Hill Tippera and the Chittagong Hill Tracts. The highest peaks are: in the former, Betling Sib (3200 feet), and in the latter, Keokradang (4034 feet) and Pyramid Hill (3017 feet). The only other elevations in Bengal worthy of being called hills are found on the fringe of the Chota Nagpur plateau; the highest are Susinia (1442 feet) and Bihārinath (1469 feet) in the Bānkura district.

In Bihar and Orissa the only hills north of the Ganges are the Sumeswar and Dūn Hills, which extend over 364 miles in the north of Champāran. The **Sumeswar Hills**, which run along the northern frontier for 46 miles, form the lowest and outermost of the Himalayan ranges. They vary from a few hundred feet in height to 2884 feet above sea level at Fort Sumeswar, which commands a majestic view of the Himalayas, the great peaks of Dhaulagiri (26,826 feet) and Gosainthān (26,305 feet) being clearly visible from it. At the eastern extremity of the range is the Bhikna Thori pass into Nepal, up to which the railway has made its way. The **Dūn Hills** stretch for 20 miles to the south of the Sumeswar range, from which they are separated by an elevated tableland known as the Dūn Valley. Skirting the hills is the unhealthy submontane tract known as the Tarai, consisting mostly of prairie land and forest in which the aboriginal Thārus have their scattered clearings.

Proceeding from west to east on the south of the Ganges, the first hills met with are the **Kaimur Hills**, an offshoot of the Vindhyan range, which cover 800 square miles in the south of Shāhābad. They form an undulating plateau that rises abruptly from the plains in bold and lofty escarpments. These escarpments, which are said to be the most prominent feature of the Vindhyan area, stamping it with a geographical character peculiarly its own, occasionally have a uniform slope from top to bottom, but generally appear as vertical precipices with an undercliff that forms a talus made up of masses of debris from above. The drainage falls northwards, by a series of waterfalls, into long winding gorges that convey it to the alluvial plains. "After a clear drop of 200 to 600 feet, the water plashes into a deep pool, scooped out by its continual falling, on leaving which it runs through a channel obstructed throughout several miles of its course with huge masses of rock fallen from above. From each side of the stream rise the undercliffs of the escarpment, covered with jungle and tangled debris, and crowned by vertical precipices." The old Mughal fort of Rohtāsgarh is situated on a spur to the west, at the top of a precipice about 1000 feet high. It has an elevation of 1490 feet above sea level, and the uplands to the west of it vary from 1000 to 1400 feet in height. Another hill fort, which is not so well known, is Shergarh, which was built by the Emperor Sher Shāh (1540–45) on a plateau on the northern face of the hills.

In the districts of Gaya, Patna and Monghyr there are a number of low ranges and isolated peaks, which

Fig. 8. Kauwādol Hill in Gaya district

strike north-eastward until they reach the Ganges at the town of Monghyr. Those in the south present the appearance of a series of spurs and gentle undulations rising up into the plateau of Chota Nagpur, and are clothed in vegetation. Others have been completely, or almost completely, denuded, the vegetation having been cleared away with the axe or disappeared with the erosion of the surface soil. Either they are as bare as the rocks of Araby, or the rock shows through a thin covering of threadbare grass and starveling scrub, useless for pasturage. Some are composed of giant boulders piled one above another as if some Titan had been at play; others are much weathered, with rounded rain-scoured sides and easy slopes; others again are steep ridges with scarped faces. The principal ranges are the Barābar Hills in Gaya, the Rājgīr Hills in Patna and the Kharagpur Hills in Monghyr.

The **Barābar Hills**, about 16 miles north of Gaya town, are composed of gneissose granite weathering into huge boulders, and contain a group of rock-cut caves dating back to the third century B.C. The **Rājgīr Hills** form part of a long range that stretches north-eastward from near Bodh Gaya for about 40 miles. They are of no great height, the highest peak having an altitude of only 1472 feet, but are of no little historical interest. In a valley enclosed by two parallel ranges stood the earliest capital of Magadha, the town of Rājagriha, of which remains are still extant. Buddha himself frequently preached here, and it was the scene of the first great Buddhist Council. The **Kharagpur Hills** form a triangular block extending from near Jamālpur to the Jamui railway station; the highest point is Māruk (1628 feet), a table-topped hill capped with a deep layer of laterite. They contain several hot springs, which are believed to be due to thermo-dynamic action. The best known is Sītakund near Monghyr, the existence of which is explained by the following legend. Rāma, after rescuing his wife Sīta from the demon king Rāvana, suspected that she might have been false to him. Sīta, to prove her chastity, entered a fiery burning furnace, from which she emerged unscathed. She then had a bath, and imparted to the pool the heat which she had absorbed from the fire. The heat of the water in the spring rises to 138° F., and the lowest on record is 92° F. To the south-west is another group of hills, which are known locally as the Gidheswar Hills from a peak of that name, but are referred to in geological works as the Gidhaur Hills.

A little further east the **Rājmahāl Hills** jut out into the Gangetic valley, forcing the Ganges to bend to the east before it finally takes its southerly course to the sea. With their outliers, they extend over some 2000 square miles; this is only an approximation, for the hills

Fig. 9. View on the Rajmahāl Hills

have never been properly surveyed. They consist of a series of hills and ridges separated by narrow ravines and wide valleys. The highest hills rise to a height of about 2000 feet above the sea. In the south the crests of the ridges broaden out into tablelands containing stretches of arable land. Throughout the rest of the range rugged peaks and ridges prevail, but the slope of the interior valleys is easy and affords scope for the plough. Wherever a plough can work Santāl settlements are found, whether in the valleys, on the slopes or even on the brow of a hill. The Santāls are, however, comparatively recent immigrants, the earliest inhabitants being the Maler or Sauria Pahārias, who cling to the hill tops; their villages are difficult of access and frequently can only be got at by a steep climb up a giant staircase of boulders. The greater part of the Rājmahāl Hills is a Government estate, known as the Dāman-i-koh, which has an area of 1356 square miles and is maintained as a reserve for the aboriginal races. The name is a Persian one, meaning the skirts of the hills, but the estate comprises not only the country at the foot or on the outer slopes of the hills, but practically the whole range from the Ganges on the north to the Brāhmani river on the south.

The Rājmahāl Hills have been described as "classic ground for the study of Indian geology." They consist of basaltic lava flows or traps, with interstratifications of shale and sandstone, which have a thickness of at least 2000 feet. The basaltic trap is quarried for road metal and railway ballast in a few places, and there are also some deposits of china clay, which are being worked for the manufacture of china and porcelain in Calcutta. Another important product is *sabai* grass (*Ischoemum angustifolium*), which is exported to the paper mills near Calcutta.

In Orissa each of the sea-board districts has a rocky backbone. The Nīlgiri Hills in Balasore project to within 16 to 18 miles of the Bay of Bengal; they are called after the State of Nīlgiri and were known to old navigators as the Nelligreen Mountains. In the Cuttack district the most important range bears the name of the Assia Hills. None of the hills is of any great height, the highest (Assiagiri) not being more than 2500 feet above the sea, but considerable interest attaches to the shrines crowning their summits and to the ruins of ancient temples, forts and sculptures which they contain. The hills in the Puri district vary in height from under 500 feet to 3115 feet above sea level. Historically, the most interesting are

Fig. 10. Caves in Khandagiri Hill

Udayagiri and Khandagiri, two low hills near Bhubaneswar, which are honeycombed by cells and cave dwellings cut out from the solid rock by the Jains over 2000 years ago.

Of the hills and mountains in Chota Nagpur it is scarcely an hyperbole to say that their name is legion. Pride of place is held by **Parasnāth**, which towers, in a perfect conical form, to a height of 4479 feet above sea level. It is so called after Parsvanāth, the twenty-fourth Jina or deified saint of the Jains, who is said to have attained Nirvana here. It is a sacred place of pilgrimage to the Jains and contains some exquisite little

Fig. 11. Parasnāth

shrines. The plateau on the top was selected as a convalescent depot for European troops in 1858, but was abandoned after ten years, for the space was confined, the water supply was not sufficient for even 100 men and the soldiers' health was affected by their isolation on the top of the hill.

In the north-west of Rānchi and the south of Palāmau there are a number of lofty, flat-topped hills, called *pāts*, which are capped by great masses of laterite. The highest are Netarhāt Pāt (3356 feet), Lamti Pāt (3777 feet) and Galgal Pāt (3823 feet). The crest of the Netarhāt Pāt is an undulating tableland 4 miles long by 2½ miles broad, with a cool climate but a sinister reputation for unhealthiness. To the east, in the district of Mānbhūm, the Bāgh-mundi or Ajodhya range strikes out from the plateau and forms the watershed between the Subarnarekha and Kasai rivers. It reaches an elevation of 2000 feet, but is less of a range than a large plateau containing a number of prosperous villages. The Dalma range in the same district rises to 3407 feet in the Dalma peak, which is really only the highest point in a long rolling ridge, reached by a gradual rise from lower hills on either side.

Singhbhūm, the southern neighbour of Mānbhūm, contains about a score of hills varying from 2000 to 3000 feet in height. The whole of the south-east of this district is known as "Sāranda of the 700 hills," a rugged region of mountains and hills covered with forest, in which there are a few scattered settlements. This recess has however been penetrated by the captains of industry, for iron mines have been opened in the hills of Buda (2738 feet) and Notu (2576 feet) by the Bengal Iron and Steel Co. The Sāranda hills are separated from the spurs of the Chota Nagpur plateau by a pass a little over 1100 feet high. The Bengal-Nagpur Railway line runs through this natural gap, but a tunnel 1400 feet long had to be bored through the hill at Goilkera below the pass.

In the Orissa States there is a succession of ranges rolling back into the Central Provinces and forming the watersheds of the three great rivers of Orissa. The river valleys between them in some places spread out into fertile plains, and elsewhere are penned into narrow gorges and wooded glens. The southernmost valley is that of the Mahānadi, between which and the Brāhmani is a watershed 2000 to 2500 feet high. From the north bank of the Brāhmani the hills rise into the watershed of Keonjhar, with peaks from 2500 feet high, culminating in Malayagiri (3895 feet) in the State of Pāl Lahara. This watershed, in its turn, slopes down into the valley of the Baitarani, from whose eastern bank rise the mountains of Mayurbhanj. The highest peak in the latter State is Meghāsini (3824 feet), a name which means "the seat of the clouds." The iron ore fields of the Tata Iron and Steel Co. are situated in another hill in this State called Gurumaisini.

In Kalāhandi to the south-east we come to a different hill system, the principal range being an extension of the Eastern Ghāts of Madras. The hill area in this State, which is known as the Dangarla, extends over 1400 square miles and is thus described in the *Orissa States Gazetteer*: "This country is a plateau land, averaging about 2500 feet above sea level, comprised of small valleys shut in on all sides by hills, which rise as high as 4000 feet and over. The tops of these ranges, in several places, form fine plateau lands, averaging about two miles wide to ten miles long. The largest and finest are the Karlapāt range (3981 feet) and Bafliamāli (3587 feet)." The highest hill in the State, and indeed in all Orissa, is Bankāsāmo (4182 feet). In these hills the Indrāvati river takes its rise and dashes down in seething cataracts to the plains, where it joins the Godāvari. Not far from the place where it flows south through the barrier of hills, the Hāti river rises on the northern slopes and flows due north to join the Tel, which discharges into the Mahānadi.

CHAPTER III

RIVERS

Experience of English rivers, with their comparatively regular flow, relatively permanent beds and fixed lines of drainage, hardly prepares one for the great seasonal variations of rivers which are dependent on the

Fig. 12. A Sikkim stream

tropical and sub-tropical "rains." While the monsoon is in force, they rush down brimful; for the remainder of the year they have a comparatively small volume of water. So much is this the case, that even in great waterways like the Ganges and the Brahmaputra, steamers may ground on sandbanks and stick there for hours or days together; while in smaller rivers nothing is left but a small sluggish stream meandering among dry wide banks of sand and mud. The rivers are destructive as well as beneficent, being apt to overflow their banks and to flood the adjoining country. The inundation sometimes causes widespread misery, and at other times is hailed with joy, according to its depth and duration and the fertilizing qualities of its silt. In the deltaic tracts the stream sways from side to side, now eroding the land and now forming it. Alluvial formations, called *diāras* and *chars*, which may be either islands or long riparian spits, are formed wherever a backwater or curve produces an eddy in the current, which thereupon becomes sufficiently checked to deposit its burden of silt. These formations may last for years or be washed away as quickly as they arise.

The actual river channels, moreover, are liable to change, the river cutting through its friable banks in flood and reappearing miles away. All these are ordinary incidents of deltaic formation. As Mr Fergusson remarked fifty years ago: "A river runs in a given course, gradually elevating its bed and the country near it to or even above the level of the adjacent delta, until one of two things happens. Either the river overflows into a lower tract of country and commences to raise a new tract, or, if that part of the delta is practically levelled up and completed, the river is gradually choked up by its own sediment and dies, and a new river is opened up in some other part of the delta where the land is lower and requires raising. The course of nature in this matter can no more be interfered with than a pendulum 39 inches in length can be made to beat once in two seconds by itself."

All stages of river life can be seen—the hill torrent, the great navigable waterway, the sluggish stream creeping to the sea through the solitudes of the Sundarbans.

Nor should the "dead river" be omitted, i.e., the distributary which has silted up at the mouth, so that it no longer receives a supply from active streams. There are various degrees of decay and decrepitude—weedy streams, choked with vegetation, that have scarcely any flow of water, channels in which only a few pools remain to mark the deeper portions of the river bed, and finally a dry bed brought under cultivation. From what

Fig. 13. A Bengal river in the dry season

has already been said it can easily be understood that the courses of the rivers do not always correspond to those entered in the old survey maps, for since the survey was made many have changed their courses or have died of inanition.

With these prefatory remarks we may pass to a brief account of the principal rivers, which belong to one or other of three systems, viz., the Ganges, the Brahmaputra and the rivers of Orissa

The **Ganges** enters Bihar a little to the west of Buxar, slightly over 1000 miles from its source, and flows through it in an easterly direction till it reaches the Rājmahāl Hills. Skirting those hills, it begins to bend to the south-east and assumes a deltaic character at the offtake of the Bhāgirathi. At this point it is about 300 miles from the Bay of Bengal, and the slope is reduced to six inches a mile, which would be a low grade even for a canal. It

Fig. 14. Morning on the Ganges

now throws off distributaries, which help to convey its flood water to the sea. The main stream continues its south-eastern direction, following the channel known as the Padma. Near Goalundo it is joined by the Jamuna, the main channel of the Brahmaputra, and the united stream flows into the Meghna estuary 1557 miles from its source

It is well known that the Ganges is a sacred river. It is not so well known, however, that, religious sentiment being intensely conservative, sanctity attaches to its old channel and not to the comparatively modern course of the Padma. The latter is not a sacred stream. The people, true to the traditions of ages, revere the Bhāgirathi and the Hooghly as far south as Calcutta, but the portion south of Calcutta is no more sacred than the Padma. The halo of sanctity then clings to a narrow channel called Tolly's Nullah (after Colonel Tolly who adapted it for navigation in the second half of the eighteenth century) and to its continuation, a silted up bed, now scarcely traceable, which runs south-east through the Sundarbans. This is still called the Adi Ganga, or original Ganges, and has all the sacred associations of that river. Saugor Island marks the point where it emerged, and a place on the island called Ganga Sāgar is peculiarly sacred as being at the junction of the Ganges and the sea. Here scores of thousands of Hindus come every year on pilgrimage to wash away their sins.

The chief tributaries of the Ganges are the Son on its right bank and the Gogra, Gandak and Kosi on its left bank. The Son drains part of the tableland of Central India. The other three rivers drain, respectively, the western, central and eastern mountain basins of Nepal. The chief deltaic distributaries are the Bhāgirathi, Bhairab, Jalangi, and Mātābhānga. Throughout its course in Bihar and Bengal the Ganges is crossed by only one bridge situated near Sāra Ghāt north of Calcutta, which was completed in 1915. The main piers are carried to a depth of 160 feet and are said to be the deepest foundations of their kind in the world. Elsewhere the railway systems on either side are connected by ferry steamers, e.g., at Digha Ghāt near Patna, Mokāmeh between Patna and Monghyr, and Goalundo. The place last named is the terminus of a large steamer traffic and has an extensive transhipment trade.

Of the numerous towns along the banks of the Ganges the most important are Patna, Monghyr and Bhāgalpur. More than one town which owed its foundation to the importance of the Ganges as a strategic route and a highway of commerce has fallen a victim to its vagaries. Not to multiply instances, Pātaliputra, the first metropolis of India, lies buried 18 to 20 feet below the surface of modern Patna. The local rate of silt deposit, as evidenced by the depth of sediment and the number of centuries which have elapsed since the disappearance of the city, is nearly a foot for every hundred years.

The **Son** (487 miles long) rises in the Amarkantak mountains of the Central Provinces, not far from the source of the Narbada, and impinges on Bihar after a course of 325 miles in the inner highlands. Flowing by the steep slopes and precipices of the Kaimur Hills, it debouches on the Gangetic valley below Rohtāsgarh, and, running north-westward for 100 miles, joins the Ganges midway between Arrah and Dinapore. At Dehri the Grand Chord Line of the East Indian Railway is carried over it by one of the largest bridges in the world; it has 93 spans of 108 feet each, and a total length of 10,044 feet—figures which suffice to show the great breadth of the river when it reaches the plains. Near its junction with the Ganges the Son is spanned by another bridge, on which runs the main line of the same railway.

The Son drains a hilly area of 21,000 square miles, and has a flood discharge of 830,000 cubic feet per second. Its waters are distributed west to Shāhābād and east to the districts of Patna and Gaya by the irrigation system of the Son canals, which derive their supply from an anicut or weir (12,500 feet long) thrown across its bed at Dehri.

The Son has been identified with the *Erannoboas*, which in the fourth century B.C. Megasthenes described as "the third river in all India and inferior to none but the Indus and the Ganges, into the latter of which it discharges its waters." *Erannoboas* is a corruption of the Sanskrit *Hiranyabahu*, a name, meaning the golden-armed, which was given to the river because of the colour of the sand it brings down in flood. Its modern name also means the golden river.

The **Gogra** or Ghagra rises near Lake Mānasarowar in Tibet, and breaking through the Himalayan barrier flows through Oudh and joins the Ganges near Chapra. In the upper portion of its course it is so much the larger of the two rivers that it is open to argument whether it is the main stream and not properly an affluent of the Ganges. It forms the boundary between Bihar and the United Provinces for about 50 miles: the upper portion of its course is outside the limits of the former province. It is navigable by light-draught steamers as far as Ajodhya in Oudh, and has a large river-borne trade.

The name is a corruption of the Sanskrit *Gharghara*, an onomatopoeic word descriptive of laughter or rattling, which may be translated as "the gurgling river." It is also called the Sarju or Sarayu, and is referred to by Ptolemy as the *Sarabos*.

The **Gandak** (the *Kondochates* of Greek geographers) rises in the central mountain basin of Nepal, which is known as the Sapt Gandaki, i.e., the country of the seven Gandaks, from the seven streams which unite to form the main river. It leaves the hills through a pass near Tribeni in the Champāran district, and, after a course of about 200 miles through North Bihar, falls into the Ganges at Sonpur nearly opposite Patna. Sonpur is a sacred site at which a Hindu bathing festival takes place every year. This is the occasion of one of the largest fairs in Northern India, the number attending it having been known to rise to 300,000.

Soon after its entry into Bihar, the Gandak loses its character of a snow-fed mountain stream and becomes a deltaic river with a shifting channel that carries on a constant work of alluvion and diluvion. It is on record that the stream was once diverted for over a mile by the sinking of a cargo boat in the channel. It conveys an enormous volume of water to the Ganges, its flood discharge being 550,000, and its minimum discharge 6000, cubic feet per second. The supply has recently been tapped by the Tribeni Canal, a work, approaching completion, which is designed to irrigate over 100,000 acres in Champāran; its offtake is at Tribeni, whence its name.

The river is also known as the Great Gandak to distinguish it from an old channel called the Little Gandak or Burh (i.e., old) Gandak, which traverses North Bihar from north-west to south-east and joins the Ganges near Monghyr.

The **Kosi** is formed by the confluence of seven rivers in the eastern mountain basin of Nepal, which is consequently known as Sapt Kosiki. It debouches on British territory in the north-east of Bhāgalpur and flows south through Purnea, joining the Ganges 84 miles from the point where it leaves Nepal. Its catchment area is greater than that of any Himalayan river except the Indus and Brahmaputra, and comprises the whole country between Kinchinjunga in Sikkim and Gosainthān in Nepal, some 24,000 square miles. Debouching on an almost level plain, it deposits masses of sandy silt in its bed and along its banks. It is subject to sudden freshets, sometimes rising 30 feet in 24 hours, and easily cuts through the friable soil, finding an outlet through new channels. Two centuries ago the main stream passed by the town of Purnea, but it has since worked westward across 50 miles of country. Between 1859 and 1875 it shifted some twenty miles, "turning fertile fields into arid wastes of sand, sweeping away factories, farms and villages, and changing the whole face of the country from a fruitful landscape to a wilderness of sand and swamp." Its silt unfortunately is an infertile micaceous sand, which destroys the productive powers of the land. There are no data as to its silt-carrying capacity, but it has been conjectured, on the analogy of the Ganges and Irrawaddy, that it carries 55 million tons of sediment a year, and that it annually deposits 37 million tons on the lands along its course. How quickly and deeply it can overlay the country is apparent from the fate of indigo factories which have been abandoned owing to its encroachments. In comparatively few years all that can be seen of them is the chimneys, for the buildings are buried deep in sand.

The **Bhāgirathi** is now merely a spill channel of the Ganges. It is known to have been silting up at least since 1666, when Tavernier wrote that Bernier was forced to go overland to Cossimbazar from near Rājmahāl, because a sandbank at its mouth made the river unnavigable. Historically it is one of the most interesting rivers in Bengal. On its left bank is the old capital of Murshidābād, close to which is Cossimbazar, once a thriving emporium with English, French, Dutch and Armenian settlements. A little further south is the battle-field of Plassey, or rather was, for the greater part of it has long since been washed away by the river.

The Bhāgirathi forms one of a group of rivers known as the **Nadia Rivers**, in which Government maintains channels for navigation, so that there may be a continuous water route from Calcutta to the Ganges. These rivers are the Bhāgirathi, the Bhairab and Jalangi (now united to form one river called the Bhairab-Jalangi), the Mātābhānga, a portion of the Hooghly and some channels between the Bhāgirathi and the Ganges; their aggregate length is 509 miles. To enable country cargo boats to use this route, there has to be a minimum depth of not less than 2½ or 3 feet. This depth can always be found during the "rains" (June to October), but during the other seven months shoals form and the current fails, so that navigation is always uncertain and often impossible by the beginning of February.

The southern continuation of the Bhāgirathi is called the **Hooghly**, though the villagers on its banks keep to the name of Bhāgirathi. The reaches below Calcutta form a tidal estuary, which will be described in the next chapter. The portion above Calcutta, as far north as Hooghly, is practically an industrial suburb of Calcutta, being lined with mills and riparian towns. On this river the European nations planted their early settlements, the Portuguese and English at Hooghly, the Dutch at Chinsura and Barnagore, the French at Chandernagore (which is still a French possession), the Danes at Serampore and the Ostend Company at Bānkibazar on the eastern bank. Near the town of Hooghly was the royal port of Sātgāon, referred to by Ralph Fitch in 1588 as "a fair city for a city of the Moors and very plentiful of all things." Some mounds of ruins, a mosque and some tombs are all that is left of what was a flourishing emporium with a considerable sea-borne trade.

Between Naihāti and Hooghly the river is spanned by a railway bridge, over which the produce of the country to the west is carried to the docks for export overseas. The depth to which the piers are sunk (73 feet below the bed of the river) sufficiently shows the engineers' fear of its scouring power.

The principal tributary of the Hooghly is the **Dāmodar,**

which has a length of 368 miles. Rising in Chota Nagpur, it flows across the plateau, selecting the easily eroded band of coal-fields, and then through the deltaic districts of Burdwān, Hooghly and Howrah, joining the Hooghly shortly before it falls into the sea. Its flood volume at the head of the deltaic portion of its course was estimated in 1853 at 584,000 cubic feet per second, while the capacity of its channel opposite the town of Burdwān was less than

Fig. 15. Dāmodar river

half of this, and fell, just above the tidal portion, to only 77,000 cubic feet per second. The difficulty therefore was to provide an escape for a discharge far too large for the lower reaches of the river. The Gordian knot was cut by maintaining embankments along the left bank and leaving the right bank, for the most part, open to inundation. In 1913 the embankments were breached by an unprecedented flood, which laid under water some 1200 square miles of country and destroyed, or more or less damaged, the houses of a quarter of a million inhabitants.

The Dāmodar is accounted a sacred river by the Santāls. It is a solemn obligation among them to cast into its waters at least some of the charred bones of the dead.

The **Brahmaputra,** as is well known, is one of the largest rivers in the world, its length being estimated—its upper portion has not all been surveyed—at 1800 miles and its drainage area at 361,000 square miles: even in the Assam Valley its flood discharge is said to be over half-a-million cubic feet per second. Only the lower section, which is locally known as the Jamuna, lies in Bengal. Sweeping round the Gāro Hills, it enters Rangpur and then flows south for 150 miles until its confluence with the Ganges. The combined stream finds an exit to the sea down the Meghna estuary. "In agricultural and commercial utility, the Brahmaputra ranks next after the Ganges, and with the Indus, among the rivers of India. Unlike those two rivers, however, its waters are not largely utilized for artificial irrigation, nor are they confined within embankments. The natural overflow of the periodic inundation is sufficient to supply a soil which receives, in addition, a heavy rainfall; and this natural overflow is allowed to find its own lines of drainage. The plains of Eastern Bengal, watered by the Brahmaputra, yield abundant crops of rice, jute and mustard, year after year, without undergoing any visible exhaustion. The Brahmaputra is navigable by steamers as high up as Dibrugarh, about 800 miles from the sea; and in its lower reaches its broad surface is covered with country craft of all sizes and rigs, down to dug-outs and timber rafts. Large cargo steamers with their attendant flats, and a daily service of smaller and speedier vessels, ply between Goalundo and Dibrugarh. The upward journey takes four and a half days to complete, the downward three." The principal river mart is Sirājganj, an important centre of the jute trade.

The chief tributary of the Brahmaputra is the **Tīsta,** which, with its tributary, the Rangīt, drains the whole of Sikkim and then flows through the Darjeeling district in a splendid strath. In this portion of its course the Tīsta is a rock-strewn mountain river. No boat can make headway against its current, while rafts are broken up in the rapids; the stream in places runs at

Fig. 16. Tīsta river

the rate of 14 miles an hour. It enters the plains in the Tarai, where it is already half a mile broad, and flows through North Bengal, joining the Brahmaputra in the Rangpur district.

Another large tributary is the **Torsa** (245 miles long), which rises below the divide between the Chumbi valley and the Tibetan plateau. It flows through that valley and through Bhutān under the name of the Amo-chu, and emerges on the plains in the Jalpaiguri district.

The chief rivers of Orissa are the Mahānadi, Brāhmani and Baitarani. The **Mahānadi** is, as its name implies, a great river, with a length of 529 miles and a catchment area of 48,000 square miles. Rising in the hilly country of the Central Provinces, it makes its way through Sambalpur and the Orissa States in a wide valley, which at one place contracts into a narrow gorge. This is the Barmul Pass in Daspalla, 14 miles long and in places not more than a quarter of a mile broad, where the river winds round magnificently wooded hills 1500 to 2500 feet high. This pass used to be known as the key to the Central Provinces. Here the Marāthas made a stand during the war of 1803, but were driven back in rout by the British forces. The Mahānadi debouches from the hills near Cuttack and after numerous ramifications enters the Bay of Bengal by two estuaries. One is known as the Devi; the other retains the name of the Mahānadi and empties itself in the sea at False Point. At Cuttack an anicut has been built across the bed of the river, which creates a head of water for the Orissa canal system. During the rains it is a fine river of great depth and breadth, but after their cessation the stream begins to dwindle. Rocks, rapids and sandbanks impede navigation in its upper reaches. In the dry season boatmen are forced to carry rakes and hoes with which to dig a narrow passage for their boats.

The **Brāhmani** and **Baitarani** rise in and drain the Orissa States and enter the delta in the Cuttack district. As they approach the sea, they unite in the Dhāmra estuary, which, passing by Chāndbāli, falls into the Bay of Bengal at Palmyras Point. The Brāhmani, with a length of 260 miles and a catchment basin of 14,000 square miles, is the larger of the two. The Baitarani is the Styx of Hindu mythology.

CHAPTER IV

ESTUARIES AND PORTS

A GLANCE at the map will show that the coast line of the Bay of Bengal is indented by a number of estuaries and silt-formed islands. In Orissa there are the estuaries of the Devi, Dhāmra and Mahānadi, and a little further north, in the district of Balasore, those of the Burabalang and Subarnarekha. All have a bar of sand across the mouth, which prevents the entrance of vessels of any considerable burden except at high tide. These sandy bars are the outcome of "the eternal war between the rivers and the sea on the monsoon-beaten coast, the former struggling to find vent for their columns of water and silt, the latter repelling them with its sand-laden currents." In spite, therefore, of its estuaries and a long sea coast, Orissa does not contain a single port worthy of the name. Perhaps the best is Chāndbāli, situated 20 miles from the mouth of the Dhāmra, but its trade, which was never more than a small coasting trade, has been seriously affected by the competition of the railway. At False Point ships can ride in an exposed anchorage, and at Puri there is another unprotected roadstead. From March to October the surf does not allow of ships being laden and unladen, but in calm weather they can lie within a mile or half a mile of the shore and land their cargoes in *masula* boats. These are surf boats, made of planks lashed together with cane strips, which enable them to give to the waves. The fishermen use still more primitive craft, the catamaran in vogue being merely four tree trunks held together by wooden pegs, the two in the middle serving as a keel.

Balasore was formerly a considerable port and was described by Bruton in 1633 as "a great sea-town, whereto much shipping belonged, and many ships and other vessels built." It has shared the fate of other ports in Orissa, the river having silted up at the mouth and new land having been formed between it and the sea. Two centuries ago it was only four miles from the sea, as the crow flies, whereas it is now seven miles inland and more than double that by water, owing to the sinuous windings of the Burhabalang, the name of which is admirably descriptive, meaning "the old twister." The ruin of the port of Pipli on the Subarnarekha has been even more complete. It contained Portuguese and Dutch settlements and was a noted slave market, to which the Portuguese and Arakanese pirates brought their captives. It has entirely disappeared and not a trace of it is left.

In Bengal there are many estuaries, but only two ports, viz., Calcutta and Chittagong. The estuaries, proceeding from west to east, are 14 in number, viz., the Hooghly, Sattarmukhi, Jāmira, Matla, Bāngāduni, Guāsuba, Raịmangal, Mālancha, Bara Pānga, Marjāta, Bāngāra, Haringhāta or Baleswar, Rabnābād and Meghna. The greatest of these is the **Meghna,** this being the name assigned to the gigantic tidal river formed by the confluence of the Ganges and Brahmaputra. The portion bearing this distinctive name is 160 miles long and varies greatly in width. In the upper reaches alluvial formation is constantly in operation, the bank advancing on one side as fast as it is washed away on the other. Shortly before its junction with the sea the Meghna splits up into a number of channels separated by low silt-formed islands. Two of these channels are 20 miles and a third is 10 miles across. Notwithstanding its vast size and enormous volume of water, navigation is difficult and often dangerous, more especially during the monsoon, when it is swept by storms and a high sea runs. Even in the calm weather which prevails from November to February, the passage of vessels is impeded by shifting sandbanks and the great rise and fall of the tide; this is 18 feet in spring tides. It may be mentioned incidentally that there is a great increase of the tidal range as one proceeds from west to east along the Bay of Bengal. The tide on the

Fig. 17. A Scene on the Hooghly

west rises only twelve or thirteen feet, but on the extreme west from forty to fifty feet, and the Meghna occupies an intermediate position. At every full moon and every new moon, more especially at the time of the equinox, there is a bore or tidal wave for several successive days. It comes up at the first of the flood tide, with a roar that is heard miles off, and presents the appearance of a wall of water, sometimes twenty feet in height, which advances at the rate of 14 miles an hour.

As a highway of commerce none of the estuaries is

comparable to the **Hooghly,** which is the channel to the **Port of Calcutta,** 80 miles from the sea. That it is navigable by sea-going steamers is one of the many triumphs of human skill over the obstacles imposed by nature, for its passage is rendered difficult not only by rapid currents and the rise and fall of the tide—the mean range is 10 to 16 feet—but also by shoals and shifting sandbanks. The most notorious of these are the James

Fig. 18. The Port of Calcutta

and Mary Sands, which owe their formation to the intrusion of the waters of the Dāmodar and Rūnārāyan. These rivers enter the Hooghly within a few miles of each other and, arresting the flow of its current by their combined discharge, deposit silt, which forms the shoal known by this name. The name itself is derived from the *Royal James and Mary,* a ship which was lost here in 1694. The skill of the Hooghly pilots, the surveying of the river bed, and the dredging operations which have been undertaken since 1907, have made the channels not only safer but also navigable by larger vessels. In 1857 the permissible draught was only 22 feet. It has been steadily increased, until at the present time the river is navigated by vessels drawing up to 29 feet, with a length exceeding 500 feet and carrying as much as 12,500 tons of cargo. In 1911–12 no less than 1700 vessels with a gross tonnage of 6¾ millions visited the port, the imports being valued at 34⅔ millions and the exports at 57¼ millions sterling. The port of Calcutta now accounts for nearly two-fifths of the foreign sea-borne trade of India and is worthy of being ranked among the greatest sea ports of the world. It may be added that at Calcutta the river forms a deep trough, so that large steamers can lie within a few feet of the bank, as shown in fig. 17.

Chittagong is a port of minor importance. It is situated on the Karnaphuli river, ten miles from its mouth, and till a few years ago was handicapped by the fact that the river was not deep enough to allow vessels of deep draught to moor in the stream. Since dredging operations were taken in hand, shoaling on the bar at its mouth has been checked and the channel considerably improved. In 1911–12 it was visited by 388 vessels with an aggregate tonnage of 367,000, the trade consisting almost entirely of tea and raw jute.

Chittagong is known to have been visited by Arab and Chinese vessels some centuries before European nations had access to it. By the end of the sixteenth century it had become familiar to the Portuguese, who called it Porto Grande, or the great port, as distinguished from Sātgāon, which was called Porto Piqueno, or the little port. The distinction is due to the fact that these widely separated places were thought to be situated on the eastern and western branches of the Ganges. De Barros, writing in 1552, described Chittagong as "the most famous and wealthy city of the kingdom of Bengal, by reason of its port, at which meets the traffic of all that eastern region."

CHAPTER V

ISLANDS

THE islands at the head of the Bay of Bengal belong to one or other of three groups. The first consists of the Sundarbans islands interspersed between the estuaries of the Gangetic delta. These are, from west to east, (1) Saugor Island, (2) Fraserganj to the west of the Sattarmukhi, (3) Lothian Island at the mouth of the Sattarmukhi, (4) Bulcherry (Balchari) Island between the Jāmira and Matla, (5) Halliday Island in the Matla, (6) Dalhousie Island between the Matla and Guāsuba, (7) Bāngaduni Island between the Guāsuba and Bāngaduni, (8) Pātni Island between the Mālancha and Bara Pānga, (9) Pārbhānga Islands (two in number) at the mouth of the Marjāta, (10) Rabnābād Island, at the mouth of the Rabnābād, and (11) Domanick Islands, a group of small islands to the east and north-east of the Rabnābād. The largest and most populous of these is Saugor, the south of which, however, is still under dense jungle. The island known as Fraserganj is shown on the Admiralty charts as Mecklenberg Island and is known locally as Nārāyantola. It was renamed by the Bengal Government in 1908 after the then Lieutenant-Governor, Sir Andrew Fraser, K.C.S.I. A scheme of reclamation was also undertaken, and it was hoped to make the place a seaside resort for the people of Calcutta; but the project was abandoned in 1910.

The second group includes the islands at the mouth of the Meghna estuary, of which the most important are Dakshin Shāhbāzpur, Sandwīp and Hātia. The third consists of the islands lying off the Chittagong coast, viz., Kutubdia, Matarbāri, Maiskhāl, and a small island called St Martin's Island at the southern extremity of the Chittagong district.

The islands are, for the most part, low-lying alluvial formations, the position of which at the head of the Bay of Bengal exposes them to the fury of cyclones and the still more destructive storm-wave which follows in their wake. The cyclone of 1864 swept away three-fourths of the inhabitants of Saugor Island, the survivors numbering less than 1500. In 1876 Hātia was submerged by a storm-wave, 40 feet high, which destroyed 30,000 persons, or more than half the population, while the number of deaths in Sandwīp was estimated at 40,000. During the cyclone of 1897, again, Kutubdia was swept by a series of storm-waves, and its effects were aggravated by a terrible epidemic of cholera, which literally decimated the population. Some of the islands in the east of the Sundarbans, such as the Rabnābād Islands, are, fortunately, protected on the sea face by a line of sand-hills, varying from 20 to 60 feet in height, which form a natural breakwater. The island of Maiskhāl, of which the highest point is 288 feet above sea level, is of a different formation from the others, for its backbone is formed by one of the Chittagong ranges of hills, which here reappears after dipping under the sea.

In historical interest **Sandwīp** has a place by itself. According to Cæsar Federici, a Venetian traveller who wrote in 1565, it was a populous and thriving centre of commerce. Two hundred ships were, he said, laden with salt there every year, and such was the abundance of timber for shipping, that the Sultan of Constantinople found it cheaper to have his ships built there than at Alexandria. In the seventeenth century it became a nest of Portuguese pirates. A bloody struggle ensued between them and the Muhammadans, in which quarter was neither asked for nor given. In 1607 the Muhammadan Governor, Fateh Khān, ordered all Christians on the island to be put to death and blazoned on his banners the ferocious scroll: "Fateh Khān, by the grace of God, Lord of Sandwīp, shedder of Christian blood and destroyer of the Portuguese nation." The Portuguese rallied again under Gonzales, a common sailor whom they elected as their leader, and recapturing the island butchered 1000 prisoners in cold blood. Gonzales commanded a fleet of eighty vessels and was undisputed master of Sandwīp and the adjoining islands until his defeat and death in battle against the king of Arakan. For fifty more years Sandwīp was held by Arakanese corsairs, who devastated the sea-board of Bengal, until they were rooted out by the Viceroy, Shaista Khān, in 1665.

Saugor Island marks the traditional place of the confluence of the Ganges and the sea and is the site of a great annual Hindu bathing festival. Here many pilgrims used to immolate themselves and their children (by drowning or death in the jaws of crocodiles) until 1802, when the practice was stopped by the Marquess Wellesley. It was this custom which inspired John Leyden (1775–1811) to write the lines:

On sea-girt Sagur's desert isle,
Mantled with thickets dark and dun,
May never morn or starlight smile
Nor ever beam the summer sun.

Not all blue Gunga's mountain flood,
That rolls so proudly round thy fane,
Shall cleanse the tinge of human blood,
Nor wash dark Sagur's impious stain.

CHAPTER VI

CLIMATE

ALTHOUGH the country lies mainly outside the tropical zone, its climate is characteristically tropical, owing to the fact that over India isothermal lines receive a large displacement to the north. The Himalayas furnish an exception to this general rule, for at the higher levels there is alpine cold, while at intermediate levels the more clement conditions of the temperate zone prevail. At Darjeeling, indeed, the average temperature of the year (53° F., or 2° lower than at Simla) is very nearly the same as in London. The highest reading recorded in this delightful hill station is 80° and the lowest is 20°. The area occupied by the Himalayan mountains is relatively so small, and conditions are so exceptional, that, except for passing references, they will be left out of consideration in the subsequent account.

The variations of temperature, both daily and seasonal, are less pronounced in the neighbourhood of the Bay of Bengal than in the inland districts; and Bengal and Orissa have a more equable climate than either Bihar or Chota Nagpur. Bengal has neither the intense summer heat of the latter nor the sharp cold of its winter nights. In the houses of Europeans fireplaces are the exception rather than the rule, whereas the reverse is the case in Bihar. Another feature which distinguishes Bengal is its high humidity—a feature which is commonly expressed by the saying that it has a damp heat like that of a hot-house. The difference in this respect between Bengal and England may be gauged by the fact that at Calcutta the quantity of vapour in the air is more than double what it is in London. Humidity is highest along the coast and diminishes the further inland one goes, but during the rainy season, when moisture-laden monsoon winds prevail, the atmosphere is nearly as humid in the interior as in the sea-board districts. Owing to its humidity, Bengal is far more relaxing and enervating than other parts of India. Even in the hot weather, though sea-winds mitigate the heat, they saturate the atmosphere, and when it is calm, there is a sultriness oppressive to persons used to drier climates.

Bengal is subject to a heavy rainfall, though there are large local variations due to the proximity of the sea and the Himalayas. The average fall ranges between 50 and 75 inches in the south-centre and west of the province, Calcutta having an average of 62 inches. It rises to between 75 and 120 inches in the south-east, east and north. The precipitation is naturally greatest in, and at the base of, the Himalayas, which arrest the rain-bearing currents from the Bay. Kurseong, at an elevation of 5000 feet, has a mean of 159 inches and Buxa, at their foot, of 209 inches a year. In the province of Bihar and Orissa, however, the average for the year is only from 50 to 58 inches, viz., 50 in Bihar, 53 in Chota Nagpur and 58 in Orissa.

There are three well-defined seasons known as the cold weather, the hot weather and the rains. The **cold weather** lasts four months, viz., from November to the end of February. January is the coldest month in Bengal, where the mean maximum is 77°. As a rule, it is cool rather than really cold, but the nights are sometimes so cold as to make the use of great coats necessary even to Europeans; the thermometer has been known to fall to 34° in the submontane country and to 39° near the sea.

Another feature of the cold weather in Bengal is the occasional occurrence of low-lying fogs, which dissipate with the rising sun.

January is also the coldest month in Bihar, but in Chota Nagpur and Orissa the lowest readings are recorded in December, when the temperature does not exceed 71° in Orissa, while it is seven degrees lower in Chota Nagpur. The average night temperatures in these two months vary from 51° in Bihar to 57° in Orissa, the lowest recorded at the meteorological stations being 34° and 40° respectively. Even lower temperatures have been observed by private individuals; at Christmas, 1912, it was only 25° in the Kaimur Hills. This is a delightful season of the year in Bihar. There is a keen but bracing sharpness in the morning, followed by bright cloudless days, and the nights are often so cold as to render fires a necessity. On the Chota Nagpur plateau there are sharp frosts, and ice, an inch thick, may be seen in basins left out in the open overnight. Ice was regularly obtained for the table of the old Nawābs of Bengal from the Rājmahāl Hills. There is an almost entire absence of rain except for showers, which occur so frequently about Christmas time, that they are referred to as "the Christmas rains."

The **hot weather** lasts from March to June and is ushered in by a rise of temperature, which is, however, neither uniform nor contemporaneous. The upward movement begins in January near the coast and in February 100 miles inland, and is established everywhere by March In Bengal there are occasional local storms, called "nor' westers," generally accompanied by rain, which affords an ephemeral relief from the heat. Hot dry westerly day-winds from the arid plains of Central India penetrate to Bihar, which feel almost like the blast from a furnace. Heavily laden with dust, they give rise, now and then, to fierce but short dust storms and whirlwinds. Low humidity is combined with very high temperatures, the maximum ranging from 109° to 118°. The fierce sun parches the vegetation and leaves the plains bare to nakedness. In some places, such as Gaya, Dehri and Sasarām, the heat forces Europeans to sleep out under the open sky. The temperature in their houses during the daytime is, to some extent, reduced by means of screens of the *khas-khas* grass; these are placed at the western windows and doors and kept constantly wet, so as to cool the air as it passes in. High temperatures are also common in the districts of south-west Bengal, which have a surface soil of laterite and are affected by the hot winds blowing down the Gangetic plain; the maximum recorded in this province is 117° at Bānkura and Midnapore.

The rains last from June to October. During these five months nine-tenths of the annual rainfall is received from the south-west monsoon, and the whole appearance of the country is transformed. Each small depression becomes a puddle, the embanked fields are under a sheet of water, and the rivers fill their channels from bank to bank. The commencement of the rains usually takes place in the second half of June, but is sometimes deferred till July. It is popularly called the "burst of the monsoon," though frequently there is no sudden incursion of the monsoon currents, but a gradual succession of cyclonic storms from the Bay of Bengal. Thenceforward the rainfall is determined by such storms or by inland depressions, which form over the central districts of Bengal and move slowly westward. The flow of the currents from the Bay is northwards over the eastern districts of Bengal, until they meet the Himalayas, by which they are deflected westward. Owing to their great ascensional motion, there is heavy precipitation on the southern slopes and spurs of those mountains: the monsoon fall at Darjeeling averages 114 inches, the heaviest monthly rainfall being 32 inches. July and August are universally the wettest months, and the strength of the currents begins to fall off about the middle of September. The succeeding four to six weeks are the most trying period of the year, as the sodden soil lies reeking under a scorching sun, and the air is still heavily charged with moisture;

Fig. 19. Scour caused by rain

even the Bengalis, habituated as they are to sultry heat, call this month "the rotten month."

The pleasantest part of the country during the rains is the Chota Nagpur plateau, where the temperature falls more rapidly than elsewhere; the fall at Hāzāribāgh, for instance, is more than twice as much as it is at Berhampore, though the two places are in the same latitude. This peculiarity is ascribed to the greater cloudiness of the plateau during the daytime and to greater radiation at night, when the skies are much freer from cloud.

The **cyclones** which come up from the Bay of Bengal are all marked by the same features of a vorticose motion (the wind moving in a direction opposite to that of the hands of a clock), a progressive advance towards the

Fig. 20. Landslip on the Darjeeling Railway, 1899

coast and very heavy rainfall over and near the area of disturbance. A remarkable instance of such rainfall was the precipitation of 24 inches at Darjeeling on 24th and 25th September, 1899, by a cyclone which was first noticed as developing to the south-east of False Point on 21st September; of this total, 14 inches fell in 12 hours. Such excessive and sudden rain, falling on slopes already saturated by an unusually heavy monsoon produced

Fig. 21. Landslip on a Darjeeling road, 1899

disastrous landslips, which caused the loss of many lives and widespread destruction of property. One landslip was 7000 feet long from top to bottom, and there were countless others of smaller size, so that the mountains looked as if some Titan's knife had been taking slices out of them. The Himalayas, it may be added, are liable to soil-cap creeps (called *schuttrutschungen* by Swiss geologists), and Sir Joseph Hooker mentions in his *Himalayan Journals* several enormous landslips that he saw during his travels among them.

Between 1737 and 1910 there were 366 cyclonic storms and cyclones in the Bay of Bengal, but only 142 were severe, of which 55 were felt in Bengal or on the coast. The cyclones which occur during the full force of the monsoon are generally of small extent and rarely attain hurricane force. The most violent, for which the name of cyclone is popularly reserved, are, as a rule, generated during the transition periods before and after the full establishment of the monsoon, i.e., during the months of April and May, October and November. Their most striking feature is an accumulation of water at and near the centre, which progresses with the storm and forms a destructive storm-wave, when it strikes the low-lying coast. It then sweeps inland, and the damage caused is terrible. In the cyclone of October, 1864, the storm-wave drowned 48,000 people and did great damage to shipping at Calcutta, while that of October, 1876, submerged a great part of Backergunge and the adjoining districts to a depth of 10 to 45 feet, causing at least 100,000 deaths.

In conclusion, brief mention may be made of the curious phenomenon called the **Barisāl guns.** This is a name given to sounds resembling the report of cannon or loud explosions, which are heard in the Sundarbans, more particularly in the vicinity of Barisāl in the Backergunge district. They are described as being like the dull, muffled boom of distant cannon, and sometimes also as like a cannonade between widely separated armies. Many explanations have been put forward, one being that they are due to the discharge of ball-lightning, and their cause is still uncertain. It is noticeable that the sound always comes from the direction of the sea and during the monsoon when there is a heavy surf; and the most probable explanation is that they are due to the great rollers, a mile or more long, beating on the coast.

CHAPTER VII

GEOLOGY

In the nomenclature of Indian geology there are four groups of rocks, of which the two oldest are unfossiliferous, while the two youngest contain fossil remains. The oldest, which is, in fact, immeasurably old, is known by the name of *Archæan* (literally ancient, from the Greek ἀρχή, meaning beginning), and consists of crystalline rocks, gneisses and schists, similar to the formations coming under the same designation in Europe and America. The second, which lies on it with marked unconformity, is distinguished by the name of *Purāna* (an Indian word meaning old) and corresponds to much of the system known as Algonkian in America. The lower and older group of fossiliferous strata is called *Dravidian* and may be correlated with the Cambrian, Ordovician, Silurian, Devonian and Carboniferous systems of the European Palæozoic. Such rocks are preserved in the Central Himalayas, but are unrepresented in the area under consideration. The upper and younger which goes by the name of *Aryan*, comprises all strata from the Permo-Carboniferous system to the present day.

For convenience of reference in the subsequent account, the different formations are shown below with their approximate ages in European and American equivalents:

Aryan	Laterite, river alluvia, sand-dunes, beach deposits	Post-Tertiary	Cainozoic
	Siwalik series of the Sub-Himalaya and Chittagong hills	Tertiary	
	Unrepresented	Cretaceous	Mesozoic
	Gondwāna system	Jurassic Triassic	
		Permian Permo-Carboniferous	Palæozoic
Dravidian	Unrepresented	Carboniferous Devonian Silurian Ordovician Cambrian	
Purāna	Vindhyan and Cuddapah systems ..	—	Algonkian
Archæan	Dharwārs, gneisses, schists and deformed (gneissose) eruptive rocks ..	—	Archæan

The hilly country of the Chota Napgur plateau belongs to the gneissic tableland of Peninsular India, and the Himalayas to the extra-Peninsular area, while the level country between the two (in which, however, there are outcrops of old gneissic and granitic rocks) is part of the Indo-Gangetic plain. In the Peninsular area the mountains are all remnants of large tablelands, the gradients of the river valleys are low, and the broad open valleys are merely denudation hollows cut by water out of the original plateau. The entire country presents the gentle undulating aspect peculiar to an ancient land surface. In the extra-Peninsular area, on the other hand, the mountains are the direct result of the disturbance the country has undergone in late geological times. As a result of this, the natural features are the very reverse of those that obtain in the Peninsular tracts; the valleys are deep and narrow, and the rivers are torrential and actively engaged in deepening their valleys.

The **Archæan system** is well represented in South Bihar, Chota Nagpur and Orissa, where it includes three classes of rocks. The first, which covers a considerable area, consists of foliated gneisses of various kinds grouped together under the name **Bengal gneiss.**

The second class consists of rocks which were originally sedimentary and volcanic, but have been altered into quartzites, schists and slates. This ancient stratified series is very similar to that designated the **Dharwār system** in Southern India (from its exposure in the district of Dharwār on the north-western border of Mysore). In South Bihar it forms several ranges and groups of hills, of which the most important are the Kharagpur Hills; in these the slate, being regularly cleaved and of good quality, is quarried to a certain extent. In Chota Nagpur a gigantic intrusion of igneous basic diorite runs through the schists, forming a lofty range, which culminates in the Dalma peak in Mānbhūm, whence the name "Dalma trap" has been derived The Dharwār rocks in Singhbhūm have a special interest on account of the valuable minerals they contain. Gold is sometimes found in the quartz veins, but has not yet been worked successfully. The copper deposits are really of greater economic importance, the ore being sometimes concentrated along special bands in the schists.

Thirdly, we find great granitic masses and innumerable veins of granitic pegmatite intruded both among the schists and the Bengal gneiss. The coarsest grained pegmatites, which cut across the schists in narrow sheets, are the most valuable because of the mica they contain;

Fig. 22. Pegmatite bands in schists

they form a rich mica-bearing belt in Hāzāribāgh, Gaya and Monghyr. In its more massive form the gneissose granite is relatively fine-grained and very homogeneous. It weathers into great rounded hummocks that have caused it to be known as "**dome gneiss.**"

The **Purāna group** is chiefly represented by the great Vindhyan tableland, of which the Kaimur Hills west of Rohtāsgarh in Shāhābād form the easternmost termination. The rocks of the **Vindhyan system** being unfossiliferous, their geological age cannot be determined exactly, but there is reason to believe that they may be partly, or wholly, older than Cambrian. In the Kaimur Hills three stratigraphical subdivisions are conspicuous, viz., in order of superimposition, Kaimur sandstone, Bijaigarh shales and Rohtās limestone. The Kaimur sandstone covers the greater part of the plateau on the top of the hills, forms the upper portion of the precipitous escarpments overlooking the Son and constitutes the whole of the northern cliffs. It is an excellent building material and has been largely quarried near Sasarām. The Bijaigarh shales and Rohtās limestone form the undercliff facing the Son, and are also seen in river gorges to the north, such as that of the Durgauti. The limestone, which is called after the old fort of Rohtāsgarh, has a thickness of 500 feet and is a fine-grained, evenly bedded rock, largely burnt for lime. The Bijaigarh shales (so called after another hill fort in the Mirzapur district of the United Provinces) are intensely brittle and frequently so black in colour as to be easily mistaken for coal. The lower Vindhyan series is found in Sambalpur, where it is an extension of the great Chhattīsgarh basin. The lowest beds are of sandstone, and the commonest rock on the surface is limestone; at one place the rocks have a thickness of perhaps 3500 feet, and there are four distinct zones of limestone. The Bārapahār Hills in the same district are an outlier of the Vindhyas and consist of an accumulation of shales, sandstones and quartzites, the relations of which are of a complicated character and indicate a region of special disturbance.

Another subdivision of the Purāna group is known as the **Cuddapah system** from the strata forming a large area in the Cuddapah district of Madras. Examples of this are found in Chota Nagpur and also in the Mahānadi valley, where they consist of a lower group, composed principally of quartzitic sandstones, and an upper group of limestones and shales.

The Purāna is separated by a huge gap in geological history from the **Aryan group,** the earliest members of which constitute the Tālcher series. These, the oldest rocks after the Vindhyas, form the lowest stage in a great system of fresh-water deposits known as the **Gondwāna system,** the age of which, as determined by fossil remains, is partly upper Palæozoic and partly Mesozoic. Gondwāna is the name given to a continent which once extended to Central and South Africa, and was bounded on the north by a great central ocean. The latter, named by geologists Tethys (after the wife of Oceanus), flowed over Central Asia, its southern limit being on the line now occupied by the Central Himalayas. The system is divided into two portions, the lower of which contains valuable coal seams, while the upper is practically devoid of coal. The former has three series, viz., Tālcher, Damuda and Pānchet, which consist almost exclusively of shales and sandstones. The Upper Gondwānas are represented by the Rājmahāl and Mahādeva series.

The Tālchers, which have been named after one of the Orissa States, in which they were first separated from the overlying beds, consist of soft sandstone and silty shales. Near the base of the series is a conglomerate of boulders, which appears to be due to ice action. Glacial action is distinctly indicated by the appearance of rounded and sometimes striated boulders and pebbles lying in a matrix of soft silt, which would not exist if they had been carried down by rapid streams. Great cold also accounts for a remarkable absence of signs of life, only a few fossil plants having been found in the upper layers.

Next in order of age comes the **Damuda series,** which is divided into three stages, called, according to their superimposition, Rāniganj, ironstone shales and Barākar. These are most important rocks from an economic point of view, for the Rāniganj and Barākars contain valuable coal measures, while the ironstone shales yield a useful iron ore. The chief coal seams are found along the Dāmodar valley, where they form the Rāniganj and Jherria coal-fields. These fields owe their preservation from denudation and their present position to a system

Fig. 23. Basalt dyke cut by river

of faults that has sunk them among the surrounding gneiss. Iron ore is obtained in the same area from clay ironstone nodules that are scattered through the shales.

The predominant member of the Upper Gondwānas is the **Rājmahāl series**, consisting of basic volcanic lava sheets that make up the greater part of the Rājmahāl Hills. Sedimentary beds are frequently intercalated between successive lava flows, and contain beautifully preserved fossil plants, mostly cycadaceous plants, with some ferns and conifers, similar to those found in the Upper Gondwānas at Jubbulpore and in Cutch. The basaltic traps, with their associated sedimentary beds, attain a thickness of at least 2000 feet, of which the

Fig. 24. Glossopteris communis

non-volcanic portion never exceeds one hundred feet. Cycads and ferns distinguish the flora of the Upper Gondwānas from that of the Lower Gondwānas, in which *Glossopteris* (*v.* figure 24) is prominent. "The remarkable agreement between the *Glossopteris* (Gondwāna) flora of India and the fossil plants of similar formation in Australia, Africa and South America can only be explained on the assumption that these lands, now separated by the ocean, once constituted a great southern continent."

Towards the end of Cretaceous and in early Tertiary times there were great convulsions which resulted in the break-up of the Gondwāna continent. Volcanic activity was accompanied by enormous flows of basic lava in the peninsula, of which the best known is that called "Deccan trap." The Eurasian ocean of Tethys was driven back, and a great folding movement gave rise to the modern **Himalayas.** It must not be imagined that this was the first appearance of these mountains. They were marked out in very early times—a range of some sort certainly existed in lower Palæozoic times—and it was only the folding, that took place in Tertiary times, which raised them to be the greatest of the world's mountain ranges. Gondwāna strata are found in Darjeeling which were included in the final folding movement. The latter is thus described by the Geological Survey Department: "The great outflow of Deccan trap was followed by a depression of the area to the north and west, the sea in eocene times spreading itself over Rajputāna and the Indus valley, covering the Punjāb to the foot of the Outer Himalayas as far east as the Ganges, at the same time invading on the east the area now occupied by Assam. Then followed a rise of the land and consequent retreat of the sea, the fresh-water deposits which covered the eocene marine strata being involved in the movement as fast as they were formed, until the Sub-Himalayan zone river deposits, no older than the pliocene, became tilted up and even overturned in the great foldings of the strata. This final rise of the Himalayan range in late Tertiary times was accompanied by the movements which gave rise to the Arakan Yoma and Nāga Hills on the east, and the hills of Baluchistān and Afghānistān on the west. The rise of the Himalayan range may be regarded as a great buckle in the earth's crust, which raised the great Central Asian plateau in late Tertiary times, folding over in the Baikal region against the solid mass of Siberia and curling over as a great wave on the south against the firmly resisting mass of the Indian peninsula."

Rocks of diverse formation are found in the different zones into which the Himalayas are divided. In the Tibetan plateau marine fossiliferous rocks are found, ranging from lower Palæozoic to Tertiary times. Granite rocks form the core of the snowy peaks and also occur in the Lower Himalayas, fringed by crystalline schists. The Outer Himalayas are formed of old unfossiliferous rocks, probably of Purāna age, while the rocks in the Sub-Himalayas are of Tertiary age. Coal is found in the Gondwāna beds in Darjeeling. Copper is very widely disseminated and forms distinct lodes of value in Sikkim. It is also found in Darjeeling in a series called Dāling, after an old Bhutanese fort to the east of the Tīsta. Another series, which is largely developed in Jalpaiguri, is known as the Buxa series from the frontier station of the same name.

The formation of the Chittagong Hills is also to be ascribed to later Tertiary times. Here a substratum of Tertiary rocks was buckled up into parallel folds by a movement connected with that which elevated the Himalayas.

Of post-Tertiary deposits the most extensive is the **Indo-Gangetic alluvium** of the plains formed by the Ganges, Brahmaputra and other large rivers, such as those of Orissa. The prevailing material is a sandy micaceous and calcareous clay. An old and new alluvium are recognized, the latter of which consists of the fluviatile deposits now in course of formation. The old alluvium generally forms high beds of clay, which are undulating from the effects of denudation. It is distinguished by nodular secretions of lime carbonate, called *kankar*, which are used for making lime and for metalling the roads. The application of *kankar* to the Grand Trunk Road during the viceroyalty of Lord William Bentinck gave rise to an atrocious pun, the Viceroy being nicknamed William the Conqueror. The alluvial deposits are of great depth. A boring at Calcutta went down 481 feet without any traces of a rocky bottom or marine deposits. Another boring at Lucknow went down nearly 1000 feet, and the only sign of an approach to the bottom was the appearance of sand near the end of the hole.

The most interesting of the recent formations, from a geological point of view, is **laterite**. This is a name derived from the Latin *later*, meaning a brick, which was given, in 1807, by Dr Francis Buchanan-Hamilton, in allusion to the way in which it can be cut up into brick-shaped blocks for building purposes. It may be defined as a surface decomposition product of a rusty red colour, which it owes to diffused ferruginous products. As pointed out in the Madras volume of this series, "the essential feature in which it differs from all ordinary rock-weathering products is due to the fact that, instead of consisting largely of ordinary clay, which is hydrous silicate of alumina, it contains the alumina largely in a free state, thus resembling in constitution the material known as bauxite, which is used as the main source of aluminium. Thus, some of the deposits of laterite in India might ultimately prove to be of commercial value as sources of the metal aluminium. They, however, differ greatly in quality from place to place, and in many cases have been mixed up with other detrital material."

There is a high-level laterite, resting on the old rocks at whose expense it has been formed, and a low-level laterite, which is merely a detrital form. The former is found as a cap on the summit of several hills, as already mentioned in Chapter II. The latter forms a broken band or mantle stretching from near the Bay of Bengal (in Orissa and Midnapore) to Rājmahāl, and generally occupying the eastern fringe of the gneissic tableland. Wherever seen in this area, it is detrital and contains pebbles of quartz, felspar and other rocks, the source of which is indicated by the way in which they increase the nearer we get to the gneiss rocks to the west. The true laterite occurs in massive beds, from which slabs are excavated for building. It is easy to cut and shape, and becomes hard and tough after exposure to the air, so that it makes an admirable building material. Some of the temples at Vishnupur in Bānkura are built of it, and in spite of its nodular structure and irregular surface, it has been used for carvings. Laterite gravels are also found, which are used for road metalling. These gravels pass by almost imperceptible gradations into solid laterite on the one hand and on the other into a coarse sandy clay, containing so few ferruginous nodules that it has scarcely a reddish tint.

Seven severe **earthquakes** are known to have occurred in the last 150 years, viz., in 1762, 1810, 1829, 1842, 1866, 1885 and 1897, while the shock of the Kāngra earthquake of 4th April, 1905, was felt as far south as False Point, and as far east as Lakhimpur (in Assam beyond the eastern boundary of Bengal). The first of these earthquakes is said to have caused a permanent submergence of 60 square miles near Chittagong, while further to the south it raised the coast of Foul Island nine feet and part of Cheduba Island 22 feet above sea level. This has not been the only change of elevation in this part. *Mohit*, a Turkish work on navigation in Indian waters, written in 1554, refers to islands, which have since entirely disappeared

The most violent earthquake on record was that of 12th June, 1897, which did extensive damage to masonry buildings within an area of 150,000 square miles, while the shock was distinctly felt over 1,200,000 square miles. The focus of the disturbance was near Cherrapunji in

Fig. 25. Railway line in North Bengal after the earthquake of 1897

Assam. The epifocal area, which extended over 10,000 square miles, was situated in Western Assam and Eastern Bengal. Here "the river channels were narrowed, railway lines were bent into sharp curves and bridges compressed, while fissures and sand-vents opened in myriads." Next year more than 5000 small shocks were recorded in the same area.

Within comparatively recent geological times there have been other **rises and subsidences of land**, particularly in a portion of the Sundarbans. "A peat bed," writes Mr R. D. Oldham, in the *Manual of the Geology of India,* "is found in all excavations round Calcutta, at a depth varying from about twenty to about thirty feet, and the same stratum appears to extend over a large area in the neighbouring country. A peaty layer has been noticed at Port Canning, thirty-five miles to the south-east, and at Khulna, eighty miles east by north, always at such a depth below the present surface as to be some feet beneath the present mean tide level. In many of the cases noticed, roots of the *sundrī* tree were found in the peaty stratum. This tree grows a little above ordinary high-water mark, in ground liable to flooding, so that, in every instance of roots occurring below the mean tide level, there is conclusive evidence of depression. This evidence is confirmed by the occurrence of pebbles, for it is extremely improbable that coarse gravel should have been deposited in water eighty fathoms deep, and large fragments could not have been brought to their present position unless the streams which now traverse the country had a greater fall formerly, or unless, which is perhaps more probable, rocky hills existed which have now been covered up by alluvial deposits. The coarse gravels and sands, which form so considerable a proportion of the beds traversed, can scarcely be deltaic accumulations, and it is therefore probable that when they were formed, the present site of Calcutta was near the margin of the alluvial plain, and it is quite possible that a portion of the Bay of Bengal was dry land."

There is also a large depression or hole, called the Swatch of No Ground, in the Bay of Bengal just off the coast of Khulna, where the soundings suddenly change from five to ten fathoms to 200 and even 300 fathoms. Its origin is uncertain, but it is probably due to the fact that sediment is carried away and deposition prevented by the strong currents which are produced by a meeting of the tides. "A very similar depression has been shown to exist in the bed of the shallow sea off the Indus delta, and the cause in both cases has probably been the same, a combination of an excess of subsidence with a deficiency of sedimentation, the latter due to the action of surface currents in sweeping away the silt-laden waters."

CHAPTER VIII

MINES AND MINERALS

IN his *Economic Geology of India* Professor Ball writes: "Were India wholly isolated from the rest of the world or its mineral productions protected from competition, there cannot be the least doubt that she would be able from within her own boundaries to supply nearly all the requirements, in so far as the mineral world is concerned, of a highly civilized community." To this wealth of mineral resources the countries dealt with in this volume contribute largely, for they contain coal and iron, those first essentials of a modern industrial State, and a large proportion of the world's supply of mica, besides copper, manganese, saltpetre, slate, steatite, pottery clays, limestone and an almost inexhaustible supply of building stone.

Nine-tenths of the coal of India is obtained from the coal-fields of Bengal and Bihar and Orissa. Here mining is advancing with rapid strides, the output having been doubled in the present century. The largest quantity is raised from the Jherria field, lying mainly in the Mānbhūm district, which was only opened in 1893, but already produces over six million tons a year. The second great coal-field, the Rāniganj field, which lies mainly in Burdwān, has been worked far longer, systematic mining

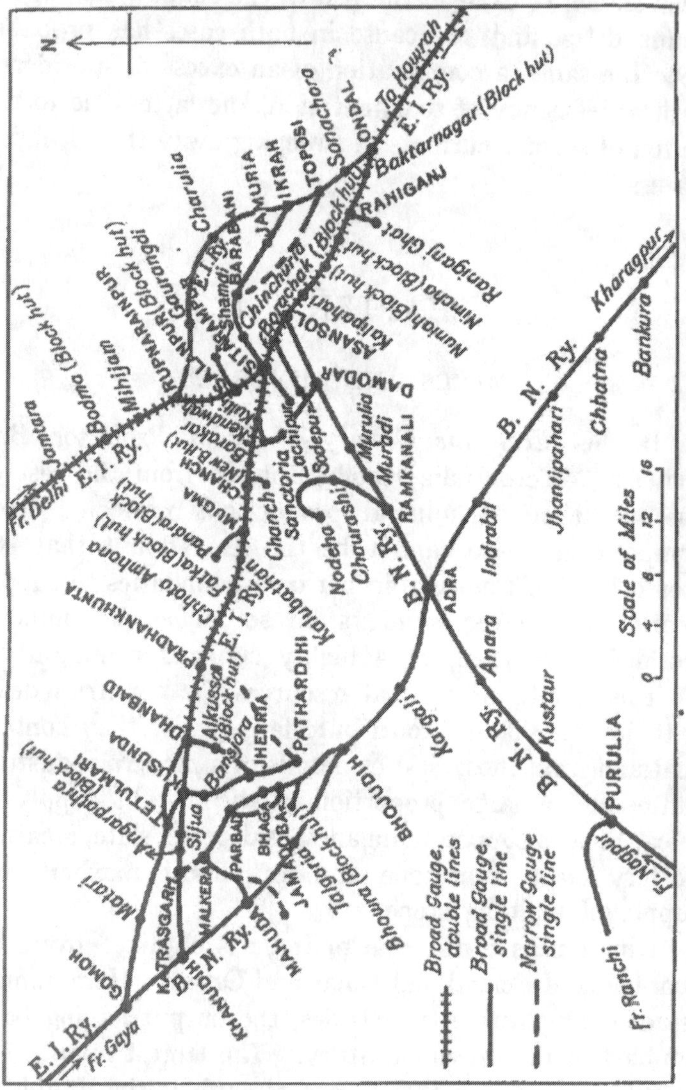

Fig. 26. Railway map of the Jherria and Rāniganj coal-fields

having been started a century ago; the annual production is now four million tons. The Giridih field, which covers

11 square miles in Hāzāribāgh and is estimated to contain 82 million tons, produces the best coal in India. The mines, which are worked by the East Indian Railway Company, have an annual output of 700,000 tons. Other collieries of minor importance are situated in the Daltonganj field in Palāmau, the outturn of which is only 70,000 tons a year.

There are also large coal seams higher up the valley ot the Dāmodar river, which have not yet been exploited owing to the absence of railway communication. Near the western boundary of the Jherria field is that of Bokāro, covering 220 square miles, with an estimated content of 1500 million tons; and close by, in the district of Hāzāribāgh, is the Rāmgarh field (40 square miles), in which, however, the coal is believed to be of inferior quality. A still larger field in the same district is that called Karanpura, which extends over 544 square miles and has an estimated capacity of 9000 million tons. The Palāmau district contains two other fields, which have also not been worked owing to their inaccessibility, viz., the Auranga and Hutar fields. The former has an area of 97 square miles, and the quantity of coal available is estimated at 20 million tons of indifferent quality. The Hutar field covers 79 square miles, and its coal is believed to be fully up to the average of Indian coals, but only three seams of a thickness that could be worked with profit have so far been discovered.

Coal deposits also exist along the valley of the Mahānadi river, notably in Sambalpur, Gangpur and Tālcher. Six thousand tons were raised in the district first named in 1911. The Santāl Parganas contain a few small mines, which merely supply local wants. Coal measures occur in the Gondwāna strata of Darjeeling, but the seams are badly crushed and the coal is so flaky, that it is of little use except for making coke or briquettes.

Coal mining is by far the most important of the mineral industries, employing a labour force of about 100,000 persons. The winning of the coal is comparatively easy, most of it being got from inclines driven into the outcrops of the seams. There are few deep shafts, and the depth of the majority of the mines varies from a few feet to 350 feet; the work consists mainly of driving galleries to extract the coal, leaving pillars to support the roof. There is, fortunately, very little fire-damp or dust, for the mines being shallow, with a superincumbent stratum of porous sandstone, most of the collieries are damp or even wet with water. Owing to the facilities of mining and the cheapness of labour, the pit-mouth price is lower than in any other mining country, the average per ton in 1912 being only Rs. 3–10 in the Rāniganj field and Rs. 2–14 in the Jherria field. The actual outturn per miner is however less than half what it is in England; in fact, it has been calculated that a Bengal mine requires 2½ times as many underground workers as an English mine. This is the inevitable result of the almost casual character of the labour force. The Indian miner has been described as being still to some extent "a miner by caprice," and alternates mining with the tillage of his fields. Even when at work, he does not work steadily and without interruption, so that the average number of working days in the year is only 220.

The coal put on the market, which is known as Bengal coal, is a good to middling steam coal, the percentage of ash ranging from 10 to 15 and of fixed carbon from 50 to 60. The greater part is consumed in the railways, jute mills and other manufacturing concerns in India. The largest consumers are the railways, which take 4½ million tons a year; a test carried out a few years ago with first class Bengal coal showed that it runs 26 lbs. per train mile, Natal coal 27 lbs., and Australian coal 30 lbs Its cheapness and the short lead to Calcutta have brought it into general use as a bunker coal for steamers, in spite of the fact that it takes 1¼ tons to do the same work as a ton of Welsh coal. The exports have now risen to nearly a million tons, mostly consigned to Ceylon and the Straits Settlements, where the competition of Japan coal has to be met.

Copper ores are found in a band, 90 miles long, in Singhbhūm; these are said to be the most widely extended deposits at present known in India. They are being worked by the Cape Copper Co., which, in the course of its prospecting operations, in 1912 produced nearly 9000 tons valued at £13,500. The latest official report states: "If this company meets with the success that its enterprise deserves, copper will soon take its place among the more important mineral products of India." Copper mining was carried on by the Jains in this district 500 to 1000 years ago. According to Professor Ball, their numerous surface workings show that they searched the country thoroughly and had considerable mining skill, while the slags conclusively prove their proficiency as practical metallurgists.

There are also copper-bearing lodes in Sikkim, the working of which is now being undertaken. Copper pyrites, mixed with lead and zinc ores, form a low-grade deposit, about 14 feet thick, in the Giridih subdivision of Hāzāribāgh. A shaft was sunk to a depth of 330 feet by a company which started work in 1882, but the undertaking proved unsuccessful and was abandoned in 1891.

Diamonds have been found in the bed of the Mahānadi in the Sonpur State and the Sambalpur district. The latter has long been famous for diamonds. Gibbon states: "As well as we can compare ancient with modern geography, Rome was supplied with diamonds from the mine of Sumelpur in Bengal." Tavernier also, in the second half of the seventeenth century, referred to "Soumelpour" as a region rich in diamonds, which contained the most ancient mines in India. Clive having been invited by the Raja to start a trade in the stones sent an agent, Mr Motte, there in 1766, as he wished to use diamonds as a means of transmitting money to England. Motte purchased several, but the scheme of trade never materialized. There is also a record of several valuable diamonds having been found at Sambalpur early in the nineteenth century; one, which the Marātha commandant confiscated, weighed 672 grains or 210 carats—a weight which places it among the largest diamonds of the world. For the last sixty years, however, few diamonds of any value have been found. Soon after 1856 a lease of the right to mine for diamonds was given out, but could not be made to pay even at the modest rental of Rs. 200 a year; and in recent times the operations of a syndicate proved a complete failure.

Chota Nagpur also appears to have been famous for its diamonds in Mughal times; they were found in the river Sankh and were occasionally paid as tribute to the Delhi Emperors. It is said that when Captain Camac came to Chota Nagpur at the head of a British force in 1772, the Raja wore a diamond worth Rs. 40,000 in his turban. With a subtlety worthy of a better cause, the Captain offered to exchange his hat for the Raja's turban as a symbol of friendship. This interested offer the Raja had reluctantly to accept.

Gold is obtained by washing the sands of the Subarnarekha and Mahānadi. The washers, who are called Jhoras, make but a poor livelihood of this business, their earnings not averaging more than four annas (*4d.*) a day. Many ancient surface workings are still extant in Singhbhūm, where there are thousands of stone crushers and mortars, which were used for grinding the vein stuffs. In

1890 there was a remarkable gold boom, when 32 companies, with a capital of nearly a million pounds, were formed for the exploitation of the deposits of Chota Nagpur. Only one mine was productive, a small bar of gold being found in it every month. When it was discovered that this mine had been regularly "salted," the boom collapsed.

A special inquiry into the value of Chota Nagpur as a gold-producing area was made by the Geological Survey Department ten years ago, and the conclusion arrived at was: "There may be, hidden away in the dense forest and covered up by the soil and by the vegetation of centuries, quartz veins rivalling those of Southern India. Certainly it was the supreme height of folly to deny the possibility. But, with the data at hand, there can be only one conclusion, viz., that with two doubtful exceptions, there is little scope for the legitimate investment of capital in the recovery of the gold of Chota Nagpur, whether from its sands or from its quartz veins."

Iron ore is found (1) in thin alluvial deposits in a number of places, (2) as masses of hæmatite and magnetite in metamorphic rocks in Singhbhūm, and (3) as nodules in the ironstone shales of the Rāniganj coal-field. It has been smelted from time immemorial in small primitive furnaces, but except in the more remote areas this industry has succumbed to the competition of cheap imported iron and steel. It still survives in Chota Nagpur, the Orissa States and the Rājmahāl Hills, where iron ore is extracted on a small scale and smelted to provide the villagers with agricultural and domestic instruments, such as ploughshares, mattocks and knives. The Santāls and other aborigines also prefer iron made in this way for their axes and the heads of their arrows. Inquiry goes to show that though the methods of smelting are wasteful and the yield is small, the iron produced is of good quality,

Fig. 27. Indigenous iron smelting

for pure wood charcoal is burnt and no flux is added, thus precluding the introduction of sulphur and phosphorus.

Hitherto the only concern which has successfully undertaken the manufacture of iron by European processes has been the Bengal Iron and Steel Co. It has large blast furnaces and a foundry at Barākar, a place which has the advantage of having iron ore and a cheap coking coal in close proximity. Manufacture is limited to pig-iron, which is produced on an extensive scale. Steel plant was laid down in 1904, but worked only for a time.

A recent development of great potential importance is the establishment of the Tata Iron and Steel Co., which proposes to make the production of steel its first object. It owes its inception to the late Mr J. N. Tata, who has been described as "the pioneer among Indians in the scientific organization of industries." The company was formed in 1907 with a capital of over £1,500,000, raised in India and with an Indian board of directors. Valuable iron-ore fields have been acquired in the Gurumaisini hill in the Mayurbhanj State, and blast furnaces and steel rolling mills have been set up at Sakchi in Singhbhūm, where a town has been laid out for 15,000 people. The first blast furnace was started at the end of 1911 and the steel plant early in 1912. The effect was immediately seen, the value of the iron ore produced in India increasing five-fold.

Limestone, of the variety known as Rohtās, is quarried in the Kaimur Hills by several firms, which have set up large kilns at Dehri on the Son. Limestone is also extracted on an extensive scale in Palāmau, Singhbhūm and Gangpur. In the State last named there are large quarries near Bisra on the Bengal-Nagpur Railway, from which lime of good quality is exported to Calcutta.

Manganese ore is found in Singhbhūm and in the

States of Gangpur and Kālāhandi. It has only recently been worked, but the output is already 25,000 tons.

Mica is quarried in the districts of Hāzāribāgh, Gaya and Monghyr, across the junctions of which stretches a mica-bearing belt, some 60 miles long and 12 miles broad. The mineral is found in the veins of a coarse-grained granite, called pegmatite, and is technically called muscovite, owing to its being used in Russia in the place of glass

Fig. 28. A mica mine

for windows. The industry, which was practically non-existent 25 years ago, has recently developed rapidly in consequence of the increasing number of uses for which mica is required, and in consequence of the invention of micanite, which has found a use for the smaller grades which used to be treated as waste. Owing to the greater demand, improved methods of working have been introduced. Ten years ago the practice was to work by hand any productive veins that were found outcropping on the surface.

A string of coolies brought up the mineral on rude bamboo ladders. Every morning, before beginning work, they baled out the water that gathered in the workings overnight. Work was at a standstill during the rains. If difficulties were met with, e.g., if the yield fell off or too much water accumulated, the mine was abandoned. It soon became so covered with debris, or so water-logged, that the vein itself was often completely obliterated. Now it is reported, "The gradual exhaustion of the outcrop workings is compelling some owners to introduce more modern methods of working. Already vertical shafts, well timbered or supported by masonry, are being sunk to reach the veins below the old workings; steam and hand-pumps are superseding the old-fashioned methods of unwatering the mines, winches are taking the place of swingpoles to raise the mineral, and manual labour is being economized generally."

Reliable statistics of output are not available, but it may be estimated that one-third of the world's present supply of mica is produced from this area; a labour force of over 16,000 persons is employed.

The chief source of **saltpetre** in India is North Bihar, where saliferous earth is found in the vicinity of the village homesteads. It occurs in the form of a white efflorescence of dried salt, which is collected and made into a crude and impure saltpetre by a rough process of filtration. It is further refined in small village refineries before being sent to Calcutta, where it is either exported or purified to a higher degree A by-product is sulphate of soda, which is used for fattening cattle, manuring certain crops and curing hides.

Saltpetre, being in great demand in Europe for the manufacture of gunpowder, was one of the principal exports from India, and the European mercantile companies competed for the trade. We find that in 1650, when the

English were meditating an advance from the sea-board, their agents who were instructed that "Patenna being on all sides concluded the best place for procuring peter, they are to make a trial how they can procure the same from thence." Tavernier, who visited Patna in 1666 with Bernier, also wrote: "The Holland Company have a house there by reason of their trade in saltpetre, which they refine at a great town called Choupar (Chapra)." He further stated that the Dutch had imported boilers from Holland and had tried to start refineries of their own, but had not succeeded because the people, afraid of losing their profits, refused to supply them with whem with which to bleach the saltpetre. Before the end of the seventeenth century the English had made a settlement at Patna and had acquired "peter godowns" at Chapra, and fleets of their boats laden with their supplies were to be seen on the Ganges. "The Court of Directors were never weary of asking for saltpetre from Patna, where it could be had so good and cheap, that the contract for it was discontinued on the west coast in 1668 and at Masulipatam in 1670."

There are six **slate** quarries in the Kharagpur Hills near Monghyr, where slate has been worked by a European firm for the last fifty years. The stone is a slightly metamorphosed phyllite, and is mainly used for roofing. It can also be employed for enamelling slate, e.g., for dadoes, so-called "marble" clocks, etc.

The **other minerals** of the country are at present of only minor economic importance and may be dismissed briefly. **Steatite** is widely distributed in Chota Nagpur in the form of potstones, which, as the name implies, are made into pots, as well as plates, cups, etc. Several minerals are found in conjunction with mica. In the pegmatite veins which are the source of mica there have been discovered (1) large crystals of **beryl** with clear fragments that might be cut into aquamarines, (2) blue, green and black varieties of tourmaline, (3) small quantities of **apatite** (a phosphate of lime), which are thrown away with the waste mica, and (4) **molybdenum**, which occurs as isolated plates.

In addition to these, the **tin** ore called cassiterite has been found in the pegmatite veins in Hāzāribāgh, where there is one considerable deposit. An attempt to work it was made by a company, which suspended operations in 1893, after it had driven an incline for 600 feet along the bed of ore. Cassiterite has also been found in the river sands of the same district by iron smelters, who have mistaken it for iron and, using it for their furnaces, have found, much to their surprise, that it produced tin. The sulphide of **lead** called galena, which is found in several places, used to be worked until the indigenous lead was supplanted by the cheap imported metal. Assay has shown a considerable proportion of **silver** in some of the argentiferous galena—in one case 50 ounces of silver were obtained from a ton of galena found in the Santāl Parganas—and an analysis of a deposit in Hāzāribāgh has shown the presence of **antimony**.

Superficial deposits of **bauxite** (from which aluminium may be made) are known to exist in laterite in some places; and **graphite** has been discovered in some of the Orissa States.

The supply of **building stone** is practically unlimited. The sandstone of the Kaimur Hills is admirably adapted for building purposes. The blocks which were used for the great buildings erected by the emperor Sher Shāh and others during the sixteenth century show little sign of decay, while the inscriptions at Rohtāsgarh are still as fresh as if they had recently been chiselled. There are enormous supplies of trap in the Rājmahāl Hills, which have been drawn on for the construction of the Ganges bridge at Sāra. This durable stone was formerly used for temples and forts in the neighbourhood. The magnificent temples at Puri, Bhubaneswar and Konārak, similarly show to what good purpose the stone of the Orissa hills can be employed. In the Himalayas, again, a gneiss is quarried, which is easily split up into blocks. Lastly, there is abundance both of laterite and of the carbonate of lime called *kaṅkar*, which have been adjudged by good authority to be "among the most valuable assets in building material possessed by the country."

Clays, which are almost ubiquitous, are utilized for the manufacture of bricks, tiles and the common unglazed pottery which is turned out on the primitive potter's wheel. A large manufacture of glazed tiles and drain-pipes is carried on in the pottery works of Messrs Burn and Co., at Rāniganj; the material is obtained from the coal measures in the neighbourhood. **Fire-clays** are plentiful on the west coast of the Rājmahāl Hills, but are mostly found, in beds, in the Dāmodar rocks of the coal-fields. Many of them are said to be perfectly infusible and their texture as fine as that of the best Stourbridge clay. It is believed that they are suitable for retorts for gas manufacture as well as for fire-bricks—in fact, that they would answer most of the requirements for which Stourbridge clay is now used. China-clay or **kaolin** is found in the white Dāmodar sandstone of the Rājmahāl Hills, where its presence is due to the decomposition of felspar. It is extracted from the sandstone by a process of crushing, washing and settling and is used by the Calcutta Pottery Company for the manufacture of china and porcelain.

CHAPTER IX

FLORA AND FORESTS

VARIETY of vegetation is the necessary resultant of great diversity of physical conditions in an area which extends from the Himalayas to the sea, which on one side verges on the tableland of Central India and on another is merely a continuation of the Gangetic plain, and which includes not only mountainous and deltaic country, but also arid and humid regions. The Himalayas are rich in the flora of a temperate climate—conifers, oaks, maples, chestnuts, walnuts, rhododendrons, etc. Bihar forms part of the upper Gangetic valley, and its indigenous species are those of a dry tropical country. For botanical purposes it is divided into two parts separated by the Ganges. The northern area of Tirhut lies from west to east between the Gandak and the Kosi; the southern portion, to which the name Bihar is given in a restricted sense, extends to the banks of the Bhāgirathi. "Greater diversity of surface and less humidity," writes Sir David Prain in *Bengal Plants*, "account for the presence in Bihar of many species that are absent from Tirhut. Another and, though an accidental, not less important factor in influencing the vegetation of Tirhut is the density of the population. So close, in consequence, is the tilth, that throughout whole districts field is conterminous with field, and the cultivated land abuts so closely on wayside and water-course as to leave no foothold for those species that form the roadside hedges and fill the weedy waste places so characteristic of Lower Bengal."

In Bengal we come to the humid region of the Gangetic delta, with a luxuriant evergreen vegetation, the villages being commonly imbedded in orchards and groves of mangoes, figs, such as banyan and *pipal,* bamboos and different kinds of palms. Over large areas the flora is aquatic or palustrine; the *bils* or marshes are covered with sedges, reeds and lilies, which are sometimes matted together into floating islets. One anomalous feature is the occurrence, on rising ground between the *bils* in Mymensingh, of a few plants typical of the Khāsi Hills, wanderers from the hilly region to the north.

In the Sundarbans the common trees and plants of Bengal are replaced by an entirely different class of vegetation. The swampy islands along the sea face are mostly covered with a dense evergreen forest of a purely Malayan type, and contain species not found elsewhere in our area except on the coast of Chittagong and Orissa, where there is a similar swampy mangrove growth. "A most remarkable character of the estuarian vegetation is the habit of several of the endemic species to send up from their subterranean roots a multitude of aerial roots, in some cases several feet long, which act as respiratory organs."

Orissa and Chittagong have two other distinctive botanical features. In the former, a peculiar littoral vegetation, with several species characteristic of the Coromandel coast, is found in the sand-hills between the alluvial rice fields and the sea. The flora of the latter is mainly that characteristic of Arakan, with a considerable admixture, however, of species typical of Cachar and a few special forms of its own.

Chota Nagpur is, for the most part, botanically unexplored, but is mainly covered with deciduous-leaved forest. Its flora contains not only representatives of dry hot countries but also, in the deep damp valleys of

Singhbhum, plants characteristic of the moist tracts of Assam; *Dillenia aurea*, a tree of the Eastern Peninsula and the tropical Himalayas, is curiously common in places. The predominant forest tree is *sal* (*Shorea robusta*), while the village lands contain a number of useful trees, e.g., the fruit-bearing mango, jack and tamarind, the *kusum* (*Schleichera trijuga*) which produces lac, the *āsan* (*Terminalia tomentosa*) which feeds the tussore silk-worm, the *harra* (*Terminalia Chebula*) which yields myrobalans, and the *mahua* (*Bassia latifolia*), the flower of which is edible as well as the fruit.

The British Government maintains a large area of forest, viz., 10,500 square miles in Bengal and 3700 square miles in Bihar and Orissa. There are also extensive forests in Native States, which have, however, suffered from reckless exploitation and the want of a proper system of sylviculture. Even in British territory forest conservancy is only sixty years old, the Forest Department having been started in 1854. The forests serve a threefold use. They bring in a considerable revenue to the State. The people in their vicinity benefit not only from the supply of timber and fuel available at their doors, but also from the grazing grounds which they afford to herds of cattle. Last, but by no means least, they are of primary importance in preventing water-erosion and in conserving and regulating the water-supply; the latter function has led to their being described as "the head-works of Nature's irrigation scheme." Where the sources of a river are protected from the sun's rays by forests, they are obviously far less liable to dry up than where the country has been denuded and the evaporation of a tropical climate is accelerated. The danger of erosion is especially great in hilly or mountainous tracts subject to a heavy rainfall. Where the slopes are protected by forest, the trees and undergrowth act like a sponge, the rain percolating through the ground gradually. On bare treeless slopes, however, the rain ploughs through the exposed soil and washes it away. The water, instead of reaching the streams and rivers gradually, swells them suddenly, with the result that there are abrupt and violent rises in their level, which cause floods, or even changes in the river courses, in the plains below.

The principal forests are those of the Himalayas, the Tarai the Sundarbans, Chittagong and Singhbhūm.

The **Himalayan forests** are found on the ridges of the mountains in Sikkim and Darjeeling and in the valleys between them. Sikkim is as well-wooded as, perhaps, any country in the world. Nearly the whole country is under virgin forest from a height of 7000 to 14,000 feet, the latter being the limit of tree growth; and the forests contain a large supply of valuable timber, mainly oaks, chestnuts, various conifers, rhododendrons and small junipers. At present, however, their economical value is very small owing to their inaccessibility, their distance from existing markets and the high price of transport. Nine-tenths of the forests are found on the higher elevations; the slopes below 7000 feet have mostly been denuded and brought under cultivation.

The forests of Darjeeling are extremely diversified, including semi-tropical, temperate and sub-alpine species according to the level of the slopes and valleys. *Sāl* (*Shorea robusta*) is at once the predominant and most valuable tree in the lowest zone, its timber being in large demand for railway sleepers. The rubber tree (*Ficus elastica*), though somewhat rare, is indigenous in this area. In the temperate zone oaks, magnolias, chestnuts, laurels, maples and a bewildering variety of other trees are found. The most conspicuous are the magnolias, which in spring, when still leafless, star the hill-sides with their gorgeous white and pink flowers.

The most useful are the following: the *champ* (*Michelia excelsa*) is used for panelling and the flooring of houses. The *tun* (*Cedrela toona*) furnishes one of the best planking woods in India; it is largely used for tea boxes, as are also the *lampatia* (*Duabanga sonneratioides*) and several kinds of laurels. Two species of oaks are available for heavy beams, while the wood of the walnut (*Juglans regia*) is equal in quality to the best English walnut.

Fig. 29. Himalayan forest (10,000 feet above sea level)

In the sub-alpine region there are forests of silver fir (*Abies Webbiana*) and rhododendrons, highly picturesque but of little economic value at present owing to difficulties of transport. Several species of aconite are found; cattle crossing into Darjeeling have to be muzzled to prevent them eating the poisonous plants. The undergrowth between 7000 and 10,000 feet consists of almost impenetrable thickets of bamboos, of which little use has hitherto been made; but an agreement has recently been concluded under which they will be exploited for the manufacture of paper pulp; a lease for the collection of nettle fibre has also been given out.

In the **Tarai forests** of Darjeeling and Jalpaiguri *sāl* is not only the most plentiful but also the most important commercial tree. It varies from canopied high forest, sometimes with 200 stems to the acre, to a thinly scattered growth. There is said to be an almost unlimited demand for its timber from the railways, and a large quantity that is not cut up into sleepers is exported to Eastern Bengal. A special difficulty encountered in these forests is the evil fertility of creepers, which, if not cut back, half strangle the trees and impede natural reproduction.

The **Sundarbans forests** supply immense quantities of timber, fuel and thatching materials to the lower deltaic districts, for which, indeed, they are practically the only source available. The predominant tree is that from which they derive their name—the *sundri* (*Heritiera littoralis*), the timber of which is in large demand for boat-building. Two gregarious palms are common, viz. the *Nipa fruticans* and the *Phoenix paludosa*. The former is a low stemless palm with a large head of nuts and tufts of feathery leaves, often 30 feet long, which are largely used for thatching. Similar use is made of the fronds of the *Phoenix*, a dwarf slender-stemmed tree, with a dense mass of foliage. Near the sea front the forest is almost entirely composed of mangroves, which extend into tidal water. At some places, however, they are separated from the sea by a line of low sand-hills, which have a few plants characteristic of other Asiatic shores, such as the *mandar* (*Erythrina indica*). The latter is a thorny leguminous tree that is used to shade young betel-nut palms in plantations and also grows thickly round village sites.

The monarch of the **Chittagong forests** is the *gurjan* (*Dipterocarpus turbinatus*), which Sir Joseph Hooker describes in his *Himalayan Journals* as "the most superb tree we met with in the Indian forests; it is conspicuous for its gigantic size, and for the straightness and graceful form of its tall, unbranched pale grey trunk and small symmetrical crown. Many individuals were upwards of 200 feet high and 15 in girth." One of the trees found here, the *chekarishi* (*Chickrassia tabularis*) yields a wood that is called Chittagong wood or Indian mahogany. Canes and bamboos grow luxuriantly; among them may be mentioned a curious berry-bearing species (*Melocanna bambusoides*).

The **Singhbhūm forests** come within the "Central Indian *Sāl* Tract" and are particularly rich in *sāl* trees, which give them a place among the most valuable forests in India. The *sāl* germinates profusely in nearly every locality—on steep rocky slopes almost devoid of soil, on upland plateaux, and in damp valleys, provided always that the soil is not water-logged. It is found at its best in the bottom of the broader valleys, where specimens over 100 feet in height and with a girth of 10 feet may be found; even in the most unfavourable areas its height is 40 feet and its girth 5 feet.

In conclusion, a brief mention may be made of some of the **common trees** of the country. Prominent among them are two members of the fig family, the banyan (*Ficus indica*) and *pipal* (*Ficus religiosa*). The banyan, according to Milton, is the tree of whose leaves Adam and Eve made aprons to hide their shame:

> "The fig-tree—not that kind for fruit renowned,
> But such as, at this day, to Indians known,
> In Malabar or Deccan spreads her arms
> Branching so broad and long that in the ground
> The bended twigs take root, and daughters grow
> About the mother tree, a pillared shade."

There is a magnificent specimen in the Botanical Gardens in Calcutta. According to the latest measurements published, the main trunk is 51 feet in girth (at 5½ feet from the ground), and 562 aerial roots have struck

Fig. 30. The parasitic pīpal

downwards into the soil. The diameter of the space covered by it is 264 to 287 feet, and the circumference of its leafy crown is just on 1000 feet. The *pīpal* is a parasitic plant that tears even solid masonry asunder—*sterilis mala robora fici*—but when standing alone is a noble and graceful tree. Like the banyan, it is accounted holy among Hindus, and it is sacrilege to cut it down.

Of greater economic use are bamboos, the utility of which is manifold, and the various palm trees. The exudation obtained by tapping the date palm (*Phoenix sylvestris*) is made into a coarse sugar in Bengal; the outturn of the sugar so manufactured is estimated at 1½ million cwts. a year, mostly produced in the district of Jessore. In Bihar it supplies a thirsty population with the liquor called toddy (a corruption of the Indian name *tārī*). When fresh and unfermented, it is a mild refreshing drink, perhaps oversweet for European palates; when fermented it is a heady liquor that steals the brains away. The betel-nut palm (*Areca catechu*), which in some places grows almost in forests, brings in a handsome revenue to the peasants in Eastern Bengal; it is estimated that in Backergunge alone there are 27 million of these trees, yielding 6000 million nuts per annum. They have a long productive life, beginning to bear when six to ten years old and continuing to do so for fifty to sixty years. The cocoanut is put to various uses. From its kernel sweetmeats are made and oil is extracted, while the milk is drunk; ropes and matting are made from the husk; the shell is used for hookahs and cups; and when the tree is past bearing, it is cut down and hollowed out into a canoe or cut up into rafters. The wood of the palmyra or fan palm (*Borassus flabellifer*), which is common both in Bihar and Bengal, is put to the same uses, while its leaves are used for thatching.

In the drier country found in Chota Nagpur and the adjoining plains the most useful tree is the *mahua* (*Bassia latifolia*), which supplies the people with food, wine, oil and timber. Its flowers are edible, and being rich in sugar, afford a fairly nutritious food, which enters largely into the diet of the aboriginals. The thin white carpet which the flowers spread over the ground, when they fall, has been compared to the fall of manna in the wilderness, and the resemblance is enhanced when the villagers turn out with their baskets to collect and carry them home. There they are spread out in the sun to dry, and then stored away for future consumption. The pulp of the fruit is also eaten, and oil is expressed from the kernel, while the tough wood of the trunk is used for

Fig. 31. View in the Royal Botanic Garden, Sibpur

the naves of cart wheels. The heart of the *kend* (*Diospyros melanoxylon*) yields the ebony of commerce; lac is propagated on the *palās* (*Butea frondosa*); tussore silk-worms feed on the *asan* (*Terminalia tomentosa*); the pods of the red cotton tree (*Bombax malabaricum*) shed a coarse cotton when they burst; and the long coarse *sabai* grass (*Ischoemum angustifolium*) is made into a strong twine or exported to the paper mills near Calcutta for manufacture into paper. The raising of this grass is of especial importance in the Rājmahāl

Hills, from which four million lbs. are exported annually Of fruit-bearing trees the most popular is the mango The mango trees of Mālda have a deservedly high reputation for the delicious flavour of their fruit ; here no less than fifty distinct varieties are recognized, the best known being those called Brindāban, Gopālbhog, Keshapat and Fasli. This is the fruit of which Bernier said : " It hath a sweetness so peculiar that I doubt whether there be any comfit in the world so pleasant." The plantain, which is allied to the banana, bears an excellent fruit when carefully cultivated. It is a tree-like plant, which, like the banana, has a lush fat stem, a crown of huge leaves falling over in curves, and below whorls of green and golden fruit, with a purple heart of flowers dangling behind them. Other common fruits are the jack, leechee, tamarind oranges (the best of which are produced in Sikkim), custard apple, guava, pine-apple, and several kinds of melon.

CHAPTER X

ZOOLOGY

INDIA falls, almost entirely, within three zoological areas, viz. (1) the Indian or Cis-Gangetic region consisting of the Indian peninsula as far east as the Bay of Bengal ; (2) the Himalo-Burmese or Trans-Gangetic sub-region, which includes the forest-clad Himalayas, Assam and Burma, and (3) the Malayan sub-region of Southern Tenasserim. The first two come within our area, the second being represented by the lower Himalayas of Sikkim and Darjeeling and by the country east of the Bay of Bengal (Chittagong, the Chittagong Hill Tracts and Hill Tippera), and the first by the remainder of Bengal and Bihar and Orissa. The higher altitudes of the Himalayas form part of a fourth sub-region, the Tibetan, which has a fauna resembling that of Central Asia and belonging to the Holarctic or Palaearctic zoological region.

The most interesting zoological areas are the Himalayas, the country to the east of the Bay of Bengal and the Sundarbans. The last has been described as "possessing an abundant pachydermatous fauna, the stronghold of gigantic and destructive saurians and peculiar fish—a curious and anomalous tract, for here we see a surface soil composed of black liquid mud supporting the huge rhinoceros, the sharp-hoofed hog, the mud-hating tiger, the delicate and fastidiously clean spotted deer—we see fishes climbing trees, wild hogs and tigers, animals generally avoiding water, swimming across the broadcast rivers, as if for amusement." Outside these areas the larger mammals have mostly disappeared owing to the spread of cultivation and human habitation, but they are still found in the sparsely inhabited hilly regions and in the forests which have not yet yielded to the axe of the pioneer and the subsequent advance of the plough.

Of the **Primates**, the long-tailed grey langur or sacred Hanumān (*Semnopithecus entellus*) and the shorter-tailed Bengal or Rhesus monkey (*Macacus rhesus*) are very widely distributed. The white-browed Gibbon, called hoolock from its cry, and one lemur are found in the country to the east of the Bay. This is also the habitat of the brown stump-tailed monkey (*M. arctoides*) of Burma, which is distinguished by a tail so short as to be almost rudimentary, and of the long-tailed capped or toque monkey (*M. pileatus*) of Ceylon. Here too the Himalayan monkey (*M. assamensis*) and a large Himalayan langur (*S. schistaceus*) are met with, as well as in the Himalayas, where the latter is hardy enough to live among the snow-laden boughs of fir trees in the higher altitudes.

The **Carnivora** include many of the **Felidae** or cat family. The tiger was once so plentiful that it is still commonly spoken of as the Bengal tiger. About 1702 a Dutchman is said to have shot 23 tigers in a week near Plassey, where the country is now entirely free from these brutes. A black tiger has been seen in Chittagong, and those frequenting the sand dunes along the sea face of the Sundarbans have almost lost their stripes in adaptation to their environment, so that their coats are of a tawny orange with only a few dark lines. In this estuarine labyrinth they commonly swim across the creeks and rivers, and one is known to have made its way across the mouth of the Hooghly, a distance of eight miles. A certain number are habitual man-eaters, more especially in Chota Nagpur and the Sundarbans; in 1911–12 the number of deaths reported as due to them in Bengal and Bihar and Orissa was 433. Of the habits of the Sundarbans man-eaters Bernier wrote in the seventeenth century: "It is in many places dangerous to land, and great care must be taken that the boat, which during the night is fastened to a tree, be kept at some distance from the shore, for it constantly happens that some person or another falls a prey to tigers. These ferocious animals are very apt, it is said, to enter into the boat itself, while the people are asleep, and to carry away some victim, who, if we are to believe the boatmen of the country, generally happens to be the stoutest and fattest of the party." It is customary for parties of woodmen entering the Sundarbans forests to take with them a *fakīr* or holy man, who is believed to have the power of driving away tigers by his spells. Unfortunately for this belief, the *fakīr* himself is sometimes carried off. In Chota Nagpur and the Orissa States man-eaters are killed by means of a huge bow, with a large poisoned arrow, which is placed by the side of paths frequented by them. It is discharged by a string stretched across the run some 18 inches from the ground. A safety string is put higher up to warn the casual passers by of their danger, but this is of no use when, as has happened before this, an aboriginal is returning home so drunk that he crawls along on his hands and feet.

Leopards, which are widely distributed, also occasionally acquire a taste for human flesh, and are more dangerous than even tigers, as they have the advantage of being able to climb trees. Their size and markings vary considerably, and black leopards are met with east of the Bay of Bengal. The snow-leopard or ounce and the lynx are peculiar to the higher altitudes in the Himalayas, while the clouded leopard is found on the lower slopes and also to the east of the Bay. A few cheetahs or hunting leopards have been shot in the Orissa States. Of other cats the most frequent is the jungle cat (*Felis Chaus*), which resembles the Indian domestic cat, but is larger and fiercer. The fishing cat (*F. viverrina*), which is so called because it feeds chiefly on fish, lives on the banks of marshes and rivers in Eastern Bengal. There are several species of civet cat, from which the civet drug is obtained—among others, the palm civet, which is also called the toddy cat from its real or imaginary liking for palm juice or toddy. The bear cat (*Arctictis binturong*) is confined to the forests east of the Bay. Alone of the animals in Europe, Asia and Africa, it has a prehensile tail, with which it can suspend itself, at least when young.

Of the **dog family,** the Indian wolf survives and still has the propensity for children which is so familiar a theme in children's story books; in the district of

Darbhanga alone, 130 deaths were caused by wolves in 1910–11. The jackal is an ubiquitous scavenger and occasionally emulates the wolf in carrying off babies. Wild dogs hunt in packs in some forests. They are extremely destructive of deer and other game, and it is credibly stated that they will even drive out the tiger from their preserves. The domestic dog is usually a half-starved mongrel, commonly called the pariah or pie-dog. He is a scavenger, "whose home is Asia, and whose food is rubbish." A nobler beast is the Tibetan mastiff, whose fame reached even the ears of Herodotus.

There are four species of the **Ursidae** or bear family. The commonest is the Indian sloth-bear (*Melursus ursinus*), which feeds on fruit, honey, the combs of white ants, the flower of the *mahua* tree, maize and sugarcane crops. The other three dwell in the Himalayas, viz., the Isabelline bear (*U. arctus*), a variety of the European bear, which is found from 11,000 to 12,000 feet, the Himalayan black bear (*U. torquatus*), which is common from that height downwards, and the Malay bear, which has been met with in Sikkim. The cat-bear (*Aelurus fulgens*), which is another denizen of the Himalayas, is neither a cat nor a bear, but belongs to the racoon family, most of which are American. It is a quaint little beast of a foxy colour merging in black with a tail 18 inches long.

The remaining carnivorous beasts may be dismissed briefly. In addition to the common mungoose (a name perhaps derived from the Tamil *munga*), there is a large species on the east of the Bay, called the crab-mungoose from its feeding on crabs; it is sometimes confounded with the badger. The carrion-eating striped hyaena is found in waste places. Otters are found both wild and tame; the latter are trained by fishermen in Bengal to drive fish into their nets.

The **Insectivora** include hedgehogs, moles and shrews. The best known is the grey musk shrew, commonly called the musk rat from its musky smell, which is due to the secretion of two glands. The tupaias or tree shrews are arboreal animals, which look like a cross between a rat and a squirrel, but are distinguished from the latter by their ears and teeth.

The **Chiroptera** have several representatives, of which the most familiar is the fruit-eating flying fox. During the day hundreds of them may be seen hanging, like great fruit, from the branches of their favourite trees; in the evening they sally forth in search of food, flying on wide membranous wings.

The rodents include rats, mice, porcupines, hares, etc. By far the most important of these is the common Indian rat (*Mus rattus*), for it harbours the plague flea, that every year slays its thousands and tens of thousands. The prevalence of plague is determined by its distribution. This fell disease is rife in Bihar, where the tiled-roofed, mud-walled houses are infested by rats. Eastern Bengal, however, is immune from the pestilence, for here the *Mus rattus* is not a domestic animal, finding little shelter in houses built of brick, bamboo-matting or wattle with roofs of corrugated iron, split bamboos or thatch. The loathsome bandicoot is a large rat, two feet in length, which burrows under houses. The name is a corruption of the Telugu *pandi-koku*, or "pig-rat," which is attributed to the animal grunting like a pig. The commonest squirrel is the prettily striped palm squirrel, which is, however, more often seen in gardens than on palm trees. Marmots are found in the higher altitudes of the Himalayas, and in the forests lower down flying squirrels may be seen, in the dusk of the evening, volplaning down from tree to tree on expanded membranes.

The order of **Ungulata** (hoofed animals) is a large one,

including elephants, rhinoceros, camels, antelopes and deer, horse, swine, sheep, goats and oxen. Tame elephants are kept by Rajas and wealthy landlords. Wild herds haunt the Tarai and the forests of Angul and the Orissa States. They sometimes ascend the Himalayas to a height of 10,000 feet, and have been seen roaming about in the snow. They are particularly mischievous and destructive in the Tarai. Here the telegraph wire has to be attached

Fig. 32. Elephants bathing

to the trees, for telegraph posts are pulled down as fast as they are put up. They are captured in kheddahs or stockades in Angul and by means of noosing in Jalpaiguri; altogether, 227 were taken in these two districts in the decennium 1902–12.

Three species of rhinoceros survive in diminished numbers, viz., the great Indian rhinoceros (*R. unicornis*) in the Tarai, the Javan rhinoceros (*R. sondaicus*), a smaller one-horned variety, in the Sundarbans and a two-horned variety (*R. sumatrensis*) in the country east of the Bay. A specimen of the hairy-eared rhinoceros (*R. lasiotis*) was captured many years ago in Chittagong and sent to the Zoological Gardens in London. Camels are confined to the hot dry climate of Bihar; a camel cart service is maintained in the Gaya district.

Fig. 33. A camel cart

The ox tribe is represented by several species, both wild and domesticated. The *gaur* (*Bos gaurus*), miscalled the bison by sportsmen, is still fairly plentiful in Singhbhūm, the Orissa States and the Tarai. The *gayāl* or *mithun* (*B. frontalis*) is found in a wild state in the country east of the Bay; a fine specimen (8 feet 7 inches in height) was shot a few years ago in Chittagong. Domesticated herds of *gayāl* and of yaks (well designated *Bos grunniens*, or the grunting ox), which make excellent milch cattle, are kept in Sikkim. The wild buffalo (*B. bubalus*), though rare, is found in a few localities; herds of domestic buffaloes are kept almost universally for the sake of their milk and their value as draught cattle. The common domestic cattle are humped animals known zoologically as zebus.

The domestic sheep are neither large nor numerous.

Fig. 34. Domestic buffaloes

Fighting rams are kept for the purpose of sport. A species of wild sheep called *bharal* (*Ovis nahura*), which climbs as nimbly as a goat, is found in the Himalayas, which are also the habitat of two goat antelopes, the *serow* (*Nemorhaedus bubalinus*) and the *goral* (*Cemas goral*). Two true antelopes are fairly common, viz., the *nilgai* or blue bull (*Boselaphus tragocomelus*) and the Indian antelope (*Antelope cervicapra*). The male of the latter is usually called the black buck: its spirally twisted horns, seen from the side or singly, have possibly given rise to the legend of the unicorn. The four-horned antelope (*Tetracerus quadricornis*) is somewhat rare. The Indian gazelle (*Gazella bennetti*), otherwise known as the *chinkāra* or ravine deer, is found in the Chota Nagpur plateau and the country at its base. The members of the deer family are many, viz., the *sāmbar*, which is the noblest of them all, the muntjac or barking deer, so-called from its dog-like bark, the *chītal* or spotted deer, the hog deer, the tiny mouse deer and the *barā-singha* (literally twelve-horned) or swamp deer. The hornless musk deer, which yields the musk of commerce, occurs in the higher elevations of the Himalayas.

Wild pigs are numerous and do great damage to the crops of rice, as they press down the stalks between their feet, so as to bring the grain to their mouths, and make long swathes in their passage. As for the horse, there is nothing to add to the account given in a recent Government publication, viz., "The only local breed is the country 'tat,' which is an object of compassion wherever one meets it owing to the cruelty to which it is subjected by the majority of owners."

The only other order of land mammals is called **Edentata** (toothless) and consists of the pangolins (*Manis*). They have an armour of horny scales and feed chiefly on ants, whence they are called scaly ant-eaters.

The aquarian mammals comprise **Cetacea**, i.e., whales, dolphins and porpoises, and **Sirenia**, of which the dugong is the only representative. In addition to the whales, dolphins and porpoises found in the Bay of Bengal, there is a fresh-water species, the Gangetic dolphin or porpoise, which is a familiar sight in the Ganges and Brahmaputra. The dugong is seen off the coast of

Chittagong, where at least one specimen has been captured. It has been suggested that this marine mammal is the original of the mermaid "with a glass and a comb in her hand," the fable having its source in the distant sight of a dugong in the shallows, half out of water, attacked by hammer-headed sharks, with their hammers shining in the sun like mirrors, and by saw-fish with their comb-like snouts.

The varieties of birds are so numerous, that all that can be attempted is a brief summary as follows:

Passeres. A large order including crows, magpies, jays, thrushes, bulbuls, the drongo or "king crow," warblers, shrikes, flycatchers, finches, swallows and martins, larks, wagtails, and the sparrow, which is as ubiquitous as the crow. This order includes the tailor and weaver birds, so called from the ingenious construction of their nests. The commonest of the babbling thrushes are known as *sāt bhai* or the seven brothers, because they go about in bands, often seven in number. The *maina* is a favourite cage-bird, and can be easily taught to talk. The handsomest are perhaps the golden oriole, the paradise flycatcher and the slender-billed irridescent sun-bird, sometimes miscalled "the humming-bird."

Eurylaemi and *Pici.* Broadbills and woodpeckers respectively.

Zygodactyli. Barbets, of which the best known is the coppersmith bird, with a monosyllabic metallic call ("took, took") resembling the hammering of copper vessels.

Ansiodactyli: Rollers, bee-eaters, kingfishers, horn-bills (miscalled toucans) and hoopoes. The Indian roller is usually called the blue jay from its colour. The plumage of some kingfishers is a blending of metallic and turquoise blue of great brilliance, but the commonest is a black and white bird. The hoopoe, like the wagtail, is a harbinger of the cold weather; the Muhammadans believe that it was a favourite bird of Solomon and consequently never molest it.

Macrochires. Swifts and nightjars or goatsuckers.

Trogones. Distinguished by the structure of their feet, the first and second toes being turned backwards.

Coccyges or cuckoos. The European cuckoo breeds in the Himalayas, where its familiar note is frequently heard in the spring. Other members of this family are the coucal or crow pheasant, the loud-voiced koel and the "brain-fever bird," which is so called from the wearisome repetition, in a high crescendo, of its call-note, which closely resembles the sound of the words "brain fever."

Psittaci or parrots. Mostly green long-tailed parroquets.

Striges or owls, one of which is regarded with superstitious dread.

Accipitres or birds of prey, including vultures, eagles, hawks, kites, etc. The Brāhmani kite is sacred to Vishnu. Vultures on the other hand are regarded with lively horror as birds of ill omen; some people will even pull down their house if a vulture alights on it.

Columbae and *Carpophaginae.* Pigeons and doves.

Pterocletes. Sand-grouse.

Gallinae or game birds proper, pea fowl, jungle fowl, pheasants, partridges, quails, etc. Pea fowl are not killed by orthodox Hindus, who hold them sacred to the god Kārtik. The red jungle fowl is said to be the bird from which the domestic fowl is derived.

Hemipodii, which resemble quails but are distinguished from them by having no hind toe.

Grallae. Rails and cranes. The great bustard has been shot in Gaya.

Limicolae. Plovers, snipes and wading birds of many kinds, which are cold-weather migrants from beyond the Himalayas. Wonderful bags of snipe are obtained in Bengal. Sandpipers are called snippets by sportsmen. This order includes the jacanas, marsh-birds with long claws which enable them to run over the floating leaves of water-lilies and other aquatic plants.

Gaviae. Gulls and terns. Inland the commonest is the Indian skimmer, or scissors-bill, which has a razor-like lower mandible, much longer than the upper, and skims over the water in search of food.

Steganopodes. Pelicans, cormorants and several sea-birds such as gannets or boobies. The Indian snake-bird, which is hunted for the sake of its scapular feathers, belongs to this order.

Tubinares. Petrels in the Bay of Bengal.

Herodiones. Ibises, spoonbills, storks, egrets and herons, the commonest being the pond heron popularly called the paddy bird. To this order belongs the adjutant bird, once common in Calcutta, where it was a useful scavenger.

Phoenicopteri. Flamingoes.

Anseres. Geese and ducks. A common species is the Brāhmani duck, which goes about in pairs.

Pygopodes. Grebes. The crested grebe has remarkable speed in diving and can travel under water for several hundred feet in a few seconds.

The **reptiles** belong to three orders, viz., crocodiles, Chelonia, or tortoises and turtles, and Squamata, or lizards and snakes.

The fresh-water **crocodile** or mugger (*C. palustris*) is common in rivers and marshes, and a salt-water species (*C. porosus*) infests the estuaries. Both have broad snub noses unlike the long-nosed fish-eating *ghariāl*, which has been Latinized, in a corrupted form, as Gavialis. The two former, which are often miscalled alligators—a name properly applicable to the American species—levy an annual toll of life. In the Sundarbans it is not safe to bathe unless the water is enclosed by palisading, and even then the wily crocodile sometimes makes his way in, during the night, from the land side and catches the early bather. Both sea and fresh-water turtles, and land and water tortoises, are found.

Of the many **lizards** the commonest is the thick-tongued little house gecko, which climbs over the walls and ceilings of houses by means of plates on the surface of its digits. The name is a Malay word imitative of its cry. A large species found in Bengal is known scientifically as *Gecko stentor*, and in the vernacular as *Touk-tai*, from its loud call. The monitors, or Varanidae, which have the nostrils half-way between the lip and the eye, are called iguanas by Europeans and *goh-sāmp* by Indians. They are popularly credited with a virulent poison, probably because they have forked tongues, whence also the name of bis-cobra (from *bish*, poison). The blood-sucker is a harmless spiny-crested lizard, also supposed to be venomous It owes its ferocious name to the red colour assumed by the male during the breeding season, and is sometimes incorrectly called a chameleon.

" India is inhabited by all the known families of living **snakes**," and our area has its full share. The largest is the python, miscalled the boa constrictor by Europeans, which is said to grow to a length of 30 feet and certainly attains 20 feet. Another large and common non-venomous snake is the *dhāman* or rat-snake, which feeds on frogs, lizards and small animals. The carpet snake (*Lycodon aulicus*), which, as its scientific name implies, frequents dwelling houses, is an innocuous little snake which is believed to be venomous, probably from its likeness to the deadly *karait*. The common poisonous snakes are either sea snakes or the following land snakes—

the cobra, the fierce *karait* (*Bungarus coeruleus*), the *rāj-sāmp* (literally king snake) or banded *karait* (*B. fasciatus*), Russell's viper, and the savage little carpet viper (*Echis carinata*). The formidable venomous snake called hamadryad or king cobra (*Naia bungarus*), which grows to a length of 12 feet, is found in some localities; it owes its scientific name of Ophiophagus to its peculiar habit of eating its own kind.

The **batrachians** include various species of frogs and toads. One species of the Caudata or tailed batrachians (newts and salamanders) has been found in Sikkim.

Fish. Sharks, skates and rays are plentiful in the Bay of Bengal and its estuaries. Hammer-headed sharks are frequently caught off the coast of Chittagong, where too a saw-fish has been captured having a saw-snout 50½ inches long and 11 inches broad at its junction with the head.

Favourite edible fish are *hilsa*, *bhekti* and mango-fish. The *hilsa* is a richly flavoured fish of the herring family (Clupeidae). It is a true shad closely allied to the Allice shad of Europe; the name Allice is indeed probably derived from the Bengali name of the fish, viz. *ilisha*. The *bhekti* (*Lates calcarifer*) is an estuarine fish. The mango-fish (*Polynemus paradiseus*) was described by Walter Hamilton in 1820 as "the best and highest flavoured fish not only in Bengal, but in the whole world." Its name is due to its smell being slightly like that of the mango fruit. The Indian name is *tapsi*, meaning a devotee, which is ascribed to the fact that it has whiskers like a Hindu ascetic. Pomfret of an excellent flavour are also caught for the table. The so-called whiting of Calcutta is not one of the cod family, like the European whiting, but one of the Sciaenidae. The curious name of "Bombay duck" or bummalo is given to dried fish of the species known as *Harpodon nehereus*, which is plentiful in the Bay. The mahseer (*Barbus tor*) is found in the rivers of the Himalayas and some other hilly regions, and affords excellent sport to fishermen. The Indian trout (*Barilius bola*) is indigenous in the streams of Chota Nagpur. Both the carp family and the Silurids are well represented; some of them grow to a length of 6 feet, and one of the larger Silurids is spoken of as the fresh-water shark.

Some fish have distinctive peculiarities of structure. The *koi* or climbing perch (*Anabas scandens*) is a small fish which climbs by means of spines along the margin of its gills, and can live for a long time out of water. In the Sundarbans hundreds of them may be seen hanging on the mangrove stems a few feet above the level of the water. Another curious fish is the Tetrodon or balloon fish, which has the power of inflating itself like a balloon, thus erecting its spines, when taken out of the water.

Prawns, shrimps and crabs are common, and there are oyster beds in the Chilka lake and along the Cuttack coast.

CHAPTER XI

ADMINISTRATION AND POPULATION

In addition to the territory under direct British administration, both Bengal and Bihar and Orissa contain some principalities, known as **Native States**, which are ruled over by Indian princes or chiefs. They are not independent, for the Governments of Bengal and Bihar and Orissa exercise a general control over their administration, but the laws that are in force in British territory do not apply to them, and their inhabitants are not British subjects.

In Bengal there are two Native States, **Cooch Behar** and Hill Tippera. The former is administered by the Maharaja, with the assistance of a State Council. A British officer, who bears the title of Superintendent of the State, acts as Vice-President of the Council and is the executive head of several departments, such as police, jails, education and public works. **Hill Tippera** is governed by a Raja, who is advised by a British Political Agent.

In Bihar and Orissa there are two groups of States known as the **Chota Nagpur Political States** and the **Orissa Feudatory States.** The former consist of two petty States, Kharsāwan and Saraikela, in the north of Singhbhūm, which taken together extend over only 600 square miles and have under 150,000 inhabitants. The latter consist of 24 States, the aggregate area and population of which are nearly as great as those of Ireland. These States are administered by their Chiefs, with the advice of a Political Agent appointed for the whole group, and in accordance with the terms of *sanads*, or agreements, which define their status and powers. The largest and most populous is Mayurbhanj (4243 square miles and 729,000 inhabitants); the smallest is Tigiria, which has an area of 46 square miles and a population of 23,000.

Sikkim is a Native State on a different footing, for it is entirely independent of local governments and has relations direct with the Government of India. It is governed by a Maharaja, with the advice and assistance of a British Political Officer, who is stationed at the capital, Gangtok.

The town of **Chandernagore** forms a French enclave in British territory. It is controlled by a French

Administrator, subordinate to the Governor of the French Possessions in India, whose headquarters are at Pondicherry.

As regards British territory, Bengal is administered by a Governor-in-Council and Bihar and Orissa by a Lieutenant-Governor-in-Council. The meaning of these terms is that the governing body in each province is an **Executive Council** presided over in one case by a

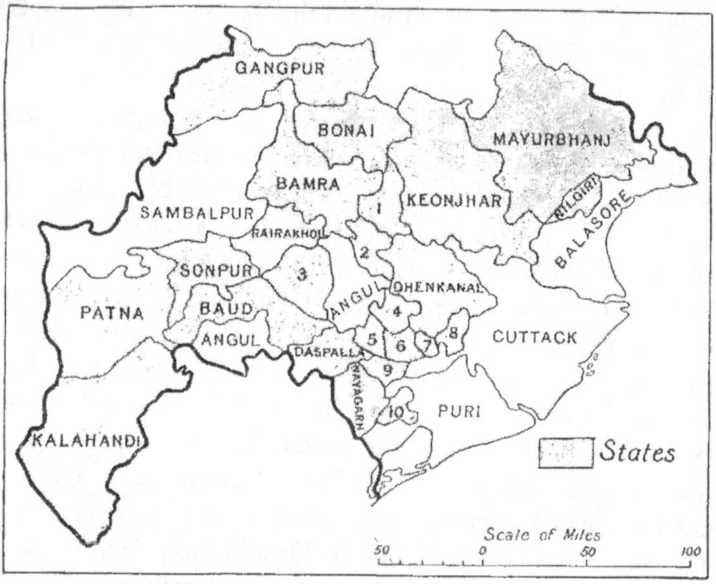

Fig. 35. Map of the Orissa States

Governor, as in Madras and Bombay, and in the other by a **Lieutenant-Governor.** The former is drawn from the ranks of English public men. The latter is a member of the Indian Civil Service, who has proved his capacity as an administrator during a long service in India. Both hold office for a term of five years, as also do the Members of Council. The number of the latter is limited to four, of whom two at least must have been twelve years in the service of the Crown in India. Up to the present, the Council has been a triumvirate, two being European members of the Indian Civil Service and the third an Indian private gentleman. The Governor and Lieutenant-Governor can overrule their Councils in matters of grave importance, but otherwise the opinion of the majority prevails. Each province has a **Legislative Council** for the enactment of laws of provincial application and for the discussion of provincial finances and administration. They are composed partly of official members and partly of non-official members, aggregating 51 in Bengal and 43 in Bihar and Orissa. The non-official members form a permanent majority; most of them are elected to represent different classes or interests, but a few are nominated by Government.

References to and from the Government of India, other governments and the local officers are dealt with by the **Secretariat**, i.e., a staff of Secretaries and Under-Secretaries. The highest revenue authority is the **Board of Revenue**, which was formerly composed of two members but now has only one. There are separate **Departments** for other special branches of administration, e.g., police, education, agriculture, public works, medical, jails, forests and excise, the heads of which deal directly with Government. Both Governments are, to a certain extent, peripatetic. Calcutta is the capital of the Bengal Government, but its summer headquarters are at Darjeeling, and it also spends a portion of the year at Dacca. Patna has been chosen as the capital of the newly created Government of Bihar and Orissa, and here buildings are being erected for the accommodation of its offices. In the meantime, it has its summer headquarters at Rānchi.

The unit of general administration is the **district.** Each district is under a District officer, who is designated Collector in respect of his authority in revenue matters and District Magistrate by virtue of other functions. He is the "handy man" of the Government, being responsible for practically every branch of administration in his district. Bengal contains 27 districts, excluding the city of Calcutta for which special arrangements are made, and Bihar and Orissa has 21 districts. Their average area is 2840 square miles in the former, and 3961 square miles in the latter province; the average population is approximately $1\frac{2}{3}$ millions in each case The largest are Rānchi and Hāzāribāgh, each of which contains over 7000 square miles, but Mymensingh has the greatest population, viz., $4\frac{1}{2}$ millions. Compared with European countries, Rānchi is very nearly as extensive as Wales, while Mymensingh has more inhabitants than Ireland. This last district, however, has proved so unwieldy that it is to be subdivided into three districts.

The districts of Chota Nagpur, the Santāl Parganas and Angul in Bihar and Orissa, and those of Darjeeling, Jalpaiguri and the Chittagong Hill Tracts in Bengal, have a simpler form of administration than the others. They are known as **Non-Regulation Districts**, because they are not subject to all the Regulations and Acts, many of which are unsuitable for aboriginals in a somewhat backward state of civilization.

The districts are grouped together by **Divisions**, the officers in charge of which are called **Commissioners**. They have powers of inspection and control over the District Officers and form intermediate authorities between them and Government. There are five divisions in each province, the number of districts in them varying from three to eight. For judicial purposes, each district, or a small group of two or sometimes three districts, is under a **District and Sessions Judge**.

The districts, with five exceptions, are subdivided

into smaller areas called **subdivisions.** That containing the district headquarters is usually directly under the District Officer, but the others are in charge of officers of the Indian Civil Service or of a subordinate service called the Provincial Civil Service, which is composed almost entirely of Indians. The average area of the subdivisions is 878 square miles in Bengal and 1110 square miles in Bihar and Orissa. The subdivisions again are split up into **thanas** or police stations, which are the units of police work. Their average area and population are 217 square miles and 125,000 persons in Bengal, and 172 square miles and 72,000 persons in Bihar and Orissa.

The system of administration is far more centralized than in a province like Madras, for practically all revenue questions are dealt with at the district headquarters, while those who have cases in the criminal courts have to go to the district or subdivisional headquarters, either of which may be scores of miles from their homes.

A limited system of **local self-government** has been introduced. For nearly every district there is a body called the District Board, composed of official, nominated and elected members. It maintains roads and bridges, provides for sanitation and water-supply, has the control of a certain number of schools, and makes grants-in-aid to others, besides keeping up dispensaries and providing medical relief. Smaller bodies, with minor powers, called Local Boards, have been constituted for the subdivisions. Local self-government is also in force in the towns, which have been made municipalities and have Boards of Municipal Commissioners to regulate their affairs.

The **revenues** consist mainly of the receipts from land revenue. Minor sources of revenue are excise duties on spirits and drugs, duties on stamps and salt, customs duties, income-tax and a public works cess. In the greater part of the country the land revenue was fixed in perpetuity in 1793 by a measure known as the Permanent Settlement. "Although," writes Sir Alfred Lyall in *The Rise of the British Dominion in India,* "the measure has cut off the Indian treasury from all share in the increase of rents and the immense spread of cultivation—although it has prevented the equitable raising of the land revenue in proportion with the fall in value of the currency in which it is paid—yet it has undoubtedly maintained Bengal as the wealthiest province of the empire." To be more precise, the rental of the landlords has increased four or five fold since 1793, but the amount contributed by them to the State has remained the same.

The land revenue is a light tax, the incidence per cultivated acre being only eight annas in Bihar and Orissa and fifteen annas in Bengal, which is much less than elsewhere in India. One-fifth of the land is temporarily settled, i.e., the amount of land revenue is periodically revised, so that the State obtains a proportion of the increased assets. In such areas the incidence is about double what it is in permanently settled areas.

The following statement shows the districts, divisions and States in each province, together with their area, population and density according to the census of 1911 :

District	Area in square miles	Population	No. per square mile
Bānkura	2,621	1,138,670	434
Birbhum	1,752	935,473	534
Burdwān	2,691	1,538,371	572
Hooghly	1,188	1,090,097	918
Howrah	510	943,502	1850
Midnapore	5,186	2,821,201	544
TOTAL—BURDWĀN DIVISION	13,948	8,467,314	607

District or State	Area in square miles	Population	No. per square mile
Calcutta	32	896,067	28,002
Jessore	2,925	1,758,264	601
Khulna	4,765	1,366,766	287
Murshidābad	2,143	1,372,274	640
Nadia	2,790	1,617,846	580
24-Parganas	4,844	2,434,104	502
TOTAL—PRESIDENCY DIVISION	17,499	9,445,321	540
Bogra	1,359	983,567	724
Darjeeling	1,164	265,550	228
Dinājpur	3,946	1,687,863	428
Jalpaiguri	2,919	902,660	309
Malda	1,899	1,004,159	529
Pabna	1,851	1,428,586	772
Rājshāhi	2,618	1,480,587	566
Rangpur	3,479	2,385,330	686
TOTAL—RAJSHĀHI DIVISION ..	19,235	10,138,302	527
Backergunge	4,642	2,428,911	523
Dacca	2,777	2,960,402	1,066
Faridpur	2,576	2,121,914	824
Mymensingh	6,249	4,526,422	724
TOTAL—DACCA DIVISION ..	16,244	12,037,649	741
Chittagong	2,492	1,508,433	605
Chittagong Hill Tracts	5,138	153,830	30
Noakhāli	1,644	1,302,090	792
Tippera	2,499	2,430,138	972
TOTAL—CHITTAGONG DIVISION	11,773	5,394,491	458
TOTAL—BRITISH TERRITORY ..	78,699	45,483,077	578
Cooch Behar	1,307	592,952	454
Hill Tippera	4,086	229,613	56
TOTAL—NATIVE STATES ..	5,393	822,565	153
Total—Bengal	84,092	46,305,642	551

District or State	Area in square miles	Population	No. per square mile
Gaya	4,712	2,159,498	458
Patna	2,069	1,609,631	778
Shahabād	4,373	1,865,660	427
TOTAL—PATNA DIVISION ..	11,154	5,634,789	505
Champāran	3,531	1,908,385	540
Darbhanga	3,348	2,929,682	875
Muzaffarpur	3,036	2,845,514	937
Sāran	2,683	2,289,778	853
TOTAL—TIRHUT DIVISION ..	12,598	9,973,359	792
Bhāgalpur	4,226	2,139,318	506
Monghyr	3,922	2,132,893	544
Purnea	4,998	1,989,637	398
Santāl Parganas ..	5,463	1,882,973	345
TOTAL—BHĀGALPUR DIVISION ..	18,609	8,144,821	441
Angul	1,681	199,451	119
Balasore	2,085	1,055,568	506
Cuttack	3,654	2,109,139	577
Puri	2,499	1,023,402	410
Sambalpur	3,824	744,193	195
TOTAL—ORISSA DIVISION ..	13,743	5,131,753	373
Hazāribāgh	7,021	1,288,609	184
Mānbhūm	4,147	1,547,576	373
Palāmau	4,914	687,267	140
Rānchi	7,104	1,387,516	195
Singhbhūm	3,891	694,394	178
TOTAL—CHOTA NAGPUR DIVISION	27,077	5,605,362	207
TOTAL—BRITISH TERRITORY ..	83,181	34,490,084	415
Kharsāwan	153	38,852	254
Saraikela	449	109,794	245
TOTAL—CHOTA NAGPUR STATES	602	148,646	247

State	Area in square miles	Population	No. per square mile
Athgarh	168	46,813	279
Athmallik	730	53,766	74
Bāmra	1,988	138,016	69
Barāmba	134	41,429	309
Baud	1,264	113,441	90
Bonai	1,296	58,309	45
Daspalla	568	57,053	100
Dhenkanal	1,463	270,175	185
Gangpur	2,492	303,829	122
Hindol	312	49,840	160
Kālāhandi	3,745	418,957	112
Keonjhar	3,096	364,702	118
Khondpāra	244	73,821	303
Mayurbhanj	4,243	729,218	172
Narsinghpur	199	39,964	201
Nayagarh	588	151,293	257
Nīlgiri	278	68,714	247
Pāl Lahara	452	25,680	57
Patna	2,399	408,716	170
Rairākhol	833	31,729	38
Ranpur	203	45,956	226
Sonpur	906	215,701	238
Tālcher	399	66,201	166
Tigiria	46	23,240	505
TOTAL—ORISSA STATES	28,046	3,796,563	135
TOTAL—NATIVE STATES ..	28,648	3,945,209	138
Total—Bihar and Orissa ..	111,829	38,435,293	344
Sikkim	2,818	87,920	31

CHAPTER XII

HISTORY

Prehistoric movements. The earliest inhabitants are believed to have been Dravidians, a prognathous curly-headed race, whose origin can only be a matter of speculation. Dravidian languages still survive in Chota Nagpur, the Orissa States and the Santāl Parganas, where they are spoken by primitive races of archaic type. The north-eastern passes and the Brahmaputra valley are believed to have afforded a passage to the next hordes of immigrants, who were tribes speaking languages of the Mon-Khmer family. The intimate connection between these languages and those of the south-eastern Pacific shows that the peoples who spoke them extended from India across Assam to Indo-China and thence across Melanesia and Polynesia as far as Easter Island. Forest tribes in Malacca, Pegu and Indo-China still use these forms of speech, with which the Nicobarese Khāsi of the central hills of Assam and the Munda tongues of Chota Nagpur are closely connected. The possibility of a common origin is further suggested by the discovery of peculiar shoulder-headed celts in the Malay Peninsula and the valley of the Irrawaddy on the one hand and in the present home of the Mundāri races on the other; while the monoliths and flat stone slabs erected as sepulchral monuments by the Khāsis in Assam and the Hos and Mundas in Chota Nagpur have a similarity that can hardly be regarded as fortuitous.

Later in the days of unchronicled antiquity came

swarms of immigrants from the west of China, who also followed the north-eastern route, descending the Brahmaputra to Assam and thence to Bengal. The Mongoloid element which they introduced is still strong in the Koches and Meches of North Bengal and is probably also to be traced in the Pods and Chandāls of the lower delta. The last notable movement was the influx of Aryans, who poured down from the north-west along the course of the Ganges. Their earliest settlement was in North Bihar, where the Videhas founded the kingdom of Mithila, a kingdom which is celebrated in legendary lore as having been a centre of civilization, culture and learning under the pious rule of king Jānaka. The wave of conquest and civilization next spread across the Ganges to South Bihar, and thence gradually extended eastwards and southwards into Bengal and Orissa. In this part of the country the numerical inferiority of the Aryans precluded wars of extermination. Conquest was followed by partial amalgamation with the earlier settlers, who learnt the arts, language, and religion of their new rulers. As late as the sixth century B.C. Baudhyayāna described the people of Magadha and Anga, i.e., South and East Bihar, as of mixed origin, while the Pundras (in North Bengal), the Vangas (in East Bengal) and the Kalingas (in Orissa and part of Madras) were regarded as outside the pale of Aryan civilization.

Early Hindu and Buddhist Period. Reliable history is first reached, in the sixth century B.C., with the rise of the kingdom of Magadha (South Bihar), which under the Mauryas was to be the nucleus of an empire stretching from sea to sea. The first capital was at Rājgīr in the Patna district, whence the Saisunāga kings extended their conquests north of the Ganges. There they established their suzerainty over the Lichchavis, one of a confederate group of tribes governed by an oligarchical republic, who had their capital at Vaisāli, the modern village of Basārh in the Muzaffarpur district. The chief interest of the Saisunāga kings, however, lies in the fact that their rule synchronized with the birth of Jainism and Buddhism, and that their territory was the cradle of both those religions. Mahāvīra, the founder of Jainism, was the son of one of the Lichchavi princes and spent his early manhood in a monastery at Vaisāli; he died, after 42 years of preaching, at Pāwāpuri in the Patna district. Gautama Buddha, though born outside the limits of Magadha, spent many years of his life in its rocky hills and warm fertile plains, attaining Buddhahood, or supreme enlightenment, under a *pīpal* tree at Bodh Gaya.

Not long after Buddha's death the capital was transferred to Pātaliputra, a city now buried deep beneath the silt of the Ganges, over which the modern town of Patna has been built. This city became the capital of the great Mauryan empire founded by Chandragupta, during whose reign it was visited by the Greek envoy Megasthenes. His account shows that the court was maintained with Oriental splendour, while the empire was divided into satrapies, its administrative system resembling that of the Persian monarchy. The city itself stretched along the bank of the Ganges for 9 or 10 miles, with a breadth of 1½ to 2 miles. It contained a population estimated at 400,000, and had a highly organized system of administration. One body had functions resembling those of the Board of Trade, another discharged the duties of foreign consuls towards foreign residents and visitors. There was an Irrigation Department to control the use of canals, while other bodies had the supervision of industries and manufactures, and enforced the registration of births and deaths. The empire developed still further under Asoka (272–31 B.C.), the monk emperor,

Fig. 36. The Bodh Gaya temple

who made Buddhism the State religion. His conversion to Buddhism is said to have been due to his horror and remorse at the bloodshed attending the conquest of Kalinga, i.e., Orissa and the northern sea-board of Madras, when 150,000 persons were made prisoners, 100,000 were slain and many more perished miserably; even allowing for exaggeration, the figures show what a teeming population the land bore and what immense forces were put into the field. With this addition to his territories, the empire of Asoka stretched from the Arabian Sea to the Bay of Bengal and comprised as large an area as the British territory in India.

After Asoka's death the Maurya dynasty was overthrown, and outlying provinces asserted and achieved their independence. The country again became part of a united empire in the fourth century A.D., when the Gupta dynasty rose to power. Some account of the state of the country under their rule is given by the Chinese traveller Fa Hien, who visited Bihar and Bengal early in the fifth century. The palace and other buildings of Asoka at Pātaliputra were still standing and of such grandeur that they appeared to be the work of genii rather than of men. The country was studded with richly endowed Buddhist monasteries, rest-houses were provided for travellers on the roads, and the sick received treatment free of charge in charitable hospitals. Maritime trade flourished, Tāmralipti (the modern Tamlūk in the Midnapore district) being the chief eastern port from which vessels traded to Ceylon and the far East. There had, indeed, long been intercourse between the sea-board districts of Kalinga and the Malay Archipelago, where the Indians introduced their writing and chronology: though Kalinga has disappeared from Indian nomenclature, Indian immigrants to the Malay States are still known as Klings.

Fig. 37. Railing and sacred tree at Bodh Gaya

Another and more famous Chinese pilgrim, Hiuen Tsiang, visited Bengal, Bihar and Orissa in the seventh century and found Buddhism and Hinduism flourishing side by side. Shortly before his visit the Buddhists had been ruthlessly persecuted by Sāsanka, king of Bengal, who sacked Pātaliputra, burnt down the sacred tree of Buddha's enlightenment at Bodh Gaya, destroyed monasteries and scattered the monks, carrying his ravages up to the foot of the Himalayas. The faith had, however, revived under the patronage of Harsha, who was the undisputed monarch of Northern India at the time of Hiuen Tsiang's visit. The prosperity of the Nālanda monastery (in the Patna district) sufficiently shows how rapid had been the recovery. It was, in fact, a university rather than a monastery, containing 10,000 monks and students, and has aptly been called the Oxford of Buddhist India. "Learned men," wrote Hiuen Tsiang, "who desire to acquire renown come in multitudes to settle their doubts, and then the streams of their wisdom spread far and wide."

The death of Harsha was followed by an invasion of the Tibetans and Nepalese, and for several centuries there was no central predominant power. Out of the general confusion the Pālas emerged in the ninth century as rulers first of North Bengal and then of Bihar. These kings continued the royal tradition of liberal patronage of Buddhism; and a splendid *vihāra* or monastery, established by the first of the line, gave its name to the town of Bihar, which was the headquarters of their Governors, and subsequently to the surrounding province. In the twelfth century the Sena kings, who had united nearly the whole of Bengal under one rule, gradually encroached on the territories of the Pālas and eventually wrested North Bengal from them. Unlike the Pālas, the Senas were devout Hindus and warm patrons of

Sanskrit learning and literature; their court attracted savànts and poets, of whom the most famous is Jayadeva, the author of that great classic, the *Gīta Govinda*.

Muhammadan Governors. At the close of the twelfth and the beginning of the thirteenth century the fabric of Hindu monarchy was swept away by the Muhammadan invasion. In 1198–99 Bakhtiyār Khilji invaded South Bihar with a body of wild horsemen, and next year a sudden raid was made on Nabadwīp (in the Nadia district), where the last Sena king held his court. Having sacked the town, Bakhtiyār Khilji retired with his booty and established himself at Gaur in the Mālda district, whence he and his successors extended the Moslem conquests. With this invasion begins the first period of Moslem rule, during which Bengal was administered for over a century by Governors, appointed by the Emperors of Delhi. The latter, however, could exercise but little real control over this outlying portion of their dominions, which, it must be remembered, was separated from the imperial court by a journey of several weeks' duration

As early as 1225 the emperor Altamish was forced to march in person against his rebellious viceroy and to install his own son in his place, but his successors left the Bengal Governors to rule practically as they pleased. Balban, the greatest of the Slave Kings, was not so complaisant. Two expeditions against the sixteenth Governor, Tughril Khān, having failed ignominiously, Balban himself marched against Gaur, declaring: "We are playing for half my kingdom, and I will never return to Delhi, nor even name it, till the blood of the rebel and his followers is poured out." Tughril Khān having been defeated and slain, Balban proceeded to teach the people of Gaur a sharp lesson on the dangers of revolt, the memory of which lasted for several generations. Gibbets were set up on both sides of the main street of the city for over two miles, and on them men, women and children were hanged, for days together, after indescribable tortures. After this, Bengal was ruled for half a century by descendants of Balban, whose subjection

Fig. 38. Firoz Minār at Gaur

to Delhi was so loose as to be merely nominal. Twice the Tughlak emperors had to lead their armies against rebellious or usurping viceroys, first in 1324 and again in 1333, when Bahādur Shāh, who had proclaimed himself king in Eastern Bengal, was overthrown and killed. Vengeance did not end with his death, for his skin was stripped from his body, stuffed with straw and paraded through the different provinces as a warning to others. Five years later Fakhr-ud-dīn Mubārak Shāh succeeded in establishing his independence, and Bengal broke away from the empire.

Independent Kings. Bengal now enters on the second stage of Musalmān domination, the period of independence, during which four dynasties and 24 kings followed each other in the course of 200 years. The first dynasty reigned for nearly a century and a half, with one brief interlude when they were supplanted by a Bengali Hindu and his descendants—a remarkable break in the long line of foreign Musalmān rulers. Next (1486–90) came a short-lived line of slave kings, who were set upon the throne by the pretorian guard of Abyssinian and negro slaves. At first the protectors of the dynasty, the guards soon became masters of the kingdom, while the palace eunuchs supplied the actual rulers: as Ferishta remarked, the people of Bengal would obey any one who killed the king and seized the throne. The tyranny of these usurpers led to a rising of the old nobility and the foundation of the Husaini dynasty, which endured for another half century. Its founder, Alā-ud-dīn, who was an Arab by descent, and his son, Husain Shāh, were able administrators and great conquerors, carrying their arms eastward into Assam, southward into Orissa and westward into Bihar, which since 1397 had been subject to the kings of Jaunpur. The last of the line was driven out by Sher Shāh, the Afghan Governor of Bihar, after which Bengal acknowledged the suzerainty of the Delhi emperors.

Bengal appears to have prospered under its independent kings. A splendid court was maintained, first

Fig. 39. Fortifications at Rohtāsgarh

at Pandua, which rivalled the old capital in magnificence, and then at Gaur, which after 1456 resumed its former position as the seat of government. Maritime trade flourished, the chief emporium being Chittagong, which traded with the Arab ports of Baghdad and Bussorah on the west and with China on the east. Embassies were also sent to and received from the Emperor of China.

A Chinese interpreter attached to the suite of the Chinese envoy (1415) gives an account of thriving trade, arts and industries, which is confirmed by the description of Di Varthema, an Italian traveller who visited Bengal 90 years later. The latter says that of all countries in the world Bengal had the greatest abundance of grain, flesh of all kinds, sugar, ginger and cotton. Cotton and silk stuffs were exported to Turkey, Arabia, Syria, and Ethiopia, and were carried to all parts of India. The rich commerce of Bengal had attracted foreign merchants, including Armenian traders, while the native merchants were the richest he had ever met.

This era of peace and prosperity witnessed an outburst of religious and literary activity. Bengali poetry had its first fruits in the lyrics composed by Chandidās, while the two great epics of India, the *Mahābharata* and the *Rāmāyana*, were translated into the vernacular by Kāsirām and Krittibās: these latter are, according to Mr R. C. Dutt, "the first great literary works in the Bengali language and the foundations on which Bengali literature is built." Early in the sixteenth century a great religious reform was initiated by Chaitanya, the founder of modern Vaishnavism in Bengal and Orissa.

Afghan supremacy. The downfall of the independent kings was followed by half a century of Afghan supremacy. The Afghan chiefs had for some time held their own in Bihar, and, though quelled for a time by the invasion of Bābar in 1629, soon rallied under Sher Shāh, an ambitious leader who combined administrative ability with military talent. His dreams of a restoration of the Afghan ascendency were realized by a series of successes which made him master of Bengal, as well as of Bihar, and in 1540 secured for him the throne of Delhi. Afghan Governors and kings ruled at Gaur until 1564, and then

Fig. 40. Tomb of the Emperor Sher Shāh at Sasarām

at Tānda, a place in the Mālda district, which has disappeared, having been swept away by floods in 1826. The most notable event of their rule was the conquest of Orissa, which in 1568 was wrested from its Hindu king with the usual rapine and iconoclasm of Musalmān invasions. The Afghan domination came to an end eight years later, when Daud Khān, the last Bengal king, was defeated and slain by Akbar's army at Rājmahāl.

Mughal rule. Bengal, Bihar and Orissa were now annexed to the Mughal empire, but many years elapsed before Akbar's rule was firmly established. A formidable rebellion broke out among the Mughal nobles, the Afghans were in a constant state of revolt, and several chieftains, Hindu as well as Musalmān, enjoyed semi-independent power, secure in the protection afforded by the swamps and morasses of the lower delta. Well might Abul Fazl, the historian of Akbar, give Bengal the name of *Bulghakkhāna* or home of revolt—a name recalling the description of it as a centre of disaffection and rebellion given by Barani three centuries before. Separate Governors were appointed for Bihar and Bengal, while Orissa was sometimes attached to Bengal and at other times was placed under a separate Governor. The Governorship of Bihar was usually the stepping-stone to the more responsible and more lucrative Viceroyalty of Bengal. Not that the former was ill paid: according to the contemporary account of Sir Thomas Roe, its incumbent in 1620 drew a fixed salary which, in modern money, would amount to nearly £80,000 a year, beside the large sums which he could make out of the taxes. The headquarters of this officer were at Patna, which had become the entrepôt of a large trade extending as far as Tibet, China, Persia and even Europe. Both he and the Viceroy (Nawāb Nāzim) of Bengal held office at the pleasure of the Emperor, and, while the empire was in full vigour, were kept under close control. They were liable to recall for inefficiency and were also frequently changed for fear that they might become too powerful.

During the first century of Mughal rule there were 22 different Governors of Bengal, and the capital was shifted more than once. At the end of the sixteenth century it was transferred from Tānda to Rājmahāl, which occupied an important strategic position, as it commanded the Teliagarhi pass, "the key of Bengal" as it was called. Thence the Viceroy moved in 1608 to Dacca, where his presence was required to direct operations against the Ahoms of Assam and to check the raids of the Maghs, or Arakanese, and of Portuguese corsairs. The last-named constituted a permanent menace to the security of the southern districts. They carried their ravages as far as Dacca, and had depopulated the sea-board, so that, as Bernier noticed, "there were many fine islands deserted, which were formerly thickly peopled, and no inhabitants but wild beasts." These pirates had their strongholds in the island of Sandwīp and at Chittagong, which had not yet been reduced by the Mughals but was subject to the king of Arakan. It was not till 1666 that the Viceroy, Shaista Khān, rooted out these nests of pirates and added them to his dominions.

The value of the trade of the country during this century, though only a fraction of what it now is, may be gathered from the pages of Bernier: "Bengal is, as it were, the general magazine not only for Hindostan or the empire of the great Moghul, but also for all the circumjacent kingdoms and for Europe itself." Bernier was astonished at the vast quantity of cotton cloth which the Dutch alone exported, especially to Java and Europe, not to mention what the English, Portuguese and Indian merchants took. The like might be said of the silk and silk stuffs: "one could not imagine the quantity exported every year." Saltpetre was brought down in flotillas of country boats from Patna and whole shiploads taken overseas by the English and Dutch. Rice was exported to Madras, Ceylon and the Maldives, sugar to the Deccan, and even to Arabia, Persia and Mesopotamia. "In a word, Bengal is a country abounding in all things."

In 1704 Murshid Kuli Khān made a new capital

at Murshidābād, which was apparently selected on account of its central position. Shortly afterwards he became Nawāb Nāzim of Bengal, Bihar and Orissa, which were thus united under one authority. His rule is chiefly notable for the administrative and financial reforms which he effected. In spite of its wealth and natural fertility, Bengal had hitherto contributed but little to the imperial exchequer and had sometimes been a drain upon it, money having to be remitted to cover the Bengal deficit. Under Murshid Kuli Khān all this was changed, and a crore and fifty lakhs of rupees were sent annually to Delhi. Bengal also lost the evil reputation it had as a kind of unhealthy penal settlement. The *Riyazu-s-Salātin* tells us that before his time the Mughal nobles had regarded Bengal as "not only fatal to human life, but an actual haunt of demons. Now, hearing that it had been turned into a fertile garden without a thorn, they eagerly sought for offices."

In the general disintegration of the Mughal Empire which followed the death of Aurangzeb, the Nawābs became more and more independent, and "paid little obedience and less revenue to Delhi." The Viceroyalty tended to become hereditary, but in 1740 the third Nawāb of Murshid Kuli Khān's line was overthrown by Ali Vardi Khān, an Afghan adventurer who had been appointed Deputy Governor of Bihār. His rule lasted for 16 troubled years and is a dismal record of wars, revolts and massacres, the land being perpetually harassed by the invasions of the Marāthas and the rebellions of Ali Vardi Khān's own relatives and generals. The Marāthas were at last bought off by the cession of Orissa and the annual payment of twelve lakhs of rupees. Sirāj-ud-daula succeeded five years later, and within three months had attacked the English and driven them out of their settlements, the capture of Calcutta culminating in the tragedy of the Black Hole. Calcutta was recaptured by Clive and Admiral Watson, and peace concluded with the Nawāb early in 1757. The peace lasted only a few months. A plot for the overthrow of Sirāj-ud-daula was formed at Murshidābād, and overtures were made to and accepted by Clive. In June 1757 he advanced with a body of 1000 Europeans and 2000 sepoys, and having routed the Nawāb's army of 50,000 men at Plassey, proceeded to install Mīr Jafar, one of the principal conspirators. Mīr Jafar, though amenable to the point of obsequiousness, soon proved inefficient. Having failed to carry out his undertaking to provide funds for the pay of the troops, on which the power of the British rested, he was deposed and Mīr Kāsim Ali set up in his place.

Mīr Kāsim, who made his headquarters at Monghyr, was not content to be merely a puppet Nawāb. His efforts to enforce the authority which properly belonged to his office brought him into conflict with the English. War broke out, but ended as soon as the trained levies of the English took the field, not, however, before 198 unfortunate English prisoners at Patna had been butchered in cold blood, under Mīr Kāsim's orders, by a renegade German officer in his service. Mīr Kāsim took refuge with the Vizier of Oudh, who was defeated by the English troops at Buxar in 1764. The success of the English brought the Emperor himself a suppliant into their camp, and next year he made the East India Company a grant of the Diwāni or financial administration of Bengal, Bihar and Orissa. This was a mere empty form of words so far as Orissa was concerned, for the Mughal writ did not run in that province, which was still in the grip of the Marāthas. As the Diwāni included the administration of civil justice and the right to maintain the army, as well as the collection of the revenues, this grant made the English masters of the country *de jure* as well as *de facto*. Warren Hastings removed the capital from Murshidābād to Calcutta in 1772, when also the direct revenue administration was made over to European officers; while in 1790 Lord Cornwallis announced that he had "resolved to accept the superintendence of criminal justice throughout the provinces." The only function of Government that still remained to the Nawāb was thus transferred to the English, and the Nawāb lost the last shadow of his authority.

Growth of the English Power. It was little more than a century and a half since the English had first appeared as humble merchants begging for permission to engage in trade and for land on which to build factories. Two English merchants, who had come overland to Patna, started business there in 1620, but left the place next year, and a second attempt to establish an agency there in 1632 ended in failure. The real advance was to be made from the sea-board. In 1633 a band of eight Englishmen under Ralph Cartwright set sail from Masulipatam in a crazy native junk and established factories first at Hariharpur in the Cuttack district and then at Balasore. In 1650 it was resolved to go further inland and found settlements in Bengal itself. The first settlement was made at Hooghly, and shortly afterwards factories were started at Cossimbazar, Patna and Dacca. All these were good centres from which to tap trade, but all had one defect, viz., that the factories were liable to attack, and their goods to confiscation, by a hostile or capricious Governor. The Directors of the East India Company at length determined to free themselves from dependence on the native authorities, who, they declared, "having got the knack of trampling upon us and extorting what they please of our estate from us, by the besieging of our factories and stopping of our boats, will never forbear from doing so till we have made them as sensible of our power as we have of our truth and justice."

The policy of securing a fortified post on or near the sea had long been urged by their officers and was at last accepted by them. The site of Calcutta was selected by Job Charnock, who "had had enough of fenceless factories and resolved to create for his masters a stronghold which would be a surer guarantee than any *farmān*." The Directors approved his choice of the place as "the best and fittest on the Main," as well they might, for it had strong natural defences, while the Hooghly river, the natural gateway of the foreign trade of Bengal, ensured easy access to the sea and could always be commanded by the sea power. The first permanent settlement was made here in August 1690, and though the pioneers suffered grievously from disease and death, 460 out of 1200 settlers dying before January 1691, the new town grew steadily. The English had thus at length a *pied à terre* of their own, and in the eighteenth century their trade and political power rapidly increased, until, as we have seen, they held Bengal in the hollow of their hand.

The secret of their success is well explained by Sir Alfred Lyall in *The Rise of the British Dominion in India*: "The inherent feebleness of our adversaries, the inability to govern or defend their possessions, obviously explains why the English, who could do both, so rapidly made room for themselves in a country, which, though rich and populous, was in a practical sense masterless. It must also be remembered that Bengal and the other provinces bordering on the sea in which the English won these facile triumphs, were far more defenceless than the inland country, partly through the dilapidation of the central power, partly because the people of these tracts are naturally less warlike than elsewhere, and partly by the accident that they were just then very ill-governed....They had only to upset a few unstable rulers of foreign descent, whose title rested on dexterous usurpation; and to disperse by their trained battalions, European and native, great bodies of hired troops who had usually no interest in the war beyond their pay. The inland country was being ruined by rapine and exactions; trade and cultivation had fallen low; and the position of the minor native powers was so unsteady through military weakness and financial embarrassments that any of them might be destroyed by the loss of one campaign or even a single battle." As regards the people, they "were becoming a masterless multitude swaying to and fro in the political storm, and clinging to any power, natural or supernatural, that seemed likely to protect them. They were prepared to acquiesce in the assumption of authority by any one who could show himself able to discharge the most elementary functions of government in the preservation of life and property."

British rule. The foregoing observations are sufficient to show that, when the British took over the administration, they succeeded to a legacy of trouble. The limits of space forbid any but a bare mention of the measures which had to be taken to hunt down bands of robbers and armed *sannyāsis*, whose numbers were swollen by swarms of masterless men, who had formerly found employment in the native armies. The difficulties of administration were increased by the famine of 1770, which caused a fearful loss of life; the margin of cultivation receded and the jungle was let in. Two years later Warren Hastings stated that at least one-third of the inhabitants had perished, and in 1789 Lord Cornwallis reported that one-third of the land was "a jungle inhabited only by wild beasts." In 1803 another distressful country was added to their charge by the conquest of Orissa, which for the last half century had suffered from the misgovernment of the Marāthas. "Their administration," wrote Mr Stirling in his *Account of Orissa* (1822), "was fatal to the welfare of the people and the prosperity of the country, and exhibits a picture of misrule, anarchy, weakness, rapacity and violence combined, which makes one wonder how society can have been kept together under so calamitous a tyranny." Here, as elsewhere, it was the task of the British to evolve order out of chaos, to substitute the settled orderly ways of peace for a reign of rapine.

One of the most fascinating but least known chapters in the history of British rule in this part of India is the pacification of semi-savage races and the conversion of restless marauders into quiet cultivators. This was effected partly by force of arms and partly by the personal influence of individual officers. Such an officer was Cleveland, who before his death, at the early age of 29 in 1874, had won over the Pahārias of the Rājmahāl Hills, hitherto known and feared as savage banditti. The epitaph on his tomb at Bhāgalpur records: "Without bloodshed or the terror of authority, employing only the means of conciliation, confidence and benevolence, he attempted and achieved the entire subjection of the lawless and savage inhabitants of the Jungleterry of Rajamahall, who had long infested neighbouring lands by their predatory incursions, inspired them with a taste for the arts of civilized life and attached them to the British government by a conquest over their minds—the most permanent as the most rational mode of dominion." The same words might be used to describe the work of many another officer unknown to fame.

The chief sphere of such work was Chota Nagpur, "the home of numerous non-Aryan tribes, who were never properly subjugated either by the early Aryan invaders or by the Pathān and Mughal emperors, or indeed by any outside power until the advent of the British." Their country was in fact almost *terra incognita* to the Musalmāns, among whom it was known as Jharkhand, i.e., the forest land, a vast unexplored tract stretching from Rohtāsgarh to the borders of Orissa. Here irritating and inglorious little wars had to be waged against elusive bands. "It is all a joke," wrote one officer in 1768, "to talk of licking these jungle fellows. They have not the least idea of fighting; they are like a parcel of wasps; they endeavour to sting you with their arrows and then fly off." Gradually, however, under the influence of a succession of firm but sympathetic officers, these restless races were tamed and civilized rather than subjugated.

Further to the south-east the British came into contact with the Khonds, who still practised human sacrifice. In spite of every effort, this horrid practice was not really put down until the despatch of an expedition in 1847, when "districts unheard of and unvisited by any European were traversed over; more gloomy pestilential regions were rarely seen."

The work among the aboriginals was checked more than once by rebellions connected with agrarian discontent. In Chota Nagpur there were risings in 1811, 1820 and 1831, which can be traced to the oppression of the aboriginals by Hindu and Musalmān landlords. A more serious rebellion broke out in 1855 among the Santāls of the Santāl Parganas, who were infuriated by the exactions of Hindu land-jobbers and usurers. Seeing their lands usurped by others, and themselves reduced to bond-servants, they rose with the idea of avenging themselves on their oppressors and found themselves arrayed, with their axes, bows and arrows, against the

British army. They themselves declared that they were warring, not against the British but against the Bengalis; on the latter they perpetrated fiendish outrages—slow roasting of men, ripping up of women, torture of children, and drinking of the blood of their victims. The rising was suppressed after a desperate but hopeless resistance, but really did good, for it drew attention to the grievances of the Santāls and led to the introduction of a system of administration suited to their needs.

On the north-east the British were forced to make small extensions of the frontier, mainly in consequence of the aggression of hill races, who mistook long-suffering for weakness and regarded concessions as proof of timidity. In 1814, during the Nepal war, the British entered into an alliance with the Raja of Sikkim, and in 1835 obtained from him a lease of the site of Darjeeling and some surrounding mountains for use as a sanatarium. His seizure in 1849 of Dr Campbell, Superintendent of Darjeeling, and of Sir Joseph Hooker, while travelling in Sikkim, led to the annexation of the land bestowed on him after the Nepal war, which now forms the Darjeeling Tarai. A succession of outrages committed by the Bhutanese, capped by insults offered to a British envoy in 1864, brought about the Bhutān war of the same year, which ended in the cession of the Duārs in Jalpaiguri and of Kalimpong in Darjeeling. The only other noteworthy event in the frontier history is the Sikkim war of 1888, in which the Tibetans were driven out of a part of Sikkim which they had occupied.

To the extreme south-east, the Chittagong Hill Tracts were long exposed to raids by savage hill tribes, who were sometimes impelled by the pangs of hunger and the hope of plunder to descend on the peaceful villages of the plains, at other times urged by a murderous thirst for blood, their sole object being to obtain heads. These raids continued without any long intermission until 1891, when the Lushai Hills were annexed.

Though there have been these small frontier troubles, the internal peace has remained undisturbed since the Mutiny of 1857. The events of this fanatical outbreak are so well known, that it is not necessary to relate how the seeds of disaffection were sown at Dum-Dum and Barrackpore and how the first overt acts of mutiny were committed at the latter place and at Berhampore, or to tell of the mutiny of the troops at Dinapore and of the gallant defence of the little house at Arrah. The people generally held aloof except in Shāhābād and Sambalpur. In the former a brave old Rājput landholder named Kuar Singh had a large following. In the latter there was a fierce and obstinate revolt. It had been annexed eight years previously by Lord Dalhousie, in pursuance of the doctrine of lapse, on the death without issue of its last native chief. The landholders had been exasperated by injudicious settlements and were only too ready to rally round the representatives of the old line.

In a few other places the Mutiny caused a temporary breakdown of the British authority, a brief interregnum, in which the bad old days of foray and plunder were renewed. The scenes described by the Collector of Gaya were not confined to that district. "Ten days of anarchy," he wrote, "had disgusted all quiet men with what they called the Hindustāni Rāj. They had seen how every element of disorder, violence and wickedness was rife, how the village ryots as well as the town *badmāsh* instinctively turned to plunder and violence." There was, he noted, a "universal identification of a Hindustāni government with license and plunder. *Hindustāni Rāj huā, Kuar Singh ke Rāj. Lut! Lut!* (We have a Hindustāni rule, the rule of Kuar Singh. Loot! Loot!) were the cries with which one zamindar attacked a weaker one, one village preyed upon a neighbouring hamlet, or a dozen scoundrels knocked down and fleeced a solitary traveller."

Bengal was directly administered by the Governor-General, or in his absence by the senior member of his council, until 1854, when it was placed under the charge of a Lieutenant-Governor. Assam was detached and placed

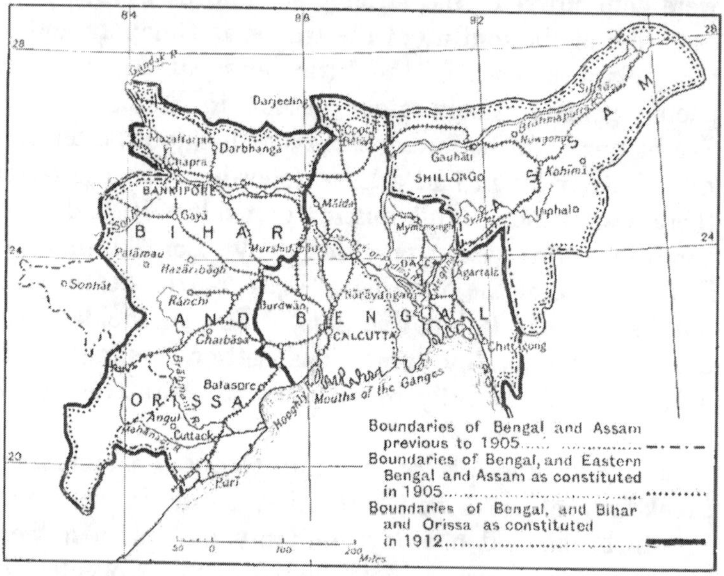

Fig. 41. Map showing redistributions of territory effected in 1905 and 1912

under a Chief Commissioner in 1874, but, even after this reduction, the province had an area but little less than that of France or the German Empire, while its population had risen by 1901 to over 78 millions and was considerably more than a quarter of that of the whole Indian Empire. This being too large a charge for one administration, Bengal was divided in 1905. The eastern portion (about one-fourth of the whole area) was separated and, with the addition of Assam, was constituted the province of Eastern Bengal and Assam under a Lieutenant-Governor with headquarters at Dacca. The remainder of the province continued to be administered from Calcutta by the Lieutenant-Governor of Bengal (who was given an executive Council in 1910), but five States on the borders of Chota Nagpur were transferred to the Central Provinces in exchange for four other States and the district of Sambalpur.

This partition aroused deep discontent among the Bengali Hindus, who resented their division between two separate administrations. It also afforded an opportunity for the development of seditious schemes previously conceived. A party hostile to British rule came into prominence, revolutionary organizations, which had been in existence long before, gained ground, and there was an outbreak of political crime, marked by the use of bombs and the assassin's pistol, and, also, in Eastern Bengal, by the plunder of defenceless villagers. In the hope of removing grievances and allaying unrest, a fresh scheme of division was carried out in 1912, when also the capital of India was moved from Calcutta to Delhi. Assam again became a Chief Commissionership, the whole of the Bengali-speaking area was constituted a Presidency under a Governor in Council, and Bihar, Chota Nagpur and Orissa were made a separate province, known as Bihar and Orissa, under a Lieutenant-Governor in Council. The map on the opposite page shows the areas affected by the partition of 1905 and the repartition of 1912.

CHAPTER XIII

ARCHAEOLOGY

THE province of Bihar and Orissa is singularly rich in remains of a date anterior to the Christian era. They belong to the Buddhist period and, for the most part, commemorate the greatness of the Mauryan empire. The oldest and most interesting are found at Patna and Bodh Gaya. In the former the remains of a great pillared hall were unearthed in 1912–13, which date back to the third century B.C. This was a stately building of nearly a hundred columns, which is said to have a remarkable similarity to the splendid Hall of a Hundred Columns at Persepolis. It was erected by the emperor Asoka, and, with the exception of *stūpas* and a *chaitya* hall recently discovered at Sānchi, is the oldest structure known to exist in India. At Bodh Gaya the oldest Buddhist memorial is a stone railing ornamented with friezes, panels and bosses, which display considerable artistic skill. The temple itself, which has a tower 180 feet high, is a modern restoration carried out by the Government, but it is claimed that in its main features it reproduces the magnificent fane on which the Chinese pilgrim Hiuen Tsiang gazed with rapt reverence and admiration in the seventh century. Here too is a large collection of *stūpas*, which pilgrims to this Mecca of the Buddhistic world left as memorials of their visits. They are of all sizes and extend over many centuries, beginning with the simple monolith of the early ages—the *stūpa* was originally a copy in brick or stone of an earthen sepulchral tumulus—and ending with the ornamented spire of the mediaeval period. The type has persisted to the present day, sepulchral monuments of a similar character, called *chortens*, being set up over the remains of the dead by the Buddhists of Darjeeling and Sikkim.

Other monuments of Asoka are the monolithic pillars which still stand in a few places. The finest is the lion-crowned pillar at Lauriya Nandangarh in Champāran, which consists of a polished block of sandstone, 33 feet

Fig. 42. Cave in the Barābar Hills

long, with a capital nearly 7 feet in length. Two other pillars are found at Rāmpurwa and Lauriya Ararāj in the same district, and a fourth at Basārh (the old Vaisāli) in Muzaffarpur. All four were set up on the imperial road from Pātaliputra (Patna) to Nepal. The edicts of the emperor are inscribed on rock at the Dhauli hill in the Puri district, and there is another inscription on a hill near Sasarām. This method of issuing proclamations may perhaps have been adopted in imitation

Fig. 43. Buddhistic remains at Kauwadol

of the great Persian king Darius. Immediately above the Dhauli inscription the rock has been carved into the likeness of an elephant, which is the oldest known stone carving of that animal in India.

To the Mauryan period also belong the so-called caves in the Barābar Hills of Gaya. These are really chambers hewn out of the solid rock, which served as hermitages. The skill with which the early Indian

Fig. 44. Carvings on railing at Bodh Gaya

mason could manipulate such intractable material as the hard granite of these hills is shown by the steely polish produced on the chiselled stone. The Khandagiri and Udayagiri Hills in Puri are also honeycombed with rock-cut chambers and cells of the Mauryan age, which are the oldest authenticated Jain remains.

Buddhistic statuary of a later date is common in the Gaya district. With the exception of the Graeco-Buddhistic sculptures of Gandhāra, these images are the only class of Indian Buddhistic art that has come down through the long procession of the ages in a fair state of completeness.

The noblest monuments of the **Hindu period** are the temples at Konārak and Bhubaneswar in Puri. The shrine at Konārak is also commonly known as the Black

Fig. 45. Chorten at Darjeeling

Pagoda, this being a name given to it by early navigators to distinguish it from the next landmark along the coast, the temple of Jagannāth at Puri, which was known as the White Pagoda. Built in the thirteenth century A.D., it has excited admiration for over six centuries and has been held to be the finest extant Hindu temple. "There is," writes Sir J. H. Marshall, Director-General of Archaeology in India, "no monument of Hinduism, I think, that is at once so stupendous and so perfectly proportioned as the Black Pagoda, and none which leaves so deep an

Fig. 46. Tiger cave on Udayagiri Hill

impression on the memory." It is remarkable both for the profusion and delicacy of its carving and also for the massiveness of its structure. The tower, which was originally 190 feet high, was crowned by a great stone slab, 25 feet thick, the weight of which is estimated at 2000 tons. A huge piece of sculpture representing a lion rampant on an elephant, 20 feet in height and 15 feet long at the base, projected from the spire, as in other Orissan temples, but has now fallen to the ground. How such enormous stones were raised is a mystery, but the tradition is that the structure

Fig. 47. Elephant cave on Udayagiri Hill

was imbedded in sand and that they were brought up the slope on rollers. The temple was dedicated to the sun-god, the wheels and horses of his chariot being carved in stone to indicate its character, and it has been described as the most exquisite memorial of sun-worship in India.

The temples at Bhubaneswar, of which about one hundred are still standing, were built at different times between the eighth and twelfth centuries A.D., and are magnificent examples of the Orissan style of architecture. Many of them are covered with richly wrought mouldings and exquisite minute carving. "Most people," wrote

Fig. 48. Temple at Bhubaneswar

Mr Fergusson, "would be of opinion that a building four times as large would produce a greater and more imposing architectural effect; but this is not the way a Hindu ever looked at the matter. Infinite labour

Fig. 49. Carving on Konärak temple

bestowed on every detail was the mode in which he thought he could render his temple most worthy of the deity; and whether he was right or wrong, the effect of the whole is certainly marvellously beautiful."

In Bengal the Hindus developed a different and peculiar local style of architecture. Its salient characteristic is a curved roof—the term "hump-backed" best expresses its shape—modelled on the form of the thatched roof

Fig. 50. Carved figure at Konārak temple

of the ordinary Bengal hut. In some cases a tower rises from the centre of the roof, in addition to which there may be four or eight, and sometimes even more, towers at the corners. Temples with five such towers are called *pāncharatna*, and those with nine towers *navaratna*. The best collection of temples of this style is to be seen at Bishnupur in the Bānkura district. They are built either of brick or laterite, and some are richly ornamented with carvings in low relief. One of them, which is called Jor Bangla (meaning the pair of bungalows), looks exactly like two Bengali huts joined together with a tower in the middle. The word bungalow, it may be added, originally meant merely a Bengal house.

In Bihar, on the other hand, the distinctive feature of temple architecture is a pyramidal spire or tower,

Fig. 51. Tomb at Gaur

the outline of which was almost certainly suggested by the natural bend of bamboos planted apart and brought together at the top.

The same imitation of the structure of the common Bengal house is observable in the Muhammadan period, when Bengal produced a peculiar style of architecture unlike the usual Saracenic. Owing to the absence of stone throughout the greater part of the country the

Muhammadan builders had recourse to brick. "The use of brick forced the builders to elaborate a local arched style of their own, and further, as Mr Fergusson pointed out, to introduce a new mode of roofing, which, though but little agreeable to our tastes, came to be regarded by the natives, whether Hindu or Muhammadan, as a most elegant form, and spread, in the seventeenth century, as far up the Gangetic valley as Delhi, and a little later even to Amritsar. The curvilinear form given to the eaves, descending at the corners of the structure, was almost certainly suggested in the form of the huts, constantly roofed with bamboos and thatch, in which the Bengalis always use a curvilinear form of roof." A typical specimen of this form of roof is shown in fig. 51.

The buildings of the pre-Mughal period are further distinguished by a massive solidity due to the use of the same building material. "The erection of large buildings of brick required heavy piers for the arches and thicker walls than those constructed entirely of stone. Such piers and walls, when enriched by a casing of moulded tiles, would appear still heavier; and for tiles, when opportunity offered, a facing of carved stone might be substituted. This Bengal style is not like any other, but a purely local one, with heavy short pillars faced, at least, with stone, supporting pointed arches and vaults of brick." The finest examples are found at the old capitals of Gaur and Pandua. At Gaur one of the most conspicuous monuments is a tower, 85 feet high, called the Firoz Minār (fig. 38). Not far off in the town of Old Mālda is a curious structure—a brick tower from which project stones cut to resemble elephants' tusks.

The Pathān style of architecture, which developed in North-West India, is far more graceful. One of the most magnificent specimens of this style is the mausoleum of the emperor Sher Shāh (1540–45) at Sasarām (fig. 40). This is an imposing structure of stone rising from a large terrace, which is built in the middle of a spacious tank almost large enough to be called a lake. The apex of the dome is 100 feet from the base, and rises to a height of 150 feet above the level of the water. The tomb, in which is the severely simple grave of the emperor, is remarkable for the great span of its dome, which is

Fig. 52. Palace buildings at Rohtāsgarh

13 feet wider than the dome of the Tāj Mahāl, and for grandeur and dignity is said to be unequalled in Northern India.

Hill fortresses of the Pathān and Mughal period are extant at Shergarh and Rohtāsgarh (fig. 39) in the Kaimur Hills. Shergarh, which was erected in the time of Sher Shāh, contains some underground chambers—a feature not found in any other building in the east of India. Rohtās-gahr contains the palace of the Mughal viceroy of Bihar, and though the buildings are of no special architectural merit, they are of interest as being the only complete specimens of Mughal civil architecture in this part of India. The finest monument of the Mughals is the mausoleum of Makhdum Daulat at Maner in the Patna district, built in 1616 in a style characteristic of the architecture of Jahāngīr's reign.

CHAPTER XIV

RACES

THE truism that India is a land of many peoples is nowhere more capable of demonstration than in Bengal, Bihar and Orissa. The people are not only distinct from those of other parts of India, but differ widely among themselves, presenting extraordinary varieties of type and standards of civilization. At the one extremity are cultured gentlemen, who have won triumphs in the fields of art, science and literature: as recently as 1913, the Nobel prize for literature was awarded to a Bengali poet, Rabindranāth Tagore. At the other extremity we find primitive races so ignorant of the elementary principles of calculation, that they cannot count above 100. The immemorial method of counting among the Santāls, for instance, consists of tying knots in pieces of string. This device had to be employed when the first census was taken in 1872. Strings of different colours were used—black for adult males, red for females, white for boys and yellow for girls—and the numbers were recorded by tying a knot for each person on the appropriate string. The Juangs of the Orissa States, again, are such a primitive race that the name of leaf-wearers is applied to them. In the more remote parts of the Orissa States the men still wear only a few leaves pinned together, while the women have nothing more than an apron of leaves. Till the nineteenth century they had no knowledge of the metals and used only stone implements. The language of these people contained no word for iron or any other metal, and similar signs of barbarism are found in the speech of other tribes. Along the Himalayas, for example, there are, as Hodgson points out, remnants of races who express agriculture by the term "felling" or "clearing the forest," who have no names for village, horse or money of any kind, and whose language is destitute of terms for almost every abstract idea. How closely the wild life of the jungle presses on modern civilization may be illustrated by two personal experiences. In the course of a morning I have been in a town with a system of electric lighting and have found in the forest sticks of wood that some man of the woods had used to obtain fire by friction. In another town I have seen a large meeting of educated Hindus listening with rapt attention to an address on Theosophy by Mrs Besant, and have been given most vivid descriptions of evil spirits by an educated Hindu, whose language recalled the account of genii familiar to readers of the *Arabian Nights*; not many miles away were villagers who told the tale of a boy who had been carried off and brought up by wolves.

In spite of diversities, the constituent elements of the population may be reduced to a few distinct types, the origin of which may be traced to the early movements of the people sketched in the preceding chapter. There are three main stocks, viz., Dravidian, Mongolian and Aryan, or more properly Indo-Aryan, which represent ethnological strata, the later being superimposed on and largely commingled with the earlier. The oldest races are the Dravidians, who survive, like an island in a sea of alien races, in the hilly country of Chota Nagpur, the Orissa States and the Santāl Parganas. Mongolians are found in the mountainous country to the extreme north and south-east of Bengal, and there is also a strong Mongoloid strain in some of the tribal castes of the plains of Bengal. Lastly, there is the Aryan element, which has modified the original type in nearly all parts, the higher castes having the strongest and the lower castes the weakest infusion of Aryan blood. That it is not more in evidence is due to the fact that not only was the Aryan invasion late chronologically, but the invaders were not numerous enough to supplant the races whom they found in possession. Generally speaking, the further one proceeds from Bihar, the first home of Aryan colonists, the more attenuated does the Aryan strain become. The Meghna is believed to have marked the limits of the wanderings of the Aryans referred to in the *Mahābhārata*, and the country to the east of it was stigmatized as *Pāndava barjita desh*, a land of utter barbarism. The popular proverb that the men of Eastern Bengal are no men, while the Oriyas are tailless monkeys, enshrines the tradition of ages and dates back to a time when the people of Eastern Bengal and Orissa had so little Aryan blood, that the Aryans higher up the Gangetic valley looked down on them as inferior races with no claims to brotherhood. The present inhabitants of the country belong either to one or other of these three main stocks or represent types formed by their fusion or admixture. Altogether, four different types are distinguished by ethnologists on the basis of anthropometrical data, viz., Aryo-Dravidian, Mongolo-Dravidian, Mongoloid and Dravidian.

The **Aryo-Dravidian** is, as the name implies, the result of the intermixture, in varying proportions, of the Indo-Aryan and Dravidian types, the former predominating in the higher and the latter in the lower social groups. It is found among the people of Bihar and is characterized by a long head with a tendency to medium, a complexion ranging from lightish brown to black, and a nose varying from medium to broad.

The **Mongolo-Dravidian** or Bengali type is peculiar to Bengal and Orissa, where it has representatives among all classes. It is a blend of the Mongolian and Dravidian races, with a strain of Indo-Aryan blood in the higher social groups. Men of this type are distinguished by broad heads and dark skins, and usually have a good crop of hair on the head, other signs of their origin being a medium stature and a medium nose. Not all are true to this type, for many of the higher classes have fair skins and fine narrow noses, which point to an Aryan ancestry. "No special theory," writes Mr J. D. Anderson, in *The Peoples of India*, "is required to account for the physical and mental qualities of the Mongolo-Dravidians of Bengal. No doubt the original population was Dravidian with a strong intermixture of Tibeto-Burmese blood, especially in the east and north-east. But the Hindu religion, developed in the sacred Midlands round Benares, spread to Bengal, bringing with it the Indo-European speech which in medieval times became the copious and supple Bengali tongue. From the west too came what we in Europe would call the gentry, the priestly and professional castes. These have acquired most of the local physical characters, dusky skin, low stature, round heads. But in nearly all cases, the fineness and sharp outline of the nose shows their aristocratic origin, and in some cases a Bengali Brahman has all the physical distinction of a western priest or sage."

The **Mongoloid** type is found in the Himalayan area to the north, among the Lepchas and several Nepalese tribes such as the Limbus, Murmis and Gurungs, and also, in the hilly country to the south-east of Bengal, among the tribes of the Chittagong Hill Tracts, who have a strong infusion of Burmese blood. The physical features of this type are well known. The head is broad; complexion dark with a yellowish tinge; hair on the face scanty; stature short or below the average; nose fine to broad; face characteristically flat; eyelids often oblique.

Lastly, we have the interesting **Dravidian** type, which pervades the Chota Nagpur plateau. Its salient characteristics are a dark, almost blackish skin, a squat figure, dark beady eyes, long heads, plentiful hair with a tendency to curl, and a nose which is of negro-like proportions: the nasal index of the Sauria Pahāria, who is regarded as the extreme type of the Dravidian race as now found in this area, is nearly the same as that of the negro.

The man in the street knows of no such scientific classification, but groups the people in a rough and ready way by language and geographical situation. He recognizes five broad groups, viz., Bengalis, Bihāris, Oriyas, hillmen of the Himalayas and the many tribes of the Chota Nagpur plateau, whom he lumps together as Kols, or simply as "aboriginals." This popular classification is based on certain common characteristics, of which a sketch may be given. It must, however, be predicated that there are such diversities between Hindus and Muhammadans, the life of the villages and the towns, the educated classes and the ignorant peasantry, that generalizations are apt to be misleading. A comprehensive analysis, which would take into account all these factors, is, however, precluded by the limits of space and the inherent complexity of the subject.

Bengalis. In the case of the Bengalis, a brief mention must first be made of the division created by religion.

There is no little truth in the saying: "Religions in the East take the place of nationalities." The line of religious cleavage is not confined to differences of creed. The Hindu, for instance, practises early marriage and regards widow marriage as disreputable. The reverse is the case among the Muhammadans, who, largely on this account, are increasing much faster than the Hindus. There is also considerable difference between their receptiveness of education. The Bengalis as a whole are the most educated people in India—not only does the province contain a larger number of literate persons than any other, but the proportion of literates to the general population is higher than elsewhere. The Muhammadans however lag far behind the Hindus. The former represent more than half the population, but contribute only three-tenths of those able to read and write; there are five literate Hindus to every two literate Muhammadans. There is even greater disparity in the case of those who have received an English education, 2 per cent. of the Hindus, but only 3 per mille of the Muhammadans having a knowledge of that language. Their superior educational qualifications have gained for the Hindus a predominating position in the professions and public service, and they also have the larger share in the industries and commerce of the country.

Considerable misconception has been caused by Macaulay's highly coloured account of the Bengalis as a compound of effeminacy, craft and subtlety. He himself had only a few years' experience of Calcutta and did not come into contact with village life. How different this is, may be realized from a brief description of the people in a typical Bengal district. "The people," according to the *Rangpur District Gazetteer*, "are generally good-natured, charitable, patient and sociable. They are usually peaceful and law-abiding. Out of the courts, that is to say when not tutored by *mukhtears* and *diwānias*, they are generally truthful in the main, though prone to exaggeration."

Love of litigation is the weak point of these patient tillers of the soil, and makes them an easy prey to the *diwānias* above mentioned, who are their professional advisers on legal and other affairs. "The *diwānia* runs his client's cases for him, drafts his petitions, and engages and instructs his *mukhtears* and pleaders. No villager will take a step or give any information without first consulting him. Were the checks imposed by a sense of duty and public opinion present, such a system would be of incalculable benefit to the people. But unfortunately they are not, and the average *diwānia* takes advantage of the ignorance and blind trust of his clients to serve his own ends. He finds it profitable to encourage and prolong litigation, to concoct false cases and tutor witnesses, to instigate crime and to hinder the investigations of the police. The majority are sea-lawyers and touts of the worst description. Almost every village has one or more of these functionaries." Other Gazetteers bear similar witness to the litigious spirit of the Bengalis.

The charge of universal effeminacy brought by Macaulay is disproved by specific instances, such as the cool courage of Bengali elephant hunters, the intrepid skill of those excellent sailors, the lascars of Chittagong, etc. Bishop Heber indeed says that Clive's army was raised chiefly from Bengal, but the sepoys he recruited in Bengal were mostly up-countrymen, and not Bengalis. It is, however, true that the Bengalis generally are not robust. Their physique is the product of their environment, for they live in a fat and fertile land, with a humid and enervating climate, in which fever is rife. Even the hardiest races would find their energies sapped by centuries of fever. The Bengali, therefore, compares unfavourably in physique with the countrymen of Northern India. He is light of bone and deficient in muscular strength, and has a low level of metabolism. His want of robustness makes him less fitted than more stalwart races for hard and exhausting labour, and produces a natural dislike for bodily drudgery. At the same time, the Bengalis generally are well-to-do, according to Indian economic standards, and can afford to employ foreign labour. They are not forced by necessity, like the Bihāris, to migrate periodically in search of employment which will eke out the income from their ancestral fields and orchards; and they leave others to supply the greater part of the labour required for the mills and mines.

As regards mental qualities, the Bengali has a quick alert intellect, which comes to maturity at an early age. He is stronger in destructive criticism and analysis than in constructive genius, and has a great command of language and argument. The up-countryman, who is better at deeds than words, is somewhat suspicious of this mental agility, and has put his estimate of it in two proverbs. One is: "The Bengali is the brother of the white ant, which builds nothing but undermines palaces"; the other is: "Go to Europe for manufactures, and to Bengal for talk."

For some time past there has been a ferment of new ideas, which stultifies the old aphorism of the "unchanging East." The idea of nationalism has taken root, and one of its products has been an effort to make the country industrially independent. The Swadeshi movement has led to the formation of companies, which however are only too often ephemeral, and the establishment of small factories, financed, organized and directed by the Bengalis themselves. A society has been formed to enable young men to be trained in modern industrial processes in Europe, America and Japan, so that on their return they may assist in the development of manufactures on modern lines. The effect of the new ideas of social service is seen in the organization of bands of volunteers for the relief of distress in time of famine or flood. During the Burdwān floods of 1913 some Brahmans even volunteered for the work of removing dead bodies, when the scavengers, whose work it was, went on strike.

The Bengali is readily adaptive, and the lesson that knowledge is power is being applied in fresh fields. There is the greatest readiness to adopt Western inventions; the bicycle, sewing machine, gramophone and cinematograph are now quite common. Physical culture is not neglected. Association football is popular, and it is not unworthy of note that in 1911 a Bengali team, many of whom played with bare feet, won the Indian Football Association Shield, defeating regimental and other European teams.

Bihāris. The Bihāris, or people of Bihar, though larger and better developed than the Bengalis, are as a rule not big or muscular. They are, however, wiry and capable of sustained endurance; four men, for instance, will carry a heavy man in a *pālki*—in itself no small weight—ten miles in three hours or even less. They are assiduous and industrious cultivators, especially in South Bihar, where they have devised an ingenious system of irrigation that taps and impounds all the available water supply. Here, till late at night, and again before dawn, one may hear the constant clang of the iron bucket in which the peasant draws up water from the well.

The Bihāris have been described as a "sluggish and depressed peasantry" far different from "the quick-witted and adaptive Bengali of the deltaic rice swamps," but the charge is too sweeping and neglects other qualities, such as stability of character and power of conduct. It is true that they are conservative, and that they have neither the mental versatility nor the education of the Bengalis, though an exception must be made of the writer caste of Kayasths, whose shrewdness and acumen are proverbial. On the whole, they are men of slow thoughts but long memories, vigorous and disciplined—traits

Fig. 53. Bihāri cultivators in a poppy field

recognized by the Bengalis themselves, who employ them to guard their persons and property in preference to their own countrymen. The Bhojpuris, or inhabitants of Sāran and Shāhābād, in particular, are wanting neither in enterprise nor resourcefulness. They are described by Sir George Grierson as "an energetic race ever ready to accommodate themselves to circumstances. An alert and active nationality, with few scruples and considerable abilities, dearly loving a fight for fighting's sake, they have spread all over Aryan India, each man ready to carve his fortune out of any opportunity which may present itself to him. They furnish a rich mine of recruitment to the Hindustāni army, and, on the other hand, they took a prominent part in the mutiny of 1857. As fond as an Irishman is of his stick, the long-boned, stalwart Bhojpuri, with his staff in his hand, is a familiar object striding over fields far from his home. Thousands of them have emigrated to British Colonies and have returned rich men; every year still larger numbers wander over Northern Bengal and seek employment, either honestly as *pālki*-bearers or otherwise as dacoits. Every Bengali zamindar keeps a posse of these men, euphemistically called *darwāns*, to keep his tenants in order. Calcutta, where they are employed, and feared, by the less heroic natives of Bengal, is full of them."

The readiness of the Bihāris to migrate is partly the result of economic necessity. In many parts the population is so dense as to be congested; there is a host of landless labourers—they and their families number $4\frac{2}{3}$ millions, or a fifth of the total population—and a considerable proportion of the peasants' holdings are too small to support them, unless supplemented by the wages of labour. There are, moreover, no large industries, now that the cultivation and manufacture of opium has been stopped and the indigo industry is moribund; and agriculture requires few hands during the greater part of the cold weather. Every year, therefore, at this season hundreds of thousands of Bihāris leave their villages to work in the mills, docks and factories or on the roads, railways and fields of Bengal. They return, for the most part, with their savings after four or five months to resume the cultivation of their own land,

and in the meantime remit money home to their relations. This annual exodus of able-bodied workers is steadily developing as the Bihāri realizes that a few months' labour in Bengal will provide him with a nest-egg for the year. It increases greatly if the crops are short in Bihar, but even in 1911, after bumper crops had been reaped, there were nearly 1¼ million Biḥāris in Bengal at the time of the census. Bengal benefits greatly from this mobility

Fig. 54. A Bihāri Brahman

of labour, and its chief manufactures depend largely on Bihar for their supply of labour.

Oriyas. The Oriyas recall the old idea of the "mild Hindu," being a kindly, peaceable and gentle race. A century ago they were described as "the most mild, quiet and inoffensive people in the Company's territories," and this account still holds good. They are somewhat unenterprising, but are not averse to leaving their homes to better their lot, and outside Orissa they have an excellent reputation as domestic servants—they have supplied the English with bearers since they first came to Bengal—and also as *chaprāsis*, gardeners and labourers; it is astonishing to see what weights Oriya coolies will carry in the jute presses of Calcutta.

Among them the old village life may be seen in all its simplicity, scarcely touched by modern influences. Nowhere else does the peasant make such deep obeisance to his superiors; men may be seen prostrating themselves at full length on the ground, or throwing dust over their heads, by way of courtesy. Of all races in the two provinces they are perhaps the most conservative and priest-ridden, but be it also added, the most devoutly religious; the rules of ceremonial purity are strictly observed, and caste rules are so rigid that mere bodily contact can cause pollution. They have long been addicted to the use of opium, which they regard as a sovereign preventive of chills and fever. The consumption to-day is greater than in any other part of the two provinces, but is no longer excessive. A century ago it was so universal, that it was officially stated that the people might be said to live on opium and could hardly exist without it. When a proclamation was issued confiscating smuggled opium, opium-eaters came before the Magistrate, with ropes round their necks, vowing that they would hang themselves if their supply was stopped. On the other hand, they are a sober race, and do not take to spirits; unlike the Bengalis and Bihāris, they smoke cigars, known as *pikas*.

Physically, the Oriyas are slightly built, slender men, somewhat effeminate in appearance. Their women have a curious sickly look due to their dyeing their skin with saffron, in order to produce a golden hue, which is supposed to enhance their beauty.

Himalayan hillmen. The Himalayan hillmen include three distinct groups, viz., the Lepchas, Bhotias and Nepalese. The **Lepchas**, who are the aborigines of Sikkim, are a peaceful and somewhat primitive people, who are

Fig. 55. A Nepali

never so happy as when they are in their native woods. They are born naturalists, learned in the lore of the jungle, and have separate names for practically every bird, orchid and butterfly. Originally they practised nomadic cultivation, and they still do so where the forests are free, but in the more settled parts they have taken to regular tillage. They still eat freely of jungle produce, from choice and not from necessity; more than 100 different kinds of forest fruits and fungi are said to enter into their fare. They live for the most part in the lower valleys, and do not stand cold well. They are averse to settled labour and fixed employment, and are being

Fig. 56. A Lepcha

largely supplanted by the virile Nepalese. They make excellent servants, however, and though generally wanting in enterprise, some have gone far afield and done excellent entomological work in far distant countries, such as Burma, the Andaman and Nicobar Islands, Sumatra, Borneo and the Malay Archipelago, the Celebes, New

Guinea and Central Africa. The Lepchas in Central Africa were left stranded by the death of their European master far from civilization, but managed to find their way back to Darjeeling with the help of the long arm of British authority.

The **Bhotias** are of Tibetan stock, the name meaning the people of Bhot, the Indian name for Tibet (which is a corruption of the Mongolian Thübot). There are four different groups of them, all of which are represented in Darjeeling and Sikkim, viz., (1) the Sikkimese Bhotias, who are the descendants of Tibetans who settled in Sikkim and intermarried with Lepchas, (2) Sharpa Bhotias, who come from the east of Nepal, *shar* meaning east, (3) Drukpa or Dharma Bhotias, whose original home was in Bhotan, and (4) Tibetan Bhotias from Tibet. They are burly mountaineers with splendid muscular development. Powerfully built, they are capable of carrying the heaviest weights—there is a story that in the days before the railway one of them carried a piano up the hills to Darjeeling 7000 feet above the plains. They are sometimes described as surly and truculent, but the writer of this volume has found them cheery merry people, quick to enjoy a joke, and most willing and resourceful workers.

The **Nepalese** met with in Darjeeling and Sikkim are immigrants or descendants of immigrants from the east of Nepal. They are more Mongolian in appearance than the Nepalese of central Nepal, being generally stuggy little men, with slanting almond-shaped eyes, an almost hairless face and a bullet head. Their character is happily described by Colonel Waddell in *Among the Himalayas*: "Though small in stature, these Nepalese have big hearts, and in many ways resemble the bright, joyous temperament of the Japanese, though lacking altogether the refinement of the latter. Naturally vigorous, excitable and aggressive, they are very law-abiding, driven as they have been to obedience by the draconic punishments of their Gurkha rulers....They are generally undersized but tough and wiry as whip-cord, and so full of energy that it is quite common to see old people scampering nimbly up and down hill

Fig. 57. Nepalese boys

in preference to walking." Though hot-tempered, they are thoroughly amenable to discipline. Their saying "There is no medicine for death, there is no answer to an order" is the proverb of a disciplined people. In this part of the country, they are cultivators and labourers rather than soldiers, and supply nearly the whole labour force of the tea-gardens in the hills. Women work as well as men, and children are taught to carry burdens almost as soon as they can toddle. Though Hindus for the most part—a few are Buddhists—they are not trammelled by caste restrictions like the Hindus of the plains, and will cheerfully accept any employment except a few that are regarded as unclean and degrading. Though no great scholars, they show considerable aptitude for work of a practical kind, e.g., they master the mysteries of the

Fig. 58. Bhotia men and women

tea-garden engine-room and quickly pick up a working knowledge of machinery in electric light and railway works. Drinking, gambling and improvidence are their weak points. They are fond of tea and of a mildly stimulating drink called *marua*, but what they really love is a good strong spirit. They are also confirmed cigarette smokers, men, women and children favouring cheap American brands at ten cigarettes a penny. They have a simple delight in good clothes, ornaments and jewelry. Women may commonly be seen dressed in velvet and decked out with heavy silver necklaces and amulets—sometimes even, on gala days, with gold nose-rings and solid but thin gold plates that serve as earrings.

Tribes of the Chota Nagpur Plateau. The name Kol is commonly used to designate the non-Aryan tribes of the Chota Nagpur plateau, which are known to the ethnologist as Dravidians. It is generally held to be a variant of a word meaning "man," by which in one form or another, such as Ho, Hor and Horo, many of these tribes designate themselves in their native tongue. The name with them is a simple but proud appellation, having the sense of the Latin *Vir*; the Hindus probably adopted the form of Kol in derision because of its similarity to a Sanskrit word meaning "pig."

Their home is in Chota Nagpur, the Orissa States and the Santāl Parganas, but there are large colonies in the districts on the fringe of Chota Nagpur. Some detached outliers are also found far afield in North Bengal, notably in Jalpaiguri, where they man the tea-gardens, and in the Barind, where they have cleared away the jungle and made themselves new homes. Altogether they number over 5 millions, the most numerous race being the Santāls (who call themselves Hor), who aggregate a little over a million. Other large and representative tribes are the Mundas (whose own name for themselves is Horo), Oraons, Hos and Khonds. One of the most primitive races consists of the Sauria Pahārias (who designate themselves Maler), who cling to the hill tops of the Rājmahāl Hills. All these have kept their purity of race and retained their tribal languages and customs, but some, such as the Gonds and Bhumij, have become largely Hinduized and have abandoned the language of their ancestors. The same is also the case with the Savars, originally a wild wandering forest tribe, who have been identified with the Suari of Pliny and the Sabaroi of Ptolemy.

These races are generally small in stature and of a light build. The average height of a man is 5 feet 3 inches and his weight 105 lbs., while a woman averages 4 feet 11 inches in height and 94½ lbs. in weight. It is not possible to give an account of all the different races, but a brief sketch may be given of the Santāls, the most interesting of all, with special reference to certain characteristics which they have in common with others.

The Santāls preserve two features of an earlier stage of civilization. Though now for the most part settled cultivators, they excel in clearing forest and have especial skill in converting jungle and waste land into fertile rice fields. "When," wrote Colonel Dalton, "through their own labour the spread of cultivation has effected denudation, they select a new site, however prosperous they may have been on the old, and retire into the back-woods, where their harmonious flutes sound sweeter, their drums find deeper echoes, and their bows and arrows may once more be utilized." In the second place, they are ardent hunters, as destructive of game as of jungle. The happiest day in the year is that on which they have a common hunt, when, armed with spears, axes, bows and arrows, clubs, sticks and stones, they beat through the jungle in thousands, killing every beast and bird they come across. In their ordinary dealings they display a cheerful straightforwardness, open bluntness and simple honesty, which are refreshing to a European accustomed to the somewhat gloomy and secretive denizen of the plains. Their word is their bond, and a knot on a string is as good as a receipt. They are plucky to a degree. A well authenticated story is told of two Santāl herdsmen, who espied the tail of a leopard sticking through the trellis-work of their cowshed. One ran in and belaboured the leopard with a thick staff, while the other held on to its tail. The leopard was soon *hors de combat* and was eventually killed outright.

Fig. 59. Santāls with a nilgai caught in the annual hunt

In the Santāl war of 1855 they showed the most reckless courage, never knowing when they were beaten and refusing to surrender. On one occasion 45 Santāls took refuge in a mud hut, which they held against the sepoys. Volley after volley was fired into it, and before each volley quarter was offered. Each time the Santāls replied with a discharge of arrows. At last, when their fire ceased, the sepoys entered the hut and found that only one old man was left alive. A sepoy called on him to surrender, whereupon the old man rushed upon him and cut him down with his battle-axe. The same war proved them to be capable of inhuman cruelty. When a Bengali money-lender fell into their hands, they first cut off his feet, with the taunt that that was four annas in the rupee, then hewed off his legs to make up eight annas, then cut his body in two to make up twelve annas, and finally lopped off his head, yelling out in chorus that he had full payment of sixteen annas in the rupee. They regarded, it must be remembered, the Bengalis as their bitter enemies, and to this day they have an intense dislike of the *dikkus*, or foreigners, as they call the Hindus and Musalmāns of the plains.

They are thriftless and careless of the morrow. Bumper crops mean increased opportunities for drinking. Like the blind watchmen of Isaiah, they say in their hearts: "We will fill ourselves with strong drink, and to-morrow shall be as this day." Their love of drink may be realized from the attitude of an old headman, whom a missionary was trying to convert. The old man asked whether the God of the Christians would allow old people to get drunk twice a week. When he heard the shocked reply of the missionary, he quietly said: "Then teach the boys and girls, but leave us alone." They enjoy a carouse, and their harvest festival is a saturnalia, in which they give themselves up to drinking, dancing, singing and sexual license. The women enjoy considerable freedom. They are not kept to house-work, but also do outdoor work, labouring in the fields and on the roads to eke out the family income.

Similar characteristics are possessed by other races,

and may be illustrated by a few typical examples. The Hos, for instance, are described as follows by Colonel Dalton: "Whilst they still retain those traits which favourably distinguish the aborigines of India from Asiatics of higher civilization—a manner free from servility, but never rude; a love, or at least the practice, of truth; a feeling of self-respect, rendering them keenly sensible under rebuke—they have become less suspicious, less revengeful, less bloodthirsty, less contumacious, and in all respects more amenable to the laws and the advice of their officers. They are still very impulsive, easily excited to rash, headlong action, and apt to resent imposition or oppression without reflection; but the retaliation, which often extends to a death-blow, is done on the spur of the moment and openly." They are as quick to admit an offence as they are rash in committing it. A few years ago one of them who had a quarrel with another man cut off his head with an axe, and then marched off several miles to the police station, with the head in his hand, and gave himself up. Another good example of their spirit is afforded in the conduct of a woman, who, when her husband had been killed by a leopard, beat in its head with a stone till she had killed it.

The Khonds furnish an interesting example of a primitive race of improvident habits. In them, however, the love of their land appears to be stronger than the love of drink. The result has been an entirely independent temperance movement. In 1908 they took a vow to give up the use of intoxicating liquor, but their good resolutions were not proof against temptation. Realizing their weakness, they petitioned Government in 1910 to close down every liquor shop in their country. It was, they declared, no use to reduce the number of shops. They would go any distance to get liquor: its mere smell gave them an intense craving for drink. Drunkenness had, they said, done enough harm already, leading to poverty, wife-beating, and—worst of all—the loss of their lands. Their request, it may be added, was granted as an experimental measure.

The same deep attachment to the land characterizes other aboriginal races, who cling to their ancestral fields with grim tenacity. It is therefore at first sight surprising that they should emigrate so freely: Assam contains over a quarter of a million emigrants from the Chota Nagpur plateau, and Bengal nearly half a million. The explanation is economic pressure. The land which they till is generally poor, and their methods of cultivation are primitive. New areas, it is true, are cleared and opened out, but they are prolific races and the extension of the area under tillage is incommensurate with the increase of population. The aboriginal, moreover, does not care to cultivate more than is required for his immediate needs. He makes no provision against bad seasons, and as his savings go in the liquor shop, he has no reserves. Their readiness to emigrate has been the gain of other parts, more especially as they are free from the caste restrictions of the Hindus and are not fastidious about their work. The tea-gardens of Assam and the Duārs have been opened out by them, and are still largely dependent on their labour. The forests of the Barind have yielded to their axes. The railways draw largely on them both for construction and maintenance. The mines find them good coal-cutters, but they are fitful workers, being content if their earnings are enough to give them food, pay off debts and enable them to get drunk fairly frequently. Even the most energetic will not work more than five days a week, and they return to their homes periodically to till their fields, enjoy a festival, etc.

Eurasians. Lastly, mention must be made of the Eurasians, who owe their origin to intermarriage or irregular unions between Europeans and Indians. They have recently been officially christened by the Government of India under the name of Anglo-Indians, which bears quite another meaning in ordinary parlance. In physique, they mostly take after the Indian, the average height being $5\frac{1}{2}$ feet, the average weight less than eight stone, and the average chest measurement only 31 inches. The higher classes have produced men with all the better qualities of the European, but the lower classes are wanting in moral stamina and grit, partly the result of racial pride, which makes them unwilling to turn their hands to work which they think beneath their dignity. The practice of early marriage also militates against social and economic progress, and many are deep sunk in poverty.

The **Armenians** are a small community mostly engaged in trade. This appears to have been their pursuit since the end of the fifteenth century, for they may be identified with the Christian merchants whom Di Varthema found trading in Bengal. They are also known to have been in Calcutta nearly a century before the English settled there. They are mostly residents of that city, where their numbers are replenished by immigrants, Armenian boys being sent there from Persia to receive an English education.

There is also a **Chinese** colony of nearly 3000 persons in Calcutta, who work for the most part as carpenters and boot and shoe makers.

CHAPTER XV

RELIGIONS

The great majority of the people are either Hindus or Muhammadans. In Bihar and Orissa the Hindus number 32 millions, or four-fifths of the population, while in Bengal the Muhammadans predominate, aggregating 24 millions and outnumbering the Hindus by a little over 3 millions. The latter province contains more Muhammadans than the whole of Turkey (as constituted before the Balkan war), Persia and Afghanistan taken together. The most distinctively Hindu areas are North Bihar and Orissa. The former was an early centre of Aryan civilization, and is to this day "a land under the domination of a sept of Brahmans extraordinarily devoted to the mint, anise and cummin of the law." Orissa has long been regarded as a holy land of Hinduism; even the Muhammadan conqueror is said to have exclaimed: "This country is no fit subject for conquest; it belongs entirely to the gods." In the isolation which it till recently enjoyed, the power of the Brahmans remained unimpaired, and of all races in the two provinces the Oriyas are the most priest-ridden. The Muhammadans form a small minority in Bihar and Orissa and are largely exceeded by the Hindus in West Bengal. In the alluvial river basins of the Ganges and Brahmaputra their strength grows more and more as one proceeds eastwards, until in Eastern Bengal they are twice as numerous as the Hindus.

Hinduism presents many aspects—as a faith, a system of philosophy and a social system—and its features are so kaleidoscopic as to defy concise definition. Perhaps the most satisfactory and comprehensive summary of its manifold nature is that given in an article which appeared recently in *The Round Table*. "Hinduism is a congeries of cults rather than a religion—less even of a religion than a social system. If it originated in a primitive nature worship, developed through an era of ritualism and metaphysical speculation into a universal pantheism of a lofty type, it only survived and spread by the admission and assimilation of aboriginal cults and ignorant superstitions. Of dogma it knows little or nothing. It has room for the philosopher and the demon-worshipper, for the ecstasies of the saint and the unspeakable orgies of the Wām-Mārgi. Having never moralized its conception of the divine, it has no sanction in religion for right and wrong conduct. Ritual is its essence and observance its test of merit. The caste system, moreover, the one solid reality which it has thrown up and its one unifying and controlling influence, though developed by the priesthood to strengthen their own authority, and now inextricably interwoven with the code of observances set up in lieu of a faith, has only been given religious sanction by a fiction. Hinduism is, in effect, a religion of caste rules and usages; its sanctions are ultimately social; its laws immemorial group customs; and its tribunal the committee of the fraternity. Thus, although it enshrines for the student and thinker a profound and impressive philosophy, it presents itself to the man in the street not as a statement of the eternal principles of morality but as a formidable code of etiquette ruling the details of his domestic life. He finds it greatly concerned that he should not marry the wrong woman or dine with the wrong man, hardly at all concerned that he should not bear false witness or lead a life of immorality. In matters of faith it is a go-as-you-please religion in which a man can believe much what he likes provided he conforms with established usage. Antiquity consecrates the usage, and the Brahman is the repository of the key to the maze, the exponent and policeman of the whole system. Acceptance of caste, of the authority of the Brahman and of the sanctity of the cow, makes the orthodox Hindu, and in practice every Hindu believes in transmigration and recognizes some god or other of the crowned pantheon in his domestic ceremonies."

As a rough and ready classification, it may be said that the mass of the Hindu people are polytheists, and that a large proportion of the educated classes are monotheists, while others of the educated minority, more especially those who have had a Brahmanical training, are pantheists. Whatever school of thought is followed, what most impresses a European observer is the non-ethical basis of Hinduism, which differentiates it sharply from such a religion as Christianity. Its gods are non-moral; they impose no moral law. It has no clear-cut definite creed; it knows no Ten Commandments. The pantheistic Hindu believes in a divine impersonality and a final absorption which have *per se* no concern with morals. The monotheist looks to his god as the means of saving him from the circle of rebirth. The polytheist regards the gods not as directors of morals, but chiefly as the dispensers of material good and evil in this temporal world.

The Hinduism of the masses is chiefly characterized by an idolatrous polytheism, of which the outward and visible sign is an anthropomorphic image-worship. Each cult and sect has its own special gods or goddesses, but all combine to revere other deities of the pantheon

Fig. 60. A Hindu temple in South Bihar

and will join in their worship. "The gods are kittle cattle and a wise man honours them all." The story of an old Brahman told by Mr Wilkins in *Modern Hinduism* is typical of this attitude. "In his private worship he first made an offering to his chosen deity, and then threw a handful of rice broadcast for the other deities, and hoped, by thus recognizing their existence and authority, to keep them in good humour towards himself." The Hindu pantheon is further very elastic. A contemporary record informs us that towards the close of the eighteenth century an English Magistrate, named Tilman Henckell, was actually deified during his lifetime by some poor salt makers whom he had protected from oppression. In the last few years the terrors of plague have led to the apotheosization of the spirit of the pestilence, this latest recruit to the legion of deities being given a place in the village shrines. At the same time, there is a vague notion, even among the polytheists, of a supreme deity, who reigns but does not govern. He is too sublime to be troubled with temporal affairs. "What is man that Thou regardest him?"

The working religion of the peasant's everyday life consists of the propitiation of jealous gods in order that they may not afflict their worshippers or may grant them material blessings. Their religion is deeply infected by Animism of the character described below, in which the main ingredient is a belief in evil spirits and godlings, who have not been admitted to the orthodox pantheon. In many parts they set up a shapeless stone or stock, or even a little heap of earth, to represent the spirit or godling. Here they themselves or non-Brahman priests make simple offerings and oblations, while hard by there may be a temple to one of the great Hindu deities with its elaborate ritual and Brahman ministrant. The primitive propitiation of spirits and the worship of the

Hindu gods go on side by side, and the same men make offerings to both.

Worship in the temples is not congregational but individual. It is also vicarious, for the sole celebrant is the Brahman priest. He repeats the *mantras* and makes the offerings; the worshipper stands apart. In family life, as apart from temple worship, the most important functionary is the *guru*, who initiates all properly brought up Hindu boys into spiritual life by whispering in their ears some mystic syllables. Without such initiation a man is not fully a Hindu; his offerings have not complete efficacy, and he himself will be condemned to the cycle of rebirth. On this account men who have put off this ceremony will have it performed when they are on their death-bed. The *gurus* act as spiritual preceptors, advise their disciples on sacred matters, hear the confessions of the penitent, and receive deep veneration. They have been described as the working clergy of Hinduism, as the one force which serves to promote an ideal of morality.

Bengal, Bihar and Orissa contain several important **places of pilgrimage,** visits to which do much to keep alive the flame of religious faith. Chief among these is Puri, which contains the far-famed shrine of Jagannāth, an incarnation of Vishnu. Here all castes may eat together of the holy rice which is distributed among them: in the presence of the god caste distinctions are obliterated, and all are equal. The Rath Jātra or **Car Festival**, in which the image of Jagannāth is placed on his car and rides in procession down a broad street, attracts immense multitudes. The image is a rude wooden block, with stumps of arms, which is renewed periodically. The festival is especially auspicious when a new body has been given to the god, as in 1912, when there were a quarter of a million pilgrims. Cases of

Fig. 61. Pilgrims at Gaya

immolation under the wheels of the great car undoubtedly used to occur, but the greater number of deaths were probably due to accidents. These were bound to occur in a dense crowd of scores, if not hundreds, of thousands pressing round and prostrating themselves before the car—a huge unwieldy structure, 45 feet high, with 16 wheels and no mechanical means of steering. Such accidents are now prevented by a cordon placed round

Fig. 62. The Car Festival of Jagannāth

the car and by the Magistrate himself directing the pulling and steering of the car to its destination.

Another celebrated place of pilgrimage is Gaya, where Vishnu is believed to have left the impress of his feet. Here pilgrims come from all parts of India to make offerings for the souls of their fathers and forefathers. The favourite place of pilgrimage among Bengalis is Kālighāt in Calcutta, where sacrifices are made to Kāli to ensure blessings or avert evil in this life. A great bathing festival is held every year at Saugor Island at the mouth of the Hooghly, which marks the spot where the holy waters of the Ganges mingle with the sea. Till a century ago, when the practice was stopped by the British Government, it was customary for parents to throw children into the sea, to be drowned or devoured by crocodiles or sharks, in order to appease, or win the favour of, the gods. Other celebrated places of pilgrimage are the shrines of Sītakund in Chittagong and Baidyanāth in the Santāl Parganas.

As regards **sects**, the unlettered peasant in many parts of Bihar and Chota Nagpur would be hard put to it to say whether he was a Vaishnava or a Saiva. Elsewhere, however, there is a sharp line of sectarian cleavage. The difference between the sects lies in the god to which a man looks to grant him *mukti* or salvation, i.e., cessation from reincarnation. This is not a matter concerned with the present life, but with the hereafter. In this respect therefore the ideas of the Hindu proper are on a different plane from those of the animistic Hindu already described. The **Saiva** looks to Siva to save him, and his idea of salvation is pantheistic in that it means the loss of identity by absorption. The **Vaishnava** or worshipper of Vishnu loathes the idea of loss of identity. His faith is based on a conception of a God Father, and he hopes to gain salvation by *bhakti*, i.e., fervent love of a personal deity. As Sir George Grierson points out, "St Augustine's commentary on faith—Quid est credere in Deum? Credendo amare, credendo diligere, credendo in eum ire et ejus membris incorporari—is almost word for word what a modern Hindu would say about *bhakti*." To the Vaishnava the first commandment is: Thou shalt love the Lord thy God—but his religion being purely personal, he omits the second Christian commandment—Thou shalt love thy neighbour as thyself. Vaishnavism is popular among the lower classes in Bengal and is almost universal in Orissa, where, however, the people have added to the worship of Krishna the worship of his beloved Rādha, so that the object of adoration has a dual personality.

A third sect, which is common only in Bengal, is that of the **Sāktas,** who worship the active female principle or power (*sakti*) as manifested in one or other of the goddess wives of Siva, viz., Durga, Kāli or Pārvati. The goddess is commonly addressed as Mother, but this denotes destructive energy rather than maternal tenderness. Their scriptures are the Tāntras, and the worship is associated with blood offerings, the sacrifice of goats, etc. One extreme branch indulges in secret orgiastic rites of indescribable indecency: even this may be said to have some scriptural sanction, for the adoration of naked women is inculcated by one of the Tāntras.

Other sects have sprung up in which the worship of the Guru, i.e., the founder of the sect. or its present head, overshadows and almost supplants the worship of the godhead, whom he interprets to, or represents among, men. The neurotic hysteria which underlies the seeming impassivity of many Bengalis has also led to the creation of small sects, in which worship, whatever its esoteric meaning, appears to verge on sexual mania. A sect of this kind, which recently gained some notoriety, combined a quasi-religious frenzy with erotic orgies, its founder having ordained the adoration of nude women, who were represented as incarnations of Kāli.

During the last century there has been a revival of Hinduism, which has found expression in two directions. On the one hand, attempts are made to rationalize Hindu customs and beliefs; on the other, there is a reactionary assertion of the excellence of old customs and ideals, which sometimes manifests itself in unexpected ways; for instance, the suicide of widows is greeted with implicit approval, as a sign of the *sati* spirit, in quarters where more enlightened views might be expected.

One outcome of the neo-Hindu movement has been the creation of new schools of thought, the earliest of which is the **Brahmo Samāj.** This is a theistic body founded by Raja Rām Mohan Ray (1774–1833) and largely moulded to its present form by Keshab Chandra Sen (1838–84). The doctrines which it professes are similar to those of Unitarianism. It has not much numerical strength, its adherents numbering only a few thousands, mostly Bengalis. There has also been a considerable dissemination of the pantheistic beliefs known as **Vedantism** by a body called the Rāmkrishna Mission. Its founder was Rāmkrishna Parahamsa (1834–86), but its chief protagonist was Swāmi Vivekananda, who died in 1902; among its members was a gifted European lady, the late Sister Nivedita (Margaret Noble). Its most characteristic features are an ardent nationalist feeling, an ideal of social service and a spirit of tolerance to foreign travel and the eating of meat. Another new religious body is the **Arya Samāj** founded by Dayanand Saraswati (1827–53), which originated in the Punjāb and the United Provinces, and has made its way into Bihar. It appeals to the Vedas as the vehicle of truth and inspiration, advocates monotheism, denounces idolatry and is in favour of social reform.

The main doctrines of **Muhammadanism** are so well known that they scarcely require explanation. Briefly they are: "There is one God. Muhammad is His prophet. The Korān contains His ordinances." Worship is congregational, and all Muhammadans are on a religious equality, though in practice this doctrine is so far departed from, that the low-born sweeper may not enter the mosque or be buried in the cemetery with other Muhammadans. A recent writer of an article "Islām in Bengal" (which appeared in the *Moslem World* of January, 1914) divides them into four classes, viz., "(*a*) The minority, read in Western thought, who live on the border line of orthodoxy and heterodoxy. (*b*) The orthodox, steeped in the Korān and traditional ideas. (*c*) The illiterate masses, who in addition to accepting the orthodox position, feed on distorted and unauthenticated traditions and superstitions, often of Hindu origin. (*d*) The heterodox, who follow the teaching of the Pīrs and Fakīrs and a corrupt form of Sufiism." These Pirs or teachers and Fakirs or ascetics, "like the Sufis, speak much of love and union with God under the figure of the lover and beloved, and they sing and perform other ceremonies under the influence of some narcotic. They also practise the ascetic exercises of the *Yoga* system of the Hindus. The number of their adherents is increasing."

The last century has witnessed a revivalist movement, almost a reformation, among the Muhammadans of Bengal, which is as remarkable as the renewed strength and vitality of Hinduism. "A century ago," wrote Sir William Hunter in his essay *England's Work in India*, "Muhammadanism seemed to be dying of inanition in Bengal. In the mosques, or amid the serene palace life of the Musalmān nobility, a few *maulavis* of piety and learning calmly carried on the routine of their faith. But the Musalmān peasantry of Bengal had relapsed into a mongrel breed of circumcised Hiṇdus, not one in ten of whom could repeat the *kalma*—a simple creed, whose constant repetition is a matter of unconscious habit with all good Muhammadans. Under our rule fervid Muhammadan missionaries have wandered from district to district, commanding the people to return to the true faith, and denouncing God's wrath on the indifferent. A great body of the Bengali Muhammadans have purged themselves of rural superstitions, and evinced such an ardour of revivalist zeal as occasionally to cause some little inconvenience to the Government."

In these last words the writer refers to the Wahābi movement, which aimed at restoring Islām to its pristine purity and simplicity by stripping it of later accretions and of anything savouring of idolatry. Politically, its doctrines were dangerous, for the *jihād* or war against infidels was preached. A series of frontier wars, for which Bengal and Bihar supplied money and recruits, awoke Government to the menace of the crusade, and the conspiracy was broken up by the trial and conviction of its ringleaders. The religious stimulus of the movement is not yet spent. Its reforming spirit is still alive in the puritanical sects known as Ahl-i-Hadis in Bihar and Farāzis in Bengal, of whom the latter have a strong following. The Farāzis claim to observe the *farāiz* or divine ordinances of God without the glosses of scholiasts, and do not adhere to any of the regular schools of doctrine of the orthodox Muhammadan world. Other Muhammadans they regard as *be-sharais*, i.e., men who do not follow the scriptures strictly. They interdict the veneration of Pīrs or saints, denounce the use of music at ceremonies and processions, and do not even observe the *maulud* or anniversary of the death of the Prophet. They may be distinguished by their dress, for they let the *dhoti* hang straight down from the waist without passing the end through the legs. Other Muhammadans tie up the *dhoti* but loosen it before praying so that it may hang down, as it is considered irreverent to expose the leg above the knees. The Farāzis carry the idea further by letting the *dhoti* hang well below the knees on all occasions. Some of them have curious economic views. They hold that the earth is the gift of God and that man is made for His service. Man should live by agriculture and never take service under others, for by so doing he will neglect the service of God.

Another schismatic sect which is beginning to make converts among the educated Muhammadans of Bihar is that of the **Ahmadias,** which was founded by Mirza Gulam Ahmad (1839–1908), a native of Kadiān in the Punjāb. The chief differences between them and orthodox Muhammadans are as follows. The latter believe that a Mahdi or Messiah will appear who will convert unbelievers at the edge of the sword. The Ahmadias deny that there will be any such advent and declare that the true Messiah is Ahmad, who came to establish Islām by peaceful means. Other Musalmāns hold that the Korān is the final divine revelation. The Ahmadias hold that divine revelation still continues, and that Ahmad was a specially favoured recipient of such revelation. Their doctrines have a strong anti-Christian bias. The orthodox Muhammadan belief is that at the end of the world Dajjāl, who is the power of evil, a kind of Anti-Christ, will hold rule until Christ appears and overthrows him, with the aid of Mahdi, when the whole world will be converted to Islām. The Ahmadias identify Dajjāl with the teachings of the Christian Church, which they declare to be false; they say that the advent of Dajjāl has come to pass with the spread of Christian missions. The Christian account of the divinity, death and resurrection of Christ is denounced as an invention. Jesus, they say, did not die on the cross, but only swooned; he did not rise from the dead, but recovered from the swoon; he did not ascend to heaven, but came to Afghanistan and India to preach to the lost tribes of Israel; and he died, and was buried, at Srīnagar in Kashmir, where his tomb may be seen to this day.

In spite of the efforts of resident and itinerary preachers and teachers, the religion of the Muhammadans of the lower, uneducated classes is debased and superstitious. They are, wrote Sir Edward Gait in the Bengal Census Report of 1901, "deeply infected with Hindu superstitions and their knowledge of the faith seldom extends beyond the three cardinal doctrines of the unity of God, the mission of Muhammad and the truth of the Korān." Some would go even further. One Muhammadan gentleman informed me that the low classes "profess to be Musalmāns, but to them Islām is only circumcision and the eating of cow's flesh." The lower classes are also divided into social groups like the Hindu castes with rigid rules regarding intermarriage and commensality. A curious instance of such caste laws is found among the Bāramāsias of Bogra, who are so called because they live in boats for the twelve (*bāra*) months (*mās*) of the year. "This manner of life is preserved by no less a sanction than absolute loss of caste for any member of the tribe who is found on shore after the jackals begin to cry." In most parts of Bengal the Muhammadans have formed associations for the advancement of their cause, and branches of the Anjumān Islāmia are to be found in the most backward villages.

The great majority of the Muhammadans are believed to be descendants of local converts from Hinduism. In Eastern Bengal, in particular, there must have been great "mass movements" resulting in the general adoption of the faith of Islām. There are, however, notable exceptions, as in Chittagong. "The high cheek bones, hook noses and narrow faces of many of the inhabitants of Chittagong proclaim their Arab origin. Again, the muscular, bull-necked strong-featured and thick-bearded dweller on the *chars* is a very different creature from the fleshless, featureless, hairless inhabitant of the interior of the district. These differences are racial, the former being descendants of soldiers of the Mughal armies, while the latter are probably of mixed origin." The general conclusion is stated as follows by Sir Edward Gait, who estimates the strength of the foreign element at four millions at the most: "There is no question as to the foreign origin of many of those of the better class; the difference between the coarse features and dark complexion of the ordinary villagers and the fair skin and fine features of some of the gentry is apparent to all....Even in places where the general appearance of the Muhammadans most closely resembles that of their Hindu neighbours, there are often cases of atavism, where the full eye, Semitic nose, high stature and strong beard show unmistakable traces of foreign blood. It is not contended that even in Bengal Proper the ordinary Muhammadans are all of purely Indian descent, but it is certain that, of the total number, those who are wholly Indian or in whom the Indian element greatly preponderates, form by far the largest proportion."

Animism is a term applied to that primitive form of religion of which the basis is "the belief which explains to primitive man the constant movements and changes in the world of things by the theory that every object which has activity enough to affect him in any way is animated by a life and will like his own." It peoples the world with spirits, nearly all of whom are malevolent and require propitiation if man is to escape their attacks. It does not exclude the belief in a supreme spirit, but this being does not concern himself with ordinary human affairs. Worship is practically demonolatry. The spirits may be wandering spirits without any local habitation and incapable of being represented, or they may take up their abode in some object, animate or inanimate.

In the latter case we have fetichism, i.e., the worship of a visible object supposed to possess active power. As a rule, the spirits are represented by some actual object. They may live in a tree, a hill, a rock, a river, etc. Or they may be represented by a little heap of earth, a log of wood or a stone, which may be left in the rough or have some crude carving; in one place I have seen a pair of wooden clogs and a low wooden seat placed at the shrine for the spirit's use. These objects are generally smeared with vermilion, and at them libations, offerings and sacrifices are made.

Natural calamities, the failure of crops and the sickness of cattle are ascribed to the anger of evil spirits. The cause of illness is demoniacal possession, not insanitary conditions or the anopheles mosquito. The remedy lies not in medicine, but in exorcism. Wizards and exorcists are consequently important personages, while witches are dreaded as the natural enemies of man. This belief gives rise to brutal murders; in Singhbhūm, when the Mutiny of 1857 caused a temporary breakdown of law and authority, the Hos made a clean sweep of all women whom they suspected to be witches. Nor is this belief to be wondered at when women themselves have a firm conviction of their supernatural powers for evil and declare themselves to be witches. A few years ago in Palāmau a cultivator, who was watching his crops by night, returned home to find that his child had just died. In front of the house an old hag was crouching on the ground. She had swept a patch of earth quite clean, and on it had placed the body of a dead vole with its head pointing to the place where the child lay. Behind it were the bodies of three grasshoppers, and behind them again five clay figures representing mice. These she was pushing forward, as if to attack the house, muttering strange incantations to herself.

Animism is still the religion of $3\frac{1}{2}$ million persons, but is confined to the aboriginal races. Even among them it is yielding to the steady advance of Hinduism, which has been aptly likened to a boa constrictor absorbing rival faiths. "It winds round its opponent, crushes it in its folds, and finally causes it to disappear in its capacious interior."

Mention may be made here of the movements, half religious and half agrarian, that from time to time occur among the people of Chota Nagpur and the Santāl Parganas. They have a direct connection with agrarian unrest, and show signs of the influence of Christian ideas, which the recipients have distorted rather than adopted. A new cult of this kind arose in Rānchi in 1897–99, its founder being a Munda named Birsa, who was an apostate from Christianity. His teaching was partly spiritual, partly revolutionary. He proclaimed that the land belonged to the people who had reclaimed it from jungle, and no rent should be paid for it. They should rise, expel all foreigners and rule themselves. The guns of their enemies would be turned to wood, and their bullets to water. There was but one God, one day a week should be observed as a sabbath, and the worship of other gods and devils must be given up. They must lead clean lives; murder, stealing and lying were to be regarded as deadly sins. Birsa himself professed to have received divine revelation during a thunderstorm—an idea based on the message delivered from Sinai amid thunder and lightning. He asserted that he was the Messiah and claimed divine powers of healing. All who did not join him were doomed to destruction in a flood, which would overwhelm the world and destroy all but those who were with Birsa. His crusade brought about an armed rising of the deluded peasantry, which was easily put down, and Birsa died in jail in 1900.

Buddhism has almost entirely disappeared from the land of its birth. Even before the Musalmān invasion the steady pressure of Brahmanism had relaxed its hold on the people, while the persecution of Hindu rulers reduced the number of its followers. One favourite device was to institute debates on the rival merits of the two religions, death being the penalty of defeat; when the judge was a Hindu prince, the verdict was a foregone conclusion. "Many of the chief princes," says the *Sankara Vijaya*, "who professed the wicked doctrines of the Buddhist and Jain religions were vanquished in scholarly controversies. Their heads were then cut off with axes, thrown in mortars, and ground to powder by pestles." The intolerant fury of the Musalmān invasion destroyed the monasteries, which were the chief centres of the faith, while the monks were either slain or sought refuge in and beyond the Himalayas. Such a clean sweep was made at Bihar, for instance, that when the rude Musalmān conqueror sought for some one to explain to him the contents of the great monastic library, not a single man could be found who could do so.

Survivals of Buddhism can be traced in the cult of Dharma among the lower castes in Bengal, but in the interior it lingers on as a religion only in Orissa. There it is professed by a few thousand weavers, whose name of Sārak indicates their descent from the Srāvakas, an order of Buddhist monks. The only places where it is the active religion of a considerable proportion of the population are the extreme south-east and north of Bengal. In the former there are nearly 200,000 Buddhists, mostly Maghs, the descendants of emigrants from Arakan. Their religion is a debased form of Buddhism infected both by Hinduism and Animism. The other centre of the faith is the mountainous region of Sikkim and Darjeeling, where its adherents consist of hill races, mostly Bhotias and Lepchas. Here the principles of Buddha's teaching are so deeply overlaid with demonolatry as to be almost unrecognizable. The lamas, or priests, who congregate in monasteries, are feared by the people as having mysterious powers to avert evil rather than revered as spiritual leaders.

The worship and ritual have several interesting features, of which an admirable description is given by Mr Claude White in *Sikhim and Bhutan*: "Most of the tenets of Buddhism have been set aside, and those retained are lost in a mass of ritual, so that nothing remains of the original religion but the name. The form of worship has a curious resemblance in many particulars to that of the Roman Catholic Church. On any of their high holy days the intoning of the chief lama conducting the service, the responses chanted by the choir, sometimes voices alone, sometimes to the accompaniment of instruments, where the deep note of the large trumpet strangely resembles the roll of an organ, the ringing of bells, burning of incense, the prostrations before the altar, the telling of beads and burning of candles, the processions of priests in gorgeous vestments, and even the magnificent altars surmounted by images and decorated with gold and silver vessels, with lamps burning before them, even the side chapels with the smaller shrines where lights burn day and night, add to the feeling that one is present at some high festival in a Roman Catholic place of worship."

Outside the temples the chief religious observances are the constant turning of prayer wheels, the erection of prayer flags, the wearing of charms and amulets and the repetition of formulae, in particular of *Om Mani Padme Hum*—mystic syllables, meaning literally "Oh, the jewel in the lotus," which are believed to ensure salvation. Worship is aided by mechanical means.

The prayer flags are merely strips of cotton cloth with prayers printed on them, which are attached to pieces of string or fastened to long bamboo poles; as they flutter in the wind, the prayers are borne to the ears of the spirits. The prayer wheels are cylinders of wood or metal containing prayers printed on slips of paper. Small wheels are carried on the person and turned by hand. Large wheels, containing thousands of prayers,

Fig. 63. Buddhist Lama with disciples

are worked by water power. There are also paper wheels inscribed with prayers which revolve over the hot air of a candle. In all cases the wheel must follow the course of the sun; if you turn it in the reverse direction, you bring down curses

Christian missionary enterprise was initiated by Augustinian and Jesuit priests, who first came to Bengal in the second half of the sixteenth century. The Capuchins followed early in the eighteenth century and succeeded in establishing stations in Nepal, and even at Lhāsa, in addition to those in Bengal and Bihar. The first Protestant missionary was Kiernander, who settled in Calcutta in 1758, and the first organized Protestant mission was the Serampore Mission, which was started by William Carey towards the close of the eighteenth century. So far the most fruitful field for the missionary has been not the plains of Bengal but the hilly country of Chota Nagpur. The neo-Hindu movement and the rise of the Brahmo Samāj have checked the spread of Christian propaganda among the higher class Hindus. More success has attended work among the lower classes, such as the Namasudras in the sultry swamps of Bengal. But the greatest progress has been made among the aboriginal races of Chota Nagpur, especially in Rānchi. Out of every 100 persons in this district thirteen are Christians, the total number of native converts being 177,000 or double the aggregate for the whole of Bengal. Here the work of the Christian missionary is facilitated by the fact that the aboriginal is not tied by the caste system like the Hindu. Conversion does not entail excommunication with consequent severance from the family circle and loss of all share in the family property. Other influences which work on the minds of such people as the Oraons are explained as follows by Colonel Dalton: "The Supreme Being, who does not protect them from the spite of malevolent spirits, has, they are assured, the Christians under his special care. They consider that, in consequence of this guardianship, the witches and *bhūts* (i.e., evil spirits) have no power over Christians; and it is, therefore, good for them to join that body. They are taught that for the salvation of Christians one great sacrifice has been made, and they see that those who are baptised do not in fact reduce their live stock to propitiate the evil spirits. They grasp at this notion and, long afterwards, when they understand it better, the mystical washing away of sin by the blood of Christ

Fig. 64. Jain shrine at Parasnāth

is the doctrine on which their simple minds most dwell."

The spread of Christianity has been very rapid in the ten years preceding the census of 1911, during which the number of converts has risen by 114,000 or 50 per cent.

The total for both provinces is now 342,000, to which the Roman Catholics contribute 142,000, the Lutherans 100,000, the Anglicans 50,000, the Baptists 34,000 and other denominations 16,000.

There are but few members of **other religions**, which are chiefly represented by immigrants, such as the Jain Mārwāris: some of these have become domiciled in the country of their adoption, and number among them some of the richest merchants in Bengal. There are, however, some celebrated shrines of the Jains and Sikhs, which attract pilgrims from far and wide. Patna was the birthplace of Govind Singh, the founder of the Sikh military brotherhood, and the site is marked by a temple containing his cradle and shoes. There are also Jain shrines at Parasnāth, which is a sacred mountain, having been the scene of the Nirvana, or beatific annihilation, of no less than ten of the twenty-four deified saints who are the object of Jain adoration; from Parsvanāth, the last of these, the mountain has taken its name.

CHAPTER XVI

LANGUAGES

THE Indian languages spoken throughout our area belong to one or other of four linguistic families, viz., Indo-European, Austro-Asiatic, Dravidian and Tibeto-Chinese. The principal Indo-European languages are Bengali, Bihāri, Hindi, Urdu, Oriya and Nepali. The Austro-Asiatic family is represented by the Munda languages, and the Dravidian by Oraon, Malto and Kandh.

The Tibeto-Chinese family comprises the Tibeto-Burman languages, which are subdivided into two branches, viz., Tibeto-Himalayan, such as Bhotia, Lepcha and Nepalese tribal languages, and Assam-Burmese, such as Burmese, Gāro, Mech and Tipura.

Bengal may be regarded as uni-lingual, for nine-tenths of its inhabitants speak Bengali. The remaining tenth are temporary or domiciled immigrants, or belong to the hill races of the Himalayas or the south-east frontier, who retain the Tibeto-Chinese speech of their forefathers. The province of Bihar and Orissa, on the other hand, is polyglot. Bihāri is the vernacular of Bihar and some adjoining districts, and Oriya of Orissa, while the Chota Nagpur plateau is the home of those early indigenous languages which go by the name of Dravidian and Munda. In a few districts the speakers of different languages dwell side by side, and the want of a common form of speech adds considerably to the difficulties of administration and education. In the Santāl Parganas, for instance, four distinct languages are current, three in Mānbhūm and Singhbhūm and two in Purnea. The following table shows the number of persons speaking the main languages according to the census of 1911.

Languages	Bengal	Bihar and Orissa	Sikkim
Indo-European ..	44,904,000	35,081,000	28,000
Bengali	*42,566,000*	*2,295,000*	..
Bihāri, Hindi and Urdu ..	*1,917,000*	*24,933,000*	..
Oriya	*294,000*	*7,820,000*	..
Nepali	*91,000*	*3,000*	*28,000*
Munda..	771,000	2,559,000	..
Dravidian	133,000	785,000	..
Tibeto-Burman ..	110,000	..	59,000
Assam-Burmese ..	261,000	..	..

Bengali is not only spoken throughout Bengal, but spreads across its borders, being the mother-tongue of two-thirds of the people of Mānbhūm and of two-fifths in Purnea. It has been described as "a language as copious and expressive as Greek itself," but the slurred consonants and broken vowels make it difficult for a foreigner to master. Sanskrit words have been introduced wholesale into the modern literary Bengali, in consequence of which some of the book language is unintelligible to the uneducated masses. Sanskritization is a foible of cultured Hindus. The Musalmāns, on the other hand, are fond of interlarding their speech with Urdu and Arabic words, producing a patois which is called Musalmāni Bengali.

Bihāri, Hindi and Urdu are distinct languages, which are grouped together simply because they are not distinguished in the census returns. Popularly they are all called Hindustāni, which is, strictly speaking, a local vernacular of Hindi spoken between Meerut and Delhi. It has, however, spread all over Northern India and become a *lingua franca*. Urdu is a Persianized form of Hindustāni, i.e., the Persian character is used for writing it and a number of Persian and Arabic words have been added to its vocabulary. The great majority of the people of Bihar, however, speak neither Hindi nor Urdu, but Bihāri, which the Hindus call Hindi and the Musalmāns Urdu. There are three dialects of Bihāri known as Bhojpuri, Māgadhi and Maithili. All three are written in the Kaithi character, which is a form of Devanāgari, the character generally used for Hindi; the latter is distinguished by a straight line at the top of the letters.

Oriya has the advantage of being pronounced as it is spelt, each letter being clearly sounded. It is "comprehensive and poetical, with a pleasant sounding and musical intonation, and by no means difficult to acquire and master." On the other hand, it has a perplexing character, due to the fact that until recent times it was written with a stylus on palm leaves—a fragile material, which is apt to split if a line follows the grain. To avoid this, the scribes discarded the long straight line of Devanāgari and substituted a series of curves round the letters. "It requires remarkably good eyes to read an Oriya printed book, for the exigencies of the printing press compel the type to be small, and the greater part of each letter is this curve, which is the same in nearly all, while the real soul of the character, by which one is distinguished from another, is hidden in the centre, and is so minute, that it is often difficult to see. At first glance an Oriya book seems to be all curves, and it takes a second look to notice that there is something inside each."

Nepali, which has affinities with Hindi, is the *lingua franca* of the Himalayas. The Nepalese are usually bilingual, speaking their tribal language among themselves and Nepali in their dealings with others.

The **Munda languages** are spoken by many tribes in Chota Nagpur, the Orissa States and the Santāl Parganas; the languages are named after the tribes, e.g., Santāli, Mundāri, Bhumij, Ho, Juang, Kharia, etc. They are, writes Sir George Grierson, the greatest living authority on Indian languages, "agglutinative, and preserve this characteristic in a very complete manner. Suffix is piled upon suffix, and helped out by infix, till we obtain words which have the meaning of a whole sentence. For instance, the word *dal* means 'strike,' and from it we form the word *da-pa-l-ocho-akan-tahen-tae-tiñ-a-e,* which signifies 'he who belongs to him who belongs to me will continue letting himself be caused to fight.' Not only *may* we, but we *must* employ this posy of speech, if, for instance, my slave's son was too often getting himself entangled in affrays."

The vocabulary is rich in terms for natural objects and the common incidents of village and jungle life—Santāli, for instance, has more than half a dozen verbs descriptive of falling, e.g., forwards, backwards, from a height, etc.; but it is practically destitute of expressions for emotions and abstract ideas.

Dravidian languages, which are akin to the Tamil and Telugu of Southern India, are spoken by other aboriginal tribes in the same area, e.g., Oraon or Kurukh by the Oraons, Mālto by the Maler or Sauria Pahārias of the Santāl Parganas and Kandh or Kui by the Khonds. Gondi, another Dravidian language, has fallen into desuetude in our area, as the Gonds have adopted the language of their Aryan neighbours.

The **Tibeto-Burman languages** are confined to Sikkim, Darjeeling and Jalpaiguri, and consist of Bhotia or Tibetan, Lepcha and a number of Nepalese tribal languages named after the tribes speaking them, such as Murmi, Mangar, Jimdār and Khambu, Limbu, Newāri, Sunuwāri and Yākha.

The **Assam-Burmese languages** belong to three groups called Bodo, Kuki-Chin and Burma. The most important of the Bodo group are (1) Tipura or Mrung, which is the mother tongue of the Tiparas of Hill Tippera, a Mongolian race who appear to be identical with the Mrungs of Arakan; (2) Gāro, which has spread to Mymensingh from the Gāro hills, and (3) Mech, which is used by the Meches of Jalpaiguri. The only languages of the Kuki-Chin group that are spoken to any extent are Manipuri, which the Manipuris of Hill Tippera speak almost to a man, and Kuki, which is current among the hill tribes of the same State and of the Chittagong Hill Tracts. The Burma group is represented by Burmese and the allied language of Mru, the latter of which is a vernacular of the Chittagong Hill Tracts. Burmese is spoken by 74,000 persons, mostly Maghs resident in the Hill Tracts and Chittagong. For the most part, the Maghs are descendants of emigrants from Arakan, and use a dialect current in Arakan, which they call Magh and others Arakanese.

CHAPTER XVII

AGRICULTURE

THE supreme economic importance of agriculture may be realized from the fact that three-fourths of the population are dependent on it for a means of livelihood. At the census of 1911 it was found that in Bengal 35 millions, and in Bihar and Orissa 30 millions, subsisted on the cultivation of land. The great majority of this vast host have no occupation apart from agriculture, while one in every twenty of those engaged in non-agricultural pursuits supplements his income by owning or tilling some land or by working, at intervals, as a field labourer. It is no exaggeration therefore to say that the success or failure of the crops every year is a matter of vital importance.

Bengal is practically free from any anxiety on this account, for its harvests are generally assured by an abundant rainfall and the periodic overflow of silt-laden rivers. Bihar and Chota Nagpur are more exposed to the vicissitudes of the seasons. Here droughts sometimes cause scarcity and have been known to culminate in famine. Provided, however, that the rainfall is adequate and timely—a fitful distribution is as dangerous as an actual deficiency in the amount—the crops are sufficient not only for the annual food-supply of the people, but also for export overseas and to other parts of India.

Agriculture, as practised in either province, may be described as petty agriculture, for the country is

Fig. 65. Threshing

parcelled out in small farms, and the fields are often so tiny as to be mere plots of land. That the land brings forth enough to feed the people and also to provide a surplus for export is due to the patient skill acquired by centuries of inherited experience, and to the frugal life of the inhabitants, as well as to the natural fertility of the soil. Its productive powers owe little to manure.

Firewood is usually so scarce that cowdung, mixed with straw, is made into cakes for the domestic fires. In Eastern Bengal, however, there is no need of artificial fertilization, for the land is annually enriched by the silt deposit of the rivers. The agricultural implements in general use are so simple as to be almost primitive—the plough, for instance, is an iron-tipped share attached to a long pole—but they serve excellently for the soil they work. Forest tribes still practise nomadic cultivation in Sikkim, the Orissa States, the Chittagong Hill Tracts and Hill Tippera. A patch of jungle is burnt down, and seeds dibbled into the soil, which is enriched by the ashes of the trees. A few crops are taken, and then the people move off and make fresh clearings.

Rice and jute predominate in Bengal, where rice is the staple food of the people; in Eastern Bengal these two crops are grown almost exclusively. There is a greater variety of crops in Bihar and Chota Nagpur, where the masses do not live on rice but on other cereals, such as maize, wheat and barley, and various pulses and millets. There are three harvests in the year, called *aghani*, *bhadoi* and *rabi*. The *aghani* harvest, consisting almost entirely of winter rice, takes place early in the cold weather; the *bhadoi* in the rains and the *rabi* in the spring.

Rice is by far the most important crop, occupying as it does from one-half (in Bihar and Orissa) to two-thirds (in Bengal) of the cropped area. "The districts of Bengal," it has been said, "a level area of nearly one hundred thousand square miles, unbroken by a single hill, rich in black mould and of boundless reproductive fertility, constitute the great rice-producing area of Northern India." The Indian name of this cereal shows the estimation in which it is held, viz., *dhān*, meaning the supporter of mankind. Among Europeans in India rice in the stalk or husk is commonly known as paddy, this being a transliteration of the Malay word *padi*. There are three main crops, viz., in order of importance: (1) winter rice, called *aghani* or *aman*, which is reaped from November to January, the greatest of the three harvests; (2) autumn or early rice, called *aus* (from the Sanskrit *asu* or early), which is cut from July to September,

Fig. 66. Treading out the grain

and (3) *boro* or spring rice, a coarse and unimportant variety, chiefly reaped in April.

As is well known, rice is almost an aquatic plant, which thrives only under a thin sheet of water. Its growth is therefore dependent on an adequate and timely supply either from the monsoon rainfall or from irrigation. The most critical period is the end of September and beginning of October, when water is essential to bring the all-important winter crop to maturity. If the supply fails then, the plants wither and the crop is a partial or complete failure.

Wheat and **barley** are not of much importance in Bengal, where they are confined to the western districts, but are cultivated extensively in Bihar, from which there are large exports of wheat. **Maize** or Indian corn is one of the chief staples of the latter sub-province and also of Chota Nagpur. *Marua* (*Eleusine coracana*) is a valuable millet which is raised in the same area during the rains; the grain is converted into flour and consumed by the lower classes. Other millets grown for local consumption are *kodo* (*Paspalum scrobiculatum*), *china* (*Panicum miliaceum*) and *juār* (*Sorghum vulgare*). **Pulses** of many different kinds are cultivated during the cold weather in both provinces, the most extensively grown being gram (*Cicer arietinum*), which furnishes a sustaining food and an excellent fodder for horses.

Among the non-food crops **jute** easily takes the first place in value, for practically all the sacks of the world are made from the fibre which it yields. Its cultivation is almost entirely a monopoly of Bengal, where it thrives on almost any soil having the necessary depth and sufficient water to keep the soil moist. Outside that province the only large jute district is Purnea, though a certain amount is produced in Orissa. The area under the crop has extended with the demand for the fibre, till it amounts to three million acres. A million tons of fibre are brought yearly to Calcutta to feed the local mills and for foreign export; and it is estimated that £25,000,000 are paid every year to the agriculturists for the raw material. The crop is cut in August and September, and the stalks, made up into bundles, are immersed in water. The steeping process is known as retting. After about three weeks, the bark is easily stripped from the stem, and the fibre is separated by washing in water and beating. It is then dried in the sun and made into hanks for despatch to market.

Other fibre crops of minor importance are *san* hemp

Fig. 67. Winnowing in the wind

(*Crotolaria juncea*) and *dhaincha* (*Sesbania aculeata*), the fibre of which is made locally into netting and cordage, The true hemp or *ganja* (*Cannabis sativa*) is cultivated for the sake of the intoxicating drugs obtained from its leaves, flowers and resin. The cultivation is carried on, under Government supervision, in a limited area in the district of Rājshāhi.

Oilseeds are grown extensively, the principal being linseed, rape-seed, and mustard. Linseed is the produce of the common flax plant, which is cultivated for the sake of the oil obtained from its seed. Sesamum or gingelly is also a common crop in nearly every district. Cotton is produced on a small scale for domestic use; the local cottons are short-stapled inferior varieties.

There is an extensive cultivation of **sugarcane,** mainly for the local manufacture of the coarse sugar called jaggery and molasses; the export trade has been almost extinguished by the competition of Java sugar. There is a larger area under **tobacco** than in any other province. It is raised almost everywhere in small patches for home use, and on an extensive scale, for trade and export, in North Bihar, Cooch Behar, Rangpur and Jalpaiguri. The leaf is exported to Burma, where it is made into cigars smoked by the Burmese themselves; the Burma cigars of the market are mostly made from Madras tobacco.

Lastly, there are three special crops, which, like jute, furnish the raw material for important industries, viz., indigo, cinchona and tea. The **opium** industry is now extinct, the cultivation of poppy for the purpose having been stopped in accordance with an agreement made by the Government with China. The crop was fairly widespread in Bihar, the drug being manufactured (from the poppy exudation produced by scarifying the poppy capsules) in the opium factory at Patna. The cultivation of **indigo,** once a large planting industry, has greatly diminished, owing mainly to the competition of the synthetic dye made in Germany, and, in a minor degree, to the good prices commanded by other crops. It has all but disappeared in Bengal, but is still carried on in North Bihar. The plant is named after the land of its growth, indigo being derived from the Greek *Indikon* meaning Indian. **Cinchona** cultivation, for the manufacture of quinine, is a Government monopoly introduced in 1861; the plantations are situated in the Darjeeling district. The cultivation of **tea** is now the principal planting industry. The tea-gardens are mostly situated in Darjeeling and Jalpaiguri, where 140,000 acres have

Fig. 68. A *pain* or irrigation channel

been planted out, but there are also two dozen gardens in Chittagong and some minor concerns in Rānchi.

Artificial **irrigation** is unnecessary in most parts of Bengal, which has no reason to complain of lack of moisture, but is essential for the cultivation of rice and other crops in Bihar and Chota Nagpur. In the tract last named the water runs quickly off the slopes, so that the higher lands are soon dry even after heavy rain. For its conservation the slopes are laid out in a series of terraced fields spreading downwards in a fan shape. They have earthen banks at the lower side to retain the water, which passes down from field to field moistening each in turn.

An ingenious system of irrigation is practised in South Bihar, and more particularly in the Gaya district, where the people impound the drainage water and also press the rivers into service by diverting the water to the land on either side. There are thousands of artificial reservoirs made by means of retaining embankments constructed across the line of drainage, and a network of artificial channels called *pains* leading from the rivers to the fields; some of the latter are ten to twenty miles in length and irrigate hundreds of villages. The whole forms a remarkable and ingenious system of artificial irrigation, which is admirably supplemented by the manner in which the water is distributed from field to field and retained in them by a network of low banks.

In Bihar and Chota Nagpur irrigation from wells is common in the cold weather, the water being raised by a simple lever appliance like that illustrated in fig. 69. This consists of a long beam or bamboo working on an upright forked post, which serves as a fulcrum. At one end the beam is weighted by a stone, a mass of dried mud or a log; at the other is a rope with a bucket attached. The rope is pulled down till the bucket is immersed; as soon as the tension is relaxed, the weight attached to the lever raises the bucket. The water is then emptied into the channel leading to the field.

There are several canal systems with a network of distributaries, which are an insurance against crop failures, scarcity and famine. The Son Canals, which take off from the river Son, irrigate the greater portion of Shāhābād and smaller areas in Patna and Gaya. The

Orissa Canals, which derive their supply mainly from the Mahānadi, perform a similar office for Cuttack. Between them, these two systems irrigate 800,000 acres. A small system is at work in Midnapore, and a large

Fig. 69. Well irrigation

scheme has recently been completed in Champāran, by which the Tribeni canal will spread the water of the Gandak over the north of the district.

CHAPTER XVIII

INDUSTRIES AND MANUFACTURES

FROM an industrial point of view the country may be regarded as in a state of transition. Agriculture monopolizes the energies of the majority of the people. The village is the main unit of economic life, the village artisans supplying the simple needs of their neighbours, though some of their products, notably their hand-woven cotton cloths, have been supplanted by machine-made imported articles. On the other hand, organized industries and manufactures of considerable importance have come into existence within the last century. A large labour force is employed in coal-mines, jute mills, tea-gardens, iron and railway works; and labour is becoming more mobile, scores of thousands of able-bodied men migrating every year to meet the demand of the manufacturing centres. Machinery is being employed to an increasing extent; factories are springing up in the towns; the joint-stock company coexists with the older and simpler form of private partnership.

The organization of manufacturing industries has not proceeded very far as yet, as may be realized from the statistics of concerns employing 20 hands or more which were obtained at the census of 1911. The result was to show that there are 1466 such concerns with 600,000 *employés* in Bengal and 583 with 180,000 *employés* in Bihar and Orissa. In the former province the jute mills and tea-gardens each account for one-third of the *employés*. No province in India has such a large factory population as Bengal, which has also many jute presses, foundries, brick and tile factories, printing presses, cotton mills, railway and engineering works, etc. In Bihar and Orissa the extraction of minerals predominates over the manufacture of finished products, two-thirds of the labour force being engaged in mining. The majority of the large manufacturing concerns are situated in Calcutta and its neighbourhood, and are not only financed by European capital, but directed and managed by Europeans. A few Indians are beginning to follow the lead thus given them and are starting various small enterprises for the manufacture of articles which were formerly imported, such as soap, matches, umbrellas, steel trunks, pencils, cigarettes, etc.

At present, the chief difficulty in the organization and development of manufactures is the absence of a regular labour supply and of a settled class of operatives. Labour in the factories and mines is intermittent rather than regular owing to the obsession of agriculture. As explained by the Indian Factory Labour Commission of 1907–08: "The habits of the Indian factory operative are determined by the fact that he is primarily an agriculturist or a labourer on the land. In almost all cases his hereditary occupation is agriculture; his home is in the village from which he comes, not in the city in which he labours; his wife and family ordinarily continue to live in that village; he regularly remits a portion of his wages there; and he returns there periodically. There is as yet practically no factory population, such as exists in European countries, consisting of a large number of operatives trained from their youth to one particular class of work and dependent upon employment at that work for their livelihood."

The indigenous industries are mainly small handicrafts worked with a few simple tools. The blacksmith works a little furnace with a goat-skin bellows such as Tubalcain may have used. The potter turns a primitive mud wheel, on which he shapes vessels of an immemorial form with his thumb. The stock-in-trade of the goldsmith and silversmith consists of a hole in the mud floor of his workshop, which serves as a furnace, an earthenware bowl, fans with which to blow up the fire, and a box of hammers, pincers, chisels and other tools.

Fig. 70. The potter

Yet some of the products are famous for fineness of workmanship. "The yarns for the gossamer-like Dacca muslins were so fine, that 1 lb. weight of cotton was spun into a thread nearly 253 miles long. This was accomplished with the aid of a bamboo spindle not much bigger than a darning needle, which was lightly weighted with a pellet of clay." Wonderful stories are told of the delicacy of the Dacca muslins. One texture called *abrawan*, or running water, was so fine that when the emperor Aurangzeb reproved his daughter for appearing in scanty clothing, she pleaded that she was wearing seven thicknesses of the cloth. Another was supposed to be as light and transparent as dew, whence its name of *shabnam* (dew). A weaver is said to have been banished from Dacca for neglecting to prevent a cow from eating a piece that had been spread out on the grass to dry, which the cow mistook either for dew or a spider's web. Again, to take the case of iron-work, a cannon made by a Dacca blacksmith in 1637, which may still be seen at Murshidābād, is 17½ feet long and weighs over 7 tons. Another, at Bishnupur in the Bānkura district, which is made of hoops or cylinders of wrought iron welded together, is 12½ feet long and has a bore of nearly a foot. With these prefatory remarks we may pass to a survey of the principal industries: the mineral industries have already been dealt with in Chapter VIII.

Jute manufacture, the chief manufacturing industry in Bengal, is nearly sixty years old, the first jute mill having been built on the bank of the Hooghly in 1854. There are now 57 mills at work, with 33,000 looms and 677,000 spindles. These mills, which are situated in Calcutta and its neighbourhood, consume fully half the jute produced in India and provide employment for 200,000 persons. The wage bill amounts to £3,000,000 a year, and the capital invested to £10,000,000. At present they produce only the coarser kinds of articles, such as gunny bags and hessian cloth. Gunny means merely sacking, for which jute fibre is the cheapest known material. There are also a large number of jute press-houses in the same locality and in the jute growing districts, in which baling is carried on, i.e., the jute is pressed into bales; the standard bale of export weighs 5 maunds or 400 lbs.

Cotton mills are of minor importance, but fourteen have been established in Bengal either for spinning and weaving or for ginning and cleaning. The first cotton mill in India was started near Calcutta in 1818. Cotton being the staple article of clothing, hand weaving is still a widespread cottage industry, though it has greatly fallen off owing to the sale of machine-made articles.

Fig. 71. The village blacksmith

As a rule only coarse fabrics are turned out, but fine muslins are produced by the weavers of Dacca. The census of 1911 shows that this industry is the means of subsistence of 850,000 persons.

Bengal is the principal **silk**-producing province in India. Its annual output is estimated at 2,400,000 lbs. of raw silk, of which less than a quarter is made up locally into piece goods, mostly those called *korahs*. The industry (of which there are three branches, viz., cocoon-rearing, spinning the new silk and weaving) was formerly of greater importance. By the end of the eighteenth century, Bengal silk had driven all competitors, except Italian and China silks, out of the English market, and in the early part of the next century silk was the largest export. Production has suffered from diseases among the silk-worms and the competition of other countries; weaving, in particular, has been seriously affected by the heavy protective tariff levied in France against manufactured silk fabrics. The industry is most important in Murshidābād, the fabrics of which have long had a high repute: here the old bandannas are still made. Mālda produces fabrics of mixed silk and cotton, which bear picturesque names derived from the woven patterns, e.g. *bulbulchasm* or nightingales' eyes, *chand-tāra* or moon and stars, *mazchar* or river ripples and *kalintarakshi* or pigeons' eyes. In addition to mulberry-worm silk, a certain amount is produced in Eastern Bengal from indigenous silk-worms called *muga* and *eri*. There is also a large output of tusser (tussore) silk from the *tasar* worm.

The manufacture of tea is the principal manufacturing industry connected with agriculture. The experimental growth of the Chinese variety of the plant was introduced into Darjeeling by Dr Campbell, the Superintendent of the district, in 1840; and the industry became established there as a commercial enterprise about 1856. Plantations quickly multiplied and spread from the hills to the Tarai of Darjeeling and the Duārs of Jalpaiguri; the first garden in the latter was opened out in 1874. There are now 372 gardens in Bengal, the output of which in 1911 was 65,000,000 lbs., almost all black tea. The Darjeeling tea has a high reputation for its fine flavour;

generally speaking, the higher the elevation of the gardens, the better the quality of the leaf. The bud makes Orange Pekoe and Broken Orange Pekoe, the young leaf next to it Souchong, and the coarser leaf Pekoe Souchong. The objectionable method of rolling the leaf by hand, which is practised by the Chinese, has long been given up, and machinery is employed for the different processes of rolling, drying, sifting, etc.

Fig. 72. A sugarcane press

Bihar has practically a monopoly of **indigo** manufacture, but the value of this monopoly has long been diminishing owing to the manufacture of a cheap synthetic dye in Germany. The production is only a third of what it was in 1896 before the artificial article came on the market. Scores of factories have been closed or have taken to other crops. The gross annual outturn of indigo dye averages about 16,000 cwts., valued at 33 lakhs of rupees.

Tobacco now occupies as large an area as indigo in Bihar and thrice as much in Bengal. The bulk is exported in a crudely cured form to Burma for manufacture into cigars, but the local manufacture of cigarettes is developing rapidly in Bengal, while in Bihar the Peninsular Tobacco Co., financed by an Anglo-American syndicate, has set up a large cigarette factory, with up-to-date machinery, at Monghyr.

Fig. 73. Drying jute

Sugar manufacture has suffered from the importation of bounty-fed sugar, but is carried on in small refineries, mostly under Indian management, in both provinces. Molasses are also made by nearly every cultivator with the aid of small roller mills worked by bullocks, as illustrated in fig. 72. The sugarcane is pressed between the rollers, and the juice extracted is boiled in shallow iron pans. When it thickens, it is poured into pots and hardens with exposure to the air.

The manufacture of **brass and copper** ware and of **bell-metal**, is a flourishing village industry carried on with simple appliances. The demand is literally enormous, for brass and copper take the place held by glass and porcelain in Europe. Not only are domestic utensils made of copper and brass in general use—the former among Muhammadans and the latter among Hindus, who have a prejudice against iron vessels—but every Hindu requires for his ablutions a brass melon-shaped vessel, called a *lota*, and every Muhammadan a spouted vessel, called a *tanti*, which is exactly like a teapot without a lid. The shape of the latter is due to the injunction in the Korān that ablutions should be performed in running water. This cannot always be got, and so, by a kind of legal fiction, water falling through a spout fulfils the letter of the law. The industry is one of the few indigenous industries which has not been affected by competition, though the use of enamelled articles is on the increase. The majority of the braziers' and coppersmiths' products are intended for practical everyday use by a frugal people, and ornamental work is rare.

Vegetable **oils** are manufactured in a few large mills and generally, on a small scale for domestic use, in small hand mills. They are also largely used for the anointment of the person: oil, in fact, takes the place of soap, the use of which is a luxury not known to or in request among the masses. Formerly castor and other vegetable oils were used for illumination, but they have been supplanted by imported kerosene oil, which may be said to have effected "a domestic revolution in the economy of the people." There are large bulk oil depots at Budge-Budge near Calcutta, where the manufacture of kerosene oil tins has recently been started. Twenty years ago not a single tin was made in Bengal, but now there are five factories, with modern stamping machines, capable of turning out 100,000 tins a day.

There is a considerable culture of lac in Chota Nagpur, the north of Orissa and the west of Bengal; and lac manufacture is carried on in the districts of Rānchi, Mānbhūm, Bānkura and Bīrbhūm. The crude lac is a cellular resinous substance deposited on the branches and twigs of certain trees by the lac insect (*Coccus lacca*), which is a relative of the cochineal. Its name, derived from the Indian numeral lakh (100,000), indicates the myriads of the young larvae which swarm from the cells. The resinous encrustation on the twigs is called stick lac. The encrusted twigs having been broken up, and the woody portion removed, the lac which is left after washing is called seed lac. It is subjected to various processes of straining and melting to produce thin sheets, which form the shellac of commerce; or it is dropped in a molten state on to smooth surfaces to produce button lac. An increasing number of uses is being found for the product from sealing-wax to gramophone records.

Of other manufacturing concerns the principal are engineering and railway works, foundries, tile and brick making, paper manufacture (in mills near Calcutta) and printing; there are over 100 printing presses in Bengal. Government itself is a large manufacturer, having a gun and shell factory at Cossipur, a rifle factory at Ichapur, and an ammunition factory at Dum-Dum—all places near Calcutta. The Dum-Dum bullet, a soft-nosed bullet which expands and lacerates when it strikes its object, was so called from its being made in the place last named. Quinine and cinchona febrifuge are produced in a Government factory in Darjeeling. Since 1892 the drug has been sold at post offices at a cheap price; twenty quinine pills of four grains each can be bought for four annas.

The **artistic industries** are neither numerous nor important. The chief centres of gold and silver work are Cuttack, Calcutta, Dacca, Murshidābād and Kharagpur in Monghyr. The speciality of Cuttack is fine filigree work, like Maltese silver filigree. The wire into which the silver is drawn out is so fine that 120 feet can be got from a rupee's weight of silver. The spidery web of wire is manipulated with great skill, and articles of

Fig. 74. Stone carving at Konārak

extreme delicacy are produced. At Calcutta and Dacca *repoussé* work is produced, and at Kharagpur the artisans make gold and silver fish with flexible bodies formed of thinly beaten overlapping scales; a small cavity in the head of the fish serves as a receptacle for perfume.

Ivory carving is carried on by a small number of workmen at Murshidābād. The carving displays the finish and minuteness characteristic of true Indian art.

One special feature is the absence of joins; the carvers so dislike having to join pieces together that they would rather make a small article in which none are required than one made of several pieces which would sell for

Fig. 75. Ivory carving at Murshidābād

twice or thrice as much. They will carve any figure but that of Krishna, as it is against their creed to create or sell the deity who is the object of their worship. The industry is languishing. It was introduced when the

Nawābs of Bengal had their court at Murshidābād and flourished with the support of the Nawābs and their entourage. Since the Nawābs ceased to rule and their court disappeared, the demand for such dainty but expensive work has fallen off.

Magnificent specimens of **stone carving** may be seen in the old temples of Orissa. In the opinion of Mr E. B. Havell, "the Orissa carvers acquired the most extraordinary technical skill in architectural decoration Hindu art has known. There is a pitiable remnant of this splendid art still struggling for existence all over the Orissa Division, but unless Government adopts some more effective measures for preserving it than those hitherto employed, it is not likely to survive many years. ....Modern Orissa carving is often not very inferior to the old work. In style it is much more interesting than the better known sand-stone carving of Rājputāna and the Punjāb, which is often monotonous and more suggestive of furniture than of architectural decoration. While the Orissa carvers are in no way inferior to those of North-West India in delicate surface ornamentation, they have not hampered themselves by the limitations of a wood-carver's technique, but have fully realized the technical possibilities of their material for producing bold effects of light and shade suitable for architectural work."

Gold and silver **embroidery** is worked at Patna and Murshidābād, gold and silver wire being worked on caps, jackets and the trappings of horses and elephants. Silk brocades heavily embroidered with gold and silver wire are known as kincobs, a corruption of *kamkhwāb*. Muslins embroidered by hand with silk or coloured cotton thread, which are known as *kasidas*, are produced at Dacca and exported to Turkey. Cotton brocades embroidered in the looms at the same place go by the name of *jamdanis*. In Bengal there is a considerable production, both for local sale and export to Europe and Australia, of hand-worked flowered muslin, called "chicken" work from the Persian *chikin* meaning cotton embroidery. Damascened work (pewter inlaid with silver and blackened) called *bidri* ware (from Bidar in the Deccan, whence it was introduced) is turned out on an insignificant scale

Fig. 76. Fish traps in Bengal

in Purnea and Murshidābād. Small clay models of figures of good design are made at Krishnagar in Nadia, and ornamental pottery at Siwān in Sāran and Sasarām in Shāhābād.

Lastly, mention should be made of **fishing**, which is an important industry in Bengal, where a million people are maintained by the capture and sale of fish. This figure, moreover, does not take into account the vast number of those who catch fish for home consumption in their own ponds, fields and ditches (as illustrated in fig. 77) at the close of the rains, when the flood-water recedes. Fish is a staple article of food in Bengal, and it is officially stated that "the fishery possibilities of the province are nowhere exceeded, except perhaps by those of the United States of America." At present, however, the supply is unequal to the demand. It comes

Fig. 77. Inland fishing in Bengal

almost entirely from the inland fisheries, and the fishing grounds in the Bay of Bengal are scarcely touched. "The fishermen generally are quite ignorant of the methods of fish-curing, and large quantities of fish are regularly lost through this cause alone. By-products are never utilized; means of transit of fish from one place to another are generally inadequate. There is no close season for any species of fish, and inconceivable numbers of eggs of many species are destroyed yearly. Anicuts are thrown indiscriminately across rivers and streams, and no fish-ladders are provided." Figure 76 shows how completely a stream may be blocked for the capture of all fish making their way up it. A Fishery Department has been started by Government in each province for the development of the industry by the investigation and improvement of the sources of supply.

CHAPTER XIX

COMMUNICATIONS

FROM the earliest times the rivers appear to have been the most important means of internal communication. Other trade routes, such as roads, railways and canals, are almost entirely modern. Until the establishment of British rule there were few roads practicable for wheeled traffic throughout the year, and merchandise was mostly conveyed by the slow-moving cargo boat or the pack-bullock. Those roads that were maintained owed their existence to their value as strategic routes, the most important being a highway, constructed by the emperor Sher Shāh (1540–5), which is said to have stretched from Bengal to the Punjāb and was the precursor of the Grand Trunk Road. In the turmoil accompanying the downfall of the Mughal Empire the roads fell into general neglect, and as late as 1833 we find an entry in Shore's *Notes on Indian Affairs* stating: "As to the roads, excepting those within the limits of civil stations, sixteen miles between Calcutta and Barrackpore is all we have to boast of."

It was not till 1854 that the first length of railway line (from Howrah to Pandua near Burdwān) was opened; three years later, when the Mutiny broke out, it extended only as far as Rāniganj. Thence the troops had to march to the north-west along the Grand Trunk Road, a long route marked at all too short intervals by little cemeteries containing the graves of cholera

Fig. 78. The country cart of the plains

victims. Even until 1891 there was no direct railway communication between Bengal and the Central Provinces, Madras and Assam. "Now the traveller can go direct to Nagpur by the great Bengal-Nagpur Railway and so on by a new and shorter route to Bombay; he can pass through the whole province of Orissa and down the east coast to Madras, instead of crossing the continent twice—first to Bombay and then back again to Madras;

and he can proceed from the port of Chittagong direct into the province of Assam, whereas previously he would have had to cross the sea to Calcutta and thence proceed by rail and steamer."

Both provinces are served by a network of **roads** maintained by three agencies. The Public Works Department is responsible for the more important highways, the District Boards for other roads and the Local Boards for village roads, which are merely fair-weather tracks.

Fig. 79. The country cart of Chota Nagpur

The vehicles mostly in use are bullock-carts like that shown in fig. 78; but in the hilly tracts of Chota Nagpur the people use a low strongly made cart with solid wooden wheels (*v.* fig. 79) suitable for rough country.

Two roads are in a class by themselves. One is the Grand Trunk Road from Calcutta to Delhi, the construction of which was taken in hand during the administration of Lord William Bentinck (1828–35). The other is the

Darjeeling Cart Road, one of the finest mountain roads in India, which mounts 7000 feet (from Siliguri to Darjeeling) in 51 miles, the ruling gradient being 1 in 31. It was commenced in 1861 to replace a military road built by Lord Napier of Magdala, which was too steep and narrow for cart traffic.

The following statement shows the **railways** in each province and the length of open line in 1912. There is no railway in Sikkim.

Railway	Bengal	Bihar and Orissa
Assam-Bengal	217	..
Bengal-Duārs..	153	..
Bengal-Nagpur	333	833
Bengal and North-Western..	..	928
Eastern Bengal ..	1264	170
East Indian	394	1040
Total	2361	2971

There are two gauges—the metre gauge of 3 feet $3\frac{3}{8}$ inches north of the Ganges and the broad gauge of 5 feet 6 inches south of it: the opening of a bridge across the Ganges near Sāra has resulted in the extension of the broad gauge up to Sāntahār on the Eastern Bengal Railway. Elsewhere connection between the two systems is effected by ferry steamers.

The **Assam-Bengal Railway** is a metre gauge line, opened in 1895, connecting Assam with Chittagong, where it has its terminus. Connection with Calcutta is effected by a branch line to Chāndpur, whence steamers run to Goalundo to meet the trains of the Eastern Bengal State Railway.

The **Bengal-Duārs Railway** was opened in 1895 and, as its name implies, serves the area in Jalpaiguri known as the Duārs. It is on the metre gauge and connects with the Eastern Bengal State Railway at Jalpaiguri and Lālmanir Hāt.

The **Bengal-Nagpur Railway** is one of the most important of all the railway systems, for it connects Bengal with Orissa and Madras on the south and with the Central Provinces and Bombay on the west. It also serves Chota Nagpur and taps the Jherria coal-

Fig. 80. Cargo boats on the Ganges

field, access to which makes it a large coal carrier. It is a broad gauge line having its terminus at Howrah and large works at Kharagpur. The latter is the junction for the coast line to Madras and the main line to Nagpur.

The **Bengal and North-Western Railway** has practically a monopoly of the traffic in North Bihar, where it has taken over the working of the Tirhut State

Railway line. It is a metre gauge line running westward into the United Provinces and connecting with the Eastern Bengal State Railway at Katihār on the east.

The **Eastern Bengal Railway** runs from Calcutta (Sealdah) to North and Eastern Bengal, and also to Assam. It was formerly known as the Eastern Bengal State Railway. It works the Cooch Behar Railway (33 miles) and has taken over the line of the Bengal Central Railway from Calcutta to Khulna.

Fig. 81. A Ganges ferry steamer

The **East Indian Railway,** the largest system in the two provinces, is the main channel of communication between Bengal, Bihar and the north-west of India. There are three principal lines. The Loop Line, the oldest of the three, was constructed to follow the Ganges. It takes off at Khāna near Burdwān and runs close to the southern bank of the Ganges from Rājmahāl to Buxar, whence it proceeds to Moghalsarai near Benares. The Chord Line strikes across the Loop Line from Khāna to Lakhisarai in Monghyr. The Grand Chord Line, which is used by the trains to Bombay, extends from near Asansol to Gaya, from which it runs westward over the Son to Moghalsarai. The terminus is at Howrah, and there are large works at Lillooah near Howrah and at Jamālpur near Monghyr.

In addition to these railways, the Port Commissioners of Calcutta maintain a line for the transport of goods to and from the docks and jetties. There are several **light railways**, as shown below:

Name	Miles	District
	Bengal	
Baraset-Basirhāt	51	24-Parganas
Howrah-Amta	44	Howrah
Howrah-Sheakhāla	20	Howrah and Hooghly
Darjeeling-Himalayan	51	Darjeeling
Tārakeswar-Māgra	33	Hooghly
	Bihar and Orissa	
Arrah-Sasarām	60	Shāhābād
Bakhtiārpur-Bihar	33	Patna
Dehri-Rohtās	24	Shāhābād

Most of them run on District Board roads and are on the 2 feet 6 inches gauge. As a rule a certain percentage, usually 4 per cent., is guaranteed by the District Board, and any profits above that figure are divided equally between the Board and the railway company.

The most interesting of the light railways is the Darjeeling-Himalayan from Siliguri to Darjeeling, a mountain railway, which at one point rises to 7407 feet. The average gradient is nearly 1 in 29, but in one portion it is as steep as 1 in 23. The gauge is only 2 feet, and the line follows the Darjeeling Cart Road already mentioned with a few diversions. In some places a quicker ascent is effected by means of loops or spirals and also of reverses, the train being taken up inclines laid out in zigzags.

Water communications are of exceptional importance in Bengal, where the river surface, even in the dry season, extends over 5000 square miles. During the rains the greater part of Eastern Bengal is flooded and under water; here the rivers and creeks serve for roads, boats take the place of carts and steamers of trains. "Every one travels by water, and on a market day in the

Fig. 82. A view on the Grand Trunk Road

flooded tracts hundreds of boats will be met coming from and going to the bazar. The vessels are of every shape and size, ranging from the earthenware pipkin in which children paddle themselves to school, or from one house to another in the village, to the huge top-heavy country boats capable of holding 1600 maunds of jute."

Steamers, both passenger and cargo, with attendant flats, ply on the Ganges and Brahmaputra as far as the United Provinces on one side and Assam on the other.

The chief centre of the steamer traffic is Goalundo, which lies near the junction of the Ganges and Brahmaputra and is the eastern terminus of the Eastern Bengal Railway system south of the Ganges. From this place steamers run to Narayanganj and Chāndpur, connecting

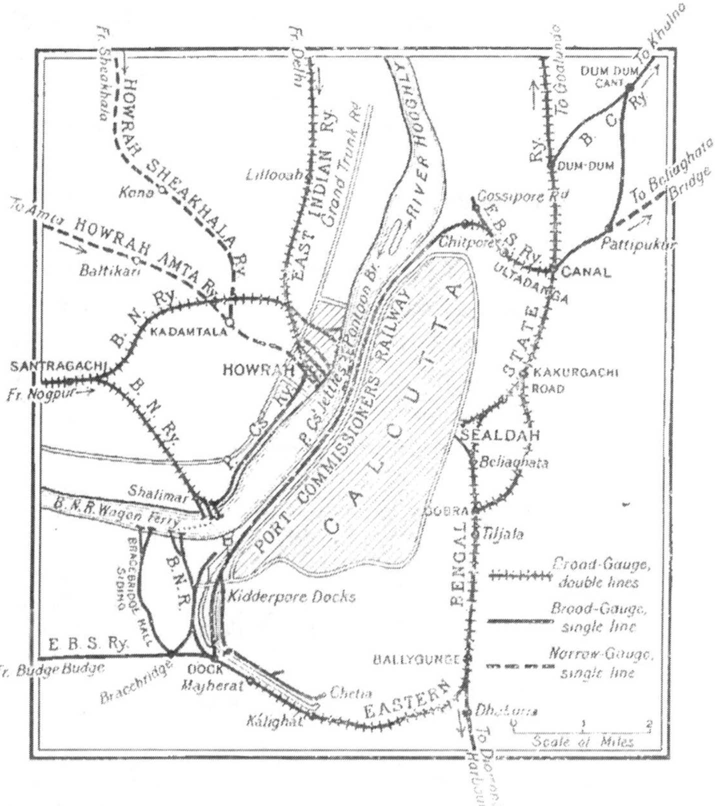

Fig. 83. Railway map of Calcutta district

at the former with the railways of Dacca and other Eastern Bengal districts and at the latter with the Assam-Bengal Railway.

There is also a continuous water route between Eastern Bengal and Calcutta, the vessels using which make their way through the Sundarbans by a succession of navigable channels known as the **Calcutta and Eastern Canals.** This is a system of natural channels, connected by a few artificial canals, by which the produce of Eastern Bengal and the Brahmaputra valley is brought to Calcutta without having to go out into the Bay of Bengal. Their length is a little over 1100 miles. The western terminus is Calcutta. Their objective to the east is Barisāl, the headquarters of the great rice-producing district of Backergunge, nearly 200 miles east of Calcutta. As the traffic passing along these channels averages a million tons a year, valued at nearly four millions sterling, this may be regarded as one of the most important systems of inland channels in the world. There is also a certain amount of navigation on the canals proper, such as the Son and Orissa Canals, and the Orissa Coast Canal. The traffic along the canals has, however, largely diminished owing to the competition of the railways.

CHAPTER XX

COMMERCE AND TRADE

As in other parts of India, the people, though independent of imports for their food, rely mainly on other countries for their clothing, their manufactured goods and their luxuries, while the bulk of the exports consists of agricultural products. The **foreign trade** centres almost entirely in Calcutta, which, though no longer the official capital of India, has a good claim to be considered its commercial capital. It is the natural entrepôt for the produce of the Gangetic and Brahmaputra valleys, and its position both as a receiving and distributing centre has been enormously improved by the construction of railways and the establishment of inland steamer services. It is, in fact, the natural port of North-East India, being the one place where river, rail and ocean traffic can be economically interchanged. The value of its foreign trade is now close on 92 millions sterling a year, or only 12 millions less than that of

Fig. 84. Village shops

Glasgow and Manchester combined; exports account for 57 millions and imports for nearly 35 millions. A small amount of foreign trade is also carried on at Chittagong, which ranks among, but is the least important of, the seven ports of India.

By far the most valuable of the exports is jute, raw and manufactured, which represents two-fifths of the exports and one-quarter of the total foreign trade. The fact that the value of the manufactured jute sometimes exceeds that of the raw fibre shows the extent to which production has been developed in the local mills. The largest supplies are shipped to the British Isles and the United States, the former taking two-fifths of the raw jute and the latter two-fifths of the manufactured jute. Grain and pulses occupy the second place in the list of exports, the best customer being Ceylon, to which two-fifths of the total quantity are consigned. Third

Fig. 85. Villagers going to market in Bengal

in importance comes tea, exported from the gardens in Darjeeling, the Duārs and Assam; Russia is the largest consumer after the United Kingdom. Other important exports are oilseeds, hides and skins and opium, the last of which is valuable rather than bulky. The United Kingdom takes altogether 30 per cent. of the exports, other British possessions 18, the United States 15 and Germany 11 per cent.

Cotton goods, which furnish the clothing of the masses of India, predominate among the imports; the United Kingdom claims all but 5 per cent. of their value. They are followed, *longo intervallo*, by metals, for India is almost entirely dependent on foreign countries for its supply of iron, steel and copper. Their value only slightly exceeds that of imported sugar, which is nearly all obtained from Java. Next come, in the order shown, mineral oils, machinery and mill work, railway plant and rolling stock, hardware and cutlery. The imports of kerosene oil in 1911–12 reached the enormous total of 32 million gallons—nearly double the figure of the preceding year—of which two-thirds came from the United States and a little under one-third from Borneo. This extraordinary rise was due to a rate war between the Standard Oil Co. and the Royal Dutch Shell Transport Combination. The shares of the import trade among the principal importing countries were—the United Kingdom 69 per cent., other British possessions 4, Java 10, Germany 5 and the United States 3.

Internal trade is concerned mainly with the same articles. Calcutta is the receiving centre for both Bengal and Bihar and Orissa, and also serves Assam, the United Provinces and, to a minor extent, the Central Provinces. Rice is exported to the United Provinces where the demand is in excess of the local supply, tobacco to Burma, silk to the Punjāb and the west of India, and coal to all parts of the continent. The **frontier trade** with Nepal, Bhutān, Sikkim and Tibet is small in volume and of no great value; the main staple of export from Tibet is raw wool.

Outside Calcutta the principal trade centres are Howrah, Chittagong, Patna, Dacca, Cuttack and Narayanganj. The place last named deals with a fifth of the total jute crop; other jute entrepôts are Chāndpur,

Goalundo, Kushtia, Madāripur and Sirājganj. In the interior a considerable trade is carried on by itinerant dealers with carts, pack-bullocks or boats, who buy up produce from the cultivators and distribute salt, oil, etc. In Eastern Bengal the markets are generally situated on the rivers, and country boats penetrate almost every river and creek bringing the villagers their supplies and

Fig. 86. A riverside mart

taking their surplus produce from them. The smaller villages contain few if any shops, and goods are mostly bought and sold in the markets held once or twice a week in the larger villages, or at the periodical fairs held in connection with the recurring religious festivals. In this respect the country is not unlike medieval England, where nearly all buying and selling took place at weekly markets or annual fairs.

CHAPTER XXI

THE ROLL OF HONOUR

IN this chapter a necessarily brief mention will be made of those who are worthy of being had in remembrance, either because they have made modern history in the two provinces or because they have distinguished themselves in science, arts, literature, etc.

Few outside India know the name of **Gabriel Boughton,** but to him the English are indebted for their first trade license, which was indeed the first step in their steady march to power. The common tradition is that he cured Jahanāra, the daughter of the Emperor Shāh Jahān, of a terrible burn, and when asked to name his reward, "with that liberality which distinguishes Britons, sought not for any private emolument, but solicited that his nation might have liberty to trade free of all duties in Bengal and to establish factories in that country." This story has been shown to be a myth, but there is no doubt that Boughton was attached as a surgeon to the court of Prince Shāh Shuja, Viceroy of Bengal from 1639 to 1660, and from him obtained a *pharmān* or trade license for his compatriots. Nor is there anything improbable in the story that he owed his favour with the Prince to having cured one of the ladies of his zenana. Of other early pioneers of British rule first place must be yielded to **Job Charnock,** the founder of Calcutta, "the man whose perseverance and foresight established this great centre of English trade in the East." He died in the city of his foundation in 1693 after 37 years of hard service in the exhausting climate of Bengal.

The annals of the next century are crowded with the

Fig. 87. Lord Clive

names of men so famous that their achievements need not be recapitulated, such as **Lord Clive, Warren Hastings,** the first Chief Justice of Bengal, **Sir Elijah Impey**

(1732–1809), and Warren Hastings' malignant enemy, **Sir Philip Francis** (1740–1818), who was almost indubitably the writer of *The Letters of Junius*. A hero who is not so well known is **John Zephaniah Holwell** (1711–98), origin-

Fig. 88. Warren Hastings

ally a surgeon, who became Zamindar of Calcutta, conducted the defence of Fort William in 1756 after Drake had fled, and was one of the 23 survivors of the Black Hole. He is called by Orme "the gallant defender of the Fort and the asserter of the reputation of the nation."

To **Lord Cornwallis**, Governor-General of India from 1786 to 1793, Bengal is indebted for the Permanent Settlement, and to **Lord Dalhousie** (1848–56) for its creation as a separate province. During Dalhousie's administration, moreover, the country began to receive the gifts of modern civilization. A cheap and uniform postage of half an anna (a halfpenny) a letter was introduced, the first telegraph line from Calcutta was set up, and the first railway line in Bengal was opened.

The following is a list of the **Lieutenant-Governors** who administered Bengal after Lord Dalhousie (with the years in which they were appointed)—Sir Frederick Halliday 1854, Sir John Peter Grant 1859, Sir Cecil Beadon 1862, Sir William Grey 1867, Sir George Campbell 1871, Sir Richard Temple 1874, Sir Ashley Eden 1877, Sir Rivers Thomson 1882, Sir Stuart Bayley 1887, Sir Charles Elliott 1890, Sir Alexander Mackenzie 1895, Sir John Woodburn 1898, Sir James Bourdillon 1902, Sir Andrew Fraser 1903, Sir Edward Baker 1908 and Sir William Duke 1911. The short-lived province of Eastern Bengal and Assam had only three Lieutenant-Governors, viz., Sir Bamfylde Fuller, Sir Lancelot Hare and Sir Charles Bayley. The last was transferred to Bihar and Orissa in 1912, when Lord Carmichael was translated from Madras to Bengal.

Of administrators working in a smaller sphere the most notable are **Augustus Cleveland** (1755–85), called "the *dulce decus* of the early Civil Service," who effected the pacification of the wild tribes of the Rājmahāl Hills, and two military officers, Major **Samuel Carteris Macpherson** (1806–60) and General **Sir John Campbell** (1802–78), by whose exertions human sacrifice was stopped among the Khonds of Orissa.

One sailor and many soldiers have distinguished

Fig. 89. Lord Dalhousie

themselves in our area. The sailor was **Admiral Watson**, who cooperated with Clive in the recapture of Calcutta in 1757 and is commemorated by a monument in Westminster Abbey. Sir **Hector Munro**, who at the age of 38 won the great victory of Buxar (1764), took over the command on the death of **Major Adams**, who with a few English veterans and a small force of sepoys, won the battles of Giria and Udhua Nullah, captured Murshidābād, Monghyr and Patna, and died, worn out by his labours, in January 1764. With him must be mentioned "the truly gallant" **Ranfurlie Knox**, who died the same year after a short but glorious career. Patna was relieved by his extraordinary forced march in 1760, when he marched from Burdwān, at the head of only 200 Europeans, and covered 294 miles in 13 days during the fierce heat of May. A gallant soldier himself, he found a kindred spirit in **Raja Shitāb Rai** (afterwards Rai Rayān and Naib Nāzim), a Kayasth general who fought by his side. "This," Knox exclaimed, pointing to Shitāb Rai covered with the dust and blood of battle, "is a real Nawāb. I never saw such a Nawāb in my life."

Three of the heroes of the Indian Mutiny may be singled out for mention, of whom two were civilians—**Herwald Wake** (1823–1901), Magistrate of Arrah, and **Vicars Boyle** (1822–1908), a railway engineer, the two leaders of the defence of the Arrah House against overwhelming odds, and **Sir Vincent Eyre** (1811–81), who organized a relief expedition on his own initiative and cut his way through to their rescue. In the early days of his service Eyre was kept as a hostage by the Afghāns (in 1841), and after his retirement he organized an ambulance service for the sick and wounded in the Franco-Prussian war. The title of **General Lloyd** to fame is based not on his success as a soldier—he was a successful general in the Santāl war, but failed when in command at Dinapore during the Mutiny—but on the fact, recorded in his epitaph, that "to his exertions and personal influence with the Raja of Sikkim the province of Bengal is indebted for the sanitarium of Darjeeling." He discovered the place in 1829 and died there in 1865.

Our knowledge of the country in early times is derived from a large number of travellers, of whom the earliest was **Megasthenes.** He resided at Pātaliputra, as an envoy from Seleucos to Chandragupta, and his account of the country "continued up to the sixteenth century to be the principal authority on India for European writers. The statements he recorded are so precise, that more is known in detail about the court and administration of Chandragupta in the fourth century B.C. than about any other Indian monarch prior to Akbar in the sixteenth century A.D., with perhaps the exception of king Harsha in the seventh century." Our knowledge of the latter is obtained from that pious and precise Chinese pilgrim, **Hiuen Tsiang,** who visited the holy places of Buddhism and left a careful and accurate record of his travels. There is also a brief but interesting account from the pen of an earlier Chinese pilgrim, **Fa Hien,** who came in quest of sacred Buddhist books and images in the fifth century. The last of the great Asiatic travellers was the Arabian **Ibn Batuta,** who left Tangiers in 1325 and visited Bengal in the course of his wanderings.

The earliest European traveller in Bengal was the Venetian nobleman, **Nicolo de Conti,** who, accompanied by his wife, sailed up the Ganges in the first half of the fifteenth century. The country was visited in the next century by two more Italians, viz., **Ludovico di Varthema** and, towards its close, **Caesar de Federici.** The first Englishman known to have reached this part of India was **Ralph Fitch,** a London merchant who made his way to it overland and about 1588 visited Patna, Hooghly,

Cooch Behar and other places in Bengal. His is the first English account of Bihar and Bengal. The first Dutch pioneer was **Linschoten** (1583–9), who gives a lurid description of the lawlessness of the Portuguese. An Augustinian friar of the latter nation, **Sebastian Manrique**, who was sent to Bengal about 1612, has left an interesting account, in which he mentions the self-immolation that took place on Saugor Island, the oppressive rule of the Mughals and the difficulty of making the landlords pay their revenue. "He who gives blows is a master. He who gives none is a dog" was his conclusion about the people. Two other famous travellers during the seventeenth century were the French physician, **Bernier**, and the French jeweller, **Tavernier**, the latter of whom first visited Bengal in 1641 and again accompanied Bernier there in 1666.

William Bruton is not so well known, but to him we are indebted for the earliest first-hand account of Orissa, to which he came with the English expedition under Ralph Cartwright in 1633. The people he found "notable ingenious men, let it be in what art or science 'soever." Very full information about the state of the country under Aurangzeb is given in the voluminous diary of **William Hedges**, Agent in Bengal from 1681 to 1688, "a simple but most quaint and interesting writer," by **Thomas Bowrey** (1669–79) in his *Countries round the Bay of Bengal*, and by **Nicolas Graaf**, a Dutch doctor who travelled up to Patna in 1670 to attend the head of the Dutch factory. On the way, having stopped to make a drawing of the fort at Monghyr, he was arrested as a spy and thrown into a dark noisome dungeon. Less important travellers are the Dutch captain **Gautier Schouten** (1658–65), **Streynsham Master**, the President of Madras, who came to Bengal on a tour of inspection in 1676 and 1679, **Captain Alexander Hamilton** (1688–1723) and **Stavorinus**, a Dutch admiral who came from Batavia in 1769.

More than one Tibetan explorer has been connected with Bengal. The famous Capuchin missionaries penetrated to Lhāsa from their headquarters at Chandernagore and Patna in the early part of the eighteenth century. **George Bogle** was sent by Warren Hastings as an envoy to Tibet in 1774, and was subsequently Collector of Rangpur. **Csoma de Köros**, a poor Hungarian student, who begged his way across Asia and spent many years in a Tibetan monastery compiling a dictionary of the Tibetan language, lived in Calcutta from 1837 to 1842, and was buried in Darjeeling, where he died while trying to make his way to Lhāsa. A later explorer, **Sarat Chandra Dās**, who entered Lhāsa in 1881, is a native of Chittagong. In the category of frontier explorers may also be mentioned **Sir Joseph Hooker**, one of the first Englishmen to explore Sikkim, whose *Himalayan Journals* is a classic. This grand old man served as surgeon and naturalist on the *Erebus* in Sir James Ross' Antarctic expedition of 1839–43 and wrote the account of Botany in the *Imperial Gazetteer of India* a few years before his death; he died in 1911 at the great age of 94.

The greatest authority on the history of Bengal, Bihar and Orissa during the latter days of the Mughal Empire is the *Sair-ul-Mutākharin* (meaning A Review of Modern Times) by **Saiyad Ghulām Husain**, a native of Bihar. It was translated into English by a French creole named Raymond, who on becoming a Musalmān adopted the name of Hāji Mustapha. The whole edition was lost at sea on the voyage to England, with the exception of a few copies circulated in Calcutta in 1789, and it was not till 1902 that it was republished by a Calcutta firm. The *Riyazu-s-Salātīn* or "King's Gardens" by **Ghulām Husain Salim**, who served as post-master at Mālda, has been described by Professor Blochmann as "the fullest account in Persian of the Muhammadan history of Bengal, which the author brings down to his own time (1786–88)." An English translation by Maulvi Abdus Salām appeared in 1904.

The fullest English history of Bengal, from the first Muhammadan invasion down to 1757, is that compiled from Muhammadan chronicles by **Major Charles Stewart,** which was published in 1813. **Professor Blochmann,** the learned translator of the *Ain-i-Akbari*, was a German who entered the English army in 1858 in order to get out to India and was engaged in educational work in Calcutta from 1860 till his death in 1878. Of modern historical writers the most graceful is **Sir William Hunter** (1840–1900), whose *Annals of Rural Bengal* appeared six years after he had joined the Bengal Civil Service. His facile pen illuminated statistics and geography as well as history, and his last work was a History of British India. Other writers on historical subjects are **Ramesh Chandra Dutt,** another versatile member of the Indian Civil Service, and **Charles Robert Wilson** (1863–1904), whose *Early Annals of the British in Bengal* is a standard work.

The vernacular literature of Bengal is rich in great names. **Jayadeva,** the writer of the *Gīta Govinda*, a Sanskrit poem, which has been called "the Indian Song of Songs," was born in **Bīrbhūm** in the twelfth century. The chief poets of the fifteenth century were **Bidyāpati,** the only great poet of Bihar, and his friend and contemporary **Chandidās,** another native of **Bīrbhūm,** the earliest vernacular Bengali poet, who is regarded as the father of Bengali lyric poetry. To the same century belong the Bengali translation of the *Mahābhārata* by **Kāsirām Dās** of Burdwān and to the sixteenth century the Bengali version of the *Rāmāyana* by **Krittibās** of

Nadia, both of which are classics. The greatest of the writers of the seventeenth century was **Mukunda Rām**, of Burdwān, commonly called Kabi Kankan or the Jewel of Bards. The theme of his poems was the goddess Chandi or Durga, whose praises were also sung in the next century by **Rām Prasād Sen** of Nadia and **Bharat Chandra Rai** of Burdwān.

In the beginning of the nineteenth century there was a revival of Bengali literature under English influence, and Bengali prose was created. Its father was the religious and social reformer Raja **Rām Mohan Ray** (1774–1833), whose successors were **Iswar Chandra Vidyāsāgar** (1820–91), also prominent in the cause of social reform, and **Akshay Kumār Datta** (1820–86). Poetic genius flourished during the same period. **Iswar Chandra Gupta** (1809–58) produced satires which earned for him the title of the greatest Bengali humorist. The chief dramatic writer was **Dinabandhu Mitra** (1829–73), whose *Nil Darpan*, dealing with the abuses of indigo planting, led to the imprisonment for libel of its translator, the Rev. James Long. Even greater than these was the epic poet, **Michael Madhusudan Datta** (1824–73), who was educated first in the Hindu College and later, after his conversion to Christianity, in Bishop's College. He is held by Mr R. C. Dutt to be "the greatest literary genius of the century," while Sir George Grierson points out that "he ranks higher in the estimation of his countrymen than any Bengali poet of this or any previous age."

Bankim Chandra Chatterji (1838–94) is the founder of the modern school of Bengali fiction, which, whether or not it deserves to be called "the best product of Bengali prose," certainly exercises immense influence. Among his successors may be mentioned **Nabin Chandra Sen**, whose recent death was deplored as a loss to Bengali literature, and **Piyāri Chānd Mitra**, who wrote under the *nom-de-plume* of Tekchānd Thākur and whose novel *Allāler Gharer Dulāl* (1858) has been compared by European critics with the best works of Molière and Fielding. The poetic genius of **Rabindranāth Tagore** has recently received international recognition with the bestowal upon him in 1913 of the Nobel prize for literature.

The intellectual activity of the end of the eighteenth and early part of the nineteenth century was shared in by many European scholars. Researches in the virgin field of Sanskrit learning and Indian antiquities were made by **Sir William Jones** (1746–94) who founded the Asiatic Society of Bengal, **Henry Thomas Colebrooke** (1765–1837), **Horace Hayman Wilson** (1786–1869) and **James Prinsep** (1799–1840), to whose memory the citizens of Calcutta erected Prinsep's Ghāt. **David Hare** (1775–1822), a philanthropic watchmaker of Calcutta, enthusiastically promoted the cause of English education for Indians and secured the foundation of the Hindu College in 1818. In this college the Eurasian poet **Derozio** (1809–31) was a teacher.

Indian archaeology has had one of its greatest exponents in **Rajendra Lāla Mitra** (1824–91), while the first systematic explorations in our area were made by **General Alexander Cunningham** (1814–93), the first Director of the Indian Archaeological Survey.

Other branches of science are well represented. **James Rennell** (1742–1830), "the father of Indian geography," was the first to make a survey of Bengal and was adjudged worthy of burial in Westminster Abbey. Most of the earlier cartographers were foreigners, such as **Gastaldi** (1516), **De Barros** (1553–1613), **Blaev** (1650) and **Valentijn** (1670). The list of Superintendents of the Royal Botanic Garden at Sibpur near Calcutta contains the names of some of the greatest Indian botanists, such as **Roxburgh** (1751–1815), the "father of Indian botany," and **Nathaniel Wallich** (1786–1854). The latter was a Dane who served as surgeon at Serampore. He was made a prisoner on its capture by the English, but released in recognition of his scientific attainments. The establishment of the Indian Museum at Calcutta in 1814 was due to his representations. Another Superintendent, Francis Buchanan (1762–1829), who took the name of **Buchanan-Hamilton** (by which he is more usually known), was a versatile scientist and the first writer of gazetteers for Bengal and Bihar districts. Extracts from his manuscript, which is preserved in the India Office, were issued by Montgomery Martin under the title of *History, Topography and Statistics of Eastern India*, which is a mine of information about agrarian conditions a century ago.

Many eminent geologists, beginning with **Dr Thomas Oldham** (1816–78), have served in the Geological Survey and have worked in our area, but they are the possession of all India rather than of either of our two provinces. The same remark applies to zoologists, such as **William Thomas Blanford** (1832–1905), and to meteorologists such as his brother **Henry Francis Blanford** (1834–93), who was originally a geologist. Among ethnologists we have **Brian Houghton Hodgson** (1800–94), an authority on the Himalayan tribes, who resided for some years at Darjeeling, **Colonel Dalton,** whose *Descriptive Ethnology of Bengal* (1872) is a first-hand authority on the tribes of Chota Nagpur, **Jogendra Nāth Bhattacharya,** the author of *Hindu Sects and Castes*, and **Sir Herbert Risley,** whose *Tribes and Castes of Bengal* is a standard ethnological work. A retired member of the Bengal Civil Service, **Sir George Grierson,** is the greatest authority on Indian languages and the author of that monumental work, *The Linguistic Survey of India*. A few painters have dealt with our area, viz., **Thomas Daniell** and his nephew

William Daniell, who spent ten years (1784–94) painting in India, **William Hodges** (1744–97) and the Bohemian portrait-painter **Johann Zoffany** (1733–1810).

Bengal has produced several religious and social reformers, of whom the greatest was **Chaitanya** (circ. 1485–1527), a native of Nadia, who for four centuries has been worshipped as an incarnation of Vishnu. In more modern times we have **Raja Rām Mohan Ray** (1772–1833), who fought against *sati* and polygamy, advocated the remarriage of widows and in 1828 founded the Brahmo Samāj. His crusade against polygamy and in favour of widow remarriage was carried on by **Iswar Chandra Vidyasāgar** (1820–91), while the Brahmo Samāj movement was developed by the saintly **Maharshi Debendra Nāth Tagore** (1818–1905), the well-known **Keshab Chandra Sen** (1838–84), who established an eclectic church, and his successor **Pratāp Chandra Mazumdar** (1840–1905).

A recent Vedantic sect owes its inspiration to **Rām Krishna Parahamsa** (1834–86), whose life and doctrines form the subject of Max Müller's *Ram Krishna: His Life and Sayings.* The chief apostle of the creed was **Swāmi Vivekananda** (1863–1902) and one of its best known adherents was the late **Sister Nivedita** (Miss Margaret Noble).

The first Protestant missionary in Bengal was a Dane, **Zachariah Kiernander** (1711–99), who was sent out to Cuddalore by the English Society for Promoting Christian Knowledge and came to Calcutta in 1758. The Baptist missionaries, **Dr William Carey** (1761–1834), **Dr Joshua Marshman** (1768–1837) and **William Ward** (1769–1823), who started the Serampore Mission in 1799, are even more famous in missionary annals. "It is on the broad foundations which they laid that the edifice of modern Indian missions has been erected." They were the first to translate the Bible into Indian languages, the first books printed in Bengali were issued from their press and they even started a Bengali newspaper. At Serampore they had close relations with **Daniel Corrie,** a Bengal chaplain who was the first Bishop of Madras, and another celebrated missionary, **Henry Martyn,** who worked both at Serampore and Dinapore and died in 1812 in Armenia; there, according to Macaulay's epitaph, "in manhood's early bloom, the Christian hero found a pagan tomb." The first missionary of the Church of Scotland was **Dr Alexander Duff** (1806–78), who first arrived in Calcutta in 1830 after being wrecked off Saugor Island and on a second visit devoted himself to the evangelization of rural districts.

The see of Calcutta has been held by several eminent divines, and in some cases peaceful careers have ended in tragic deaths. The first Bishop, **Dr Middleton,** described by Charles **Lamb,** a fellow-student at Christ's Hospital, as "a scholar and a gentleman in his teens," founded Bishop's College and died of fever in Calcutta in 1822, eight years after his arrival. There is a monument erected to him in St Paul's Cathedral in London. His successor, the well-known **Bishop Heber,** author of some of the best hymns in the English language and of many indifferent poems, died four years later from bursting a blood-vessel in a swimming bath at Trichinopoly. **Dr Daniel Wilson** built the cathedral at Calcutta and was buried there in 1858, and his successor, **Bishop Cotton,** who started schools in the hills for European and Eurasian children, was drowned at Kushtia in the Nadia district in 1866, through the simple accident of slipping on a steamer gangway and falling into the river.

CHAPTER XXII

VILLAGES, TOWNS AND CITIES

OUT of every 100 persons 94 live in villages in Bengal, and 97 in Bihar and Orissa, while Sikkim contains no place sufficiently large and populous to be dignified with the appellation of a town. Even the towns are, to a large extent, rural in character. Many of them are little more than overgrown villages in which the people may be seen grazing their cattle and tilling their fields. Others are collections of villages, with a central urban area, grouped together for municipal purposes; but others, such as the mill towns along the Hooghly, are busy industrial centres resounding with the whir of machinery.

In Bengal there are 124 towns, of which only three (Calcutta, Howrah and Dacca) have a population exceeding 100,000, while two more, viz. Maniktala and Bhātpāra, have a population of over 50,000. The most distinctively urban areas are the metropolitan districts of the 24-Parganas, Howrah and Hooghly; outside their limits there are only three towns with over 30,000 inhabitants. Two-fifths of the entire urban population are residents of Calcutta and its suburbs, including Howrah.

Bihar and Orissa contains only 76 towns, of which Patna alone has over 100,000 inhabitants, while Bhāgalpur, Cuttack, Darbhanga and Gaya have over 50,000.

The following is a list of the chief towns and cities: the bracketed figures after each name show the population at the census of 1911.

Agartala (6831). Headquarters of Hill Tippera State containing the palace of the Raja.

Alipore (19,749). Headquarters of the 24-Parganas.

Fig. 90. A Sikkim village

It is part of Calcutta (*q.v.*) for municipal and other administrative purposes and structurally cannot be distinguished from it.

Arrah (38,549). Headquarters of Shāhābād. Famous

for the defence, during the Mutiny of 1857, of the Little House, a small building built for use as a billiard room, which was held against an overwhelming force of mutineers (estimated at 10,000) by 9 Europeans, 6 Eurasians, 3 Indian civilians and 50 Sikhs. "As long as Englishmen love to hear of fidelity and constancy and courage bearing up against frightful odds, there is no fear lest they forget the name of the Little House at Arrah."

Asansol (38,549). A subdivisional headquarters, in the Burdwān district. An important railway junction and one of the chief centres of the coal industry.

Baidyabāti (20,516), on the Hooghly river in Hooghly district.

Baidyanāth. See Deoghar.

Balasore (21,362). Headquarters of Balasore district on the Burhabalang river. Formerly a large port and emporium, it contained English, Dutch, Danish and French factories; there are old English and Dutch cemeteries with monuments dating back to the seventeenth century. The name is a corruption of Baleswar.

Bally (22,394), in the Howrah district, on the river Hooghly adjoining Howrah.

Bankipore. See Patna.

Bānkura (23,453). Headquarters of Bānkura district.

Barisāl (22,473). Headquarters of Backergunge. An important inland steamer station and centre of the rice trade.

Barnagore (25,895), in the 24-Parganas on the Hooghly. It was the seat of a Dutch factory in the seventeenth century and is now an industrial town with large jute mills.

Barrackpore (39,452). A subdivisional headquarters in the 24-Parganas on the river Hooghly. It is a favourite place of residence for Europeans and contains two municipalities, North and South Barrackpore, and a cantonment.

The last was the scene of one of the first overt acts of mutiny in 1857, when it was the headquarters of the Presidency division of the army. South of the cantonment is Barrackpore Park with a country house of the Governor of Bengal. It was originally the residence of the Commander-in-Chief, but about a century ago became the country house of the Governors-General of India beginning with the Marquess Wellesley.

Berhampore (26,143). Headquarters of Murshidābād,

Fig. 91. A Darjeeling village with Nepalese merry-go-round

situated on the river Bhāgirathi. It was made a British cantonment after the deposition of Mīr Kāsim, and troops were stationed in it till 1870. The first outbreak during the Mutiny of 1857 took place here. The barracks are now used for civil purposes. It has waterworks and a large college. It was the headquarters of the Rājshāhi Division till 1875, when the district was transferred to the Presidency Division.

Bettiah (25,793). A subdivisional headquarters in Champāran. It is also the headquarters of the Bettiah

Rāj and of the Prefecture Apostolic of Bettiah and Nepal. A Capuchin Mission has been established here since 1745, when the Capuchins abandoned their work in Tibet.

Bhadreswar (24,353), in Hooghly district on the river Hooghly. A rapidly growing mill town, the population of which has been trebled since 1872.

Bhāgalpur (74,349). Headquarters of the Bhāgalpur district and Division, situated on the Ganges. It contains two monuments to Augustus Cleveland. At Sabaur, a few miles off, is the Agricultural College of Bihar and Orissa.

Bhātpāra (50,414), in the 24-Parganas on the river Hooghly. It was once a centre of Sanskrit learning, and is now a thriving mill town: its jute mills (chiefly in the quarter called Kankināra) employ over 25,000 hands. Its population has increased fivefold in the last thirty years owing to the labour recruited by the mills.

Bihar (35,151). A subdivisional headquarters in Patna district. It was a capital of the Pāla kings, one of whom founded a large Buddhist monastery or *vihāra*, from which the town and province derived their names. The monastery was destroyed when the place was taken and sacked in the first Muhammadan invasion. It contains a ruined fort, a sandstone pillar with inscriptions dating back to the fifth century and some tombs of Muhammadan saints.

Bishnupur or **Vishnupur** (20,478). A subdivisional headquarters in Bānkura district. It was the capital of some chiefs, called the Rajas of Mallabhūm, who ruled over a considerable tract. Remains of their rule are seen in some shallow artificial lakes, the fort with some old cannon, and twelve temples, built between 1622 and 1758, which are fine specimens of the Bengali type of temple architecture.

Bogra (9113). Headquarters of Bogra district.

Brāhmanbaria (22,295). A subdivisional headquarters in Tippera district.

Budge-Budge (17,982), in the 24-Parganas on the river Hooghly. It is the oil depot of Calcutta, at which oil ships discharge, and contains some large mills. A fort here was captured by Clive's force during the advance on Calcutta in 1756, but was dismantled in 1793.

Fig. 92. A Bihar village

Burdwān (35,921). Headquarters of Burdwān district. It has waterworks and a fine modern hospital, and contains the palace and gardens of the Maharaj-Adhirāj of Burdwān, one of the chief landowners in Bengal, to the munificence of whom and of his family the town and Province owe much. The founder of the line was a Punjābi, who settled here in the seventeenth century. The most interesting remains in the town are the tombs of Sher Afghān, the first husband of the Empress Nur Jahān (meaning the light of the world) and of Kutub-ud-din, the foster-brother of Jahāngīr, who met his death while helping in the assassination of Sher Afghān. Her husband having been removed in this summary fashion, Jahāngīr married the widow and made her his consort in empire.

Buxar (11,309). A subdivisional headquarters in Shāhābād. Here was fought the decisive battle of Buxar in 1764. The old fort overlooking the Ganges, which is now used as a residence, passed into the hands of the English after this victory.

Calcutta. The capital of Bengal and until 1912 of India. With its suburbs and Howrah, it is not only the largest city in India, but also, next to London, the most populous city in the British Empire. As explained in the Census Report of India—"Just as, when speaking of London, we may mean either the Municipal and Parliamentary City of London with a night population of less than 20,000, or the administrative County of London with 4½ millions, or Greater London including the Outer Ring, that is, the Metropolitan and City Police districts, with 7¼ millions; so also in speaking of Calcutta we may mean Calcutta proper, or the area administered by the Calcutta Municipal Corporation with the port, fort and canals, the population of which is 896,967, or this area *plus* the suburban municipalities of Cossipur-Chitpur, Maniktala and Garden Reach with 1,043,307 inhabitants, or lastly Greater Calcutta, which also includes Howrah, with an aggregate population of 1,222,313. The suburban municipalities differ only from Calcutta in respect of their municipal government. From a structural point of view they cannot be distinguished. The buildings are continuous throughout, and there is nothing to show where one municipality begins and the other ends. The suburban water-supply is drawn from the Calcutta mains. Howrah again is separated from Calcutta proper only by the river

Hooghly. It is just as much a part of Calcutta as Southwark is of London. Like the suburban municipalities it is the dormitory of many persons who earn their living in Calcutta proper; and its industrial life is inseparable from that of the metropolis."

Calcutta proper has an area of 32 square miles, and the suburbs, i.e. the three municipalities above mentioned, of 10 square miles. The area administered by the

Fig. 93. A village school

Calcutta Corporation is nearly 19 square miles, the Port extends over 11 square miles, and Fort William and the large open space called the Maidān over two square miles.

To use a trite phrase, Calcutta is one of the many triumphs of science over nature, for originally it was a fever-infested swamp-girdled spot that seemed marked out by nature as unfit for human habitation. The mortality among the early European settlers was fearful;

out of 1250 inhabitants, 450 died in six months. Its name was identified with Golgotha, a place of skulls, and it was long regarded as a tropical pest-house. It is indeed not so long since Rudyard Kipling dubbed it "the city of dreadful night." Now it has been purified and rendered sanitary and is as healthy a place as any in Bengal.

Being a city of modern growth, it has no pretensions to the archaeological interest of the old capitals of departed dynasties. Its chief glories are natural—the Hooghly, a river broad and deep enough to be a highway for ocean commerce, and the Maidān, a great park-line plain between the river and the city. It has been often called "a city of palaces" but it must be admitted that those who so described it must have had either an imperfect acquaintance with palaces or a very inadequate conception of what palaces are. The greatness of Calcutta lies not in its buildings but in its commerce, of which the visible representations are the shipping in the Hooghly, the prosaic docks and jetties, the banks and the offices of its merchant princes, to some of which the term palatial might properly be applied. The original "village of palaces" is Chowringhee, a noble thoroughfare running parallel to the river and bounding the Maidān. The principal residential quarter of Europeans and wealthy Indians is approximately bounded by this road, by Park Street (so called because it passed the park-like garden of Sir Elijah Impey), and Lower Circular Road, which follows part of the alignment of the Marātha Ditch, which the English constructed as a defence against Marātha raids. There are a number of other fine streets and squares, many commemorating the names of India's great statesmen, such as Clive Street, Cornwallis Street, Wellesley Street and Dalhousie Square, the last a fitting termination of another fine street, Old Court House

Street. The greater part of the city is, like other Oriental towns, a maze of mean streets, the improvement of which on modern lines is now being effected by a large Improvement Trust.

One of the most imposing and historically interesting buildings is Government House, which was built in response to the Marquess Wellesley's plea that "India should be governed from a palace, not from a counting house." The residence of the Governors-General of India for over a century, it was made over to the Governor of Bengal in 1912, when the Government of India abandoned Calcutta in favour of the more ancient Delhi. The design of the building is based on that of Kedleston Hall, the seat of the Curzons in Derbyshire. According to Sir Thomas Holdich (*India*, 1904), who holds that Calcutta has "not a public building worth looking at," it "can only be described as the ugliest viceregal residence in the Empire." Belvedere in Alipore, the residence of the Lieutenant-Governors of Bengal from 1854 to 1912, is older, having been originally a country house of Warren Hastings. A lane leading to the Meteorological Observatory close by, is called Duel Lane in commemoration of the duel which he fought here with the vindictive Philip Francis. The favourite residence of this "great Proconsul" was Hastings House, which is maintained by Government.

The Cathedral owes its construction (1839–47) to the exertions of Bishop Wilson; its spire, 207 feet high, was rebuilt after the earthquake of 1897, in which it was seriously damaged. The old Cathedral, which it replaced, was St John's Church, dating back to 1784. The most conspicuous monument in Calcutta is the Ochterlony Monument on the Maidān, a pillar crowned by a kind of pepper-box 165 feet high, which was raised to the memory of Sir David Ochterlony (1758–1825), the general who brought

Fig. 94. Government House, Calcutta

the Nepal War of 1814–15 to a victorious conclusion. There are also a number of statues on the Maidān erected in honour of many Viceroys, a few soldiers and one sailor (Sir William Peel, the leader of the Naval Brigade in the Mutiny). The finest is an equestrian statue, by Foley, of Outram sitting bareheaded on his horse and looking back to cheer on his troops to victory. In another part of the Maidān the Victoria Memorial Hall is in course of erection; this will be a noble building commemorating the great Queen-Empress. Of other buildings the most noticeable are the High Court (1872), the design of which was suggested by the Town Hall at Ypres, the Town Hall next it (1804)—a building characteristic of the period—the Indian Museum, founded in 1814, and the Imperial Library, formerly called the Metcalfe Hall after Lord Metcalfe, Governor-General in 1835–36 and afterwards Governor of Jamaica and Governor-General of Canada.

There are many large Government offices recently vacated by the Government of India, while the Government of Bengal Secretariat is located in Writers' Buildings in Dalhousie Square. This is a modern building, but its name is a survival of the time when the officers of the East India Company were known as Writers. The Indian name is Company Barrack, which dates back to the time when the site was occupied by a building in which the young officers of the Company resided when they first arrived from England. Close to it is a monument in memory of the victims of the Black Hole, a replica in marble of one erected by Holwell, which Calcutta owes to Lord Curzon. The Post Office, a few yards off, was built over the chamber in which they were done to death and occupies part of the site of old Fort William. The present fort was completed in 1773. The small bronze dome, set on a marble base, between it and the river, is the Ellenborough Monument, which was made out of old cannon under the orders of Lord Ellenborough, Governor-General from 1842 to 1844.

Calcutta is the seat of a University and has a goodly number of educational institutions, of which the largest is the Presidency College. The Madrasa, the principal Muhammadan college in Bengal, was founded by Warren Hastings in 1781, and Bishop's College by Bishop Middleton in 1820. The buildings at Sibpur, on the other side of the Hooghly, which the latter originally occupied, now accommodate a Civil Engineering College. With their Gothic architecture, turrets and smooth lawns, they recall an Oxford or Cambridge college. La Martinière, opened in 1835, owes its existence to a legacy of General Claud Martin (1735–1800), a French military adventurer and philanthropist. The oldest and finest of the many hospitals is the Presidency General Hospital; the original buildings (now demolished) belonged to Kiernander, the first Protestant missionary in Bengal, and were made over to the East India Company in 1769–70 for use as a hospital for European soldiers, Indian sepoys and the civil population.

Last but not least of the buildings of Calcutta may be mentioned Kāli Ghāt, the shrine of Kāli, a far-famed place of pilgrimage, which is especially dear to Bengali Hindus. It has a sacred site, being built on Tolly's Nullah, an old channel of the Ganges, which was canalized by Colonel Tolly in 1776–7.

The Zoological Gardens in Alipore were opened in 1876 by the Prince of Wales, afterwards Edward VII. The Eden Gardens, close to Government House, are named after the Misses Eden, sisters of Lord Auckland, Governor-General from 1836 to 1842. The Botanic Gardens at Sibpur were started in 1787 at the instance of Colonel Robert Kyd, Military Secretary of Government, an ardent horticulturist, who was their first Superintendent.

According to the imaginative Bishop Heber, they "would perfectly answer to Milton's idea of Paradise if they were on a hill instead of a dead flat."

The docks at Kidderpore, which provide for the whole export trade of Calcutta, were opened in 1882; the dock area alone is over a square mile. They are connected with the railway system on the east of the Hooghly by a steam ferry working to and from Shalimār. Ordinary passenger and cart traffic passes over the Howrah bridge, opened in 1874, prior to which date there was no bridge across the Hooghly. It is a pontoon bridge, 1528 feet between abutments, the middle section of which is movable so as to allow of the passage of vessels up and down the river. It is proposed to replace it by a more modern structure.

Chaibāsa (9009). Headquarters of Singhbhūm district.

Chandernagore (25,293). A French town on the river Hooghly. The French first settled here about 1674, and the town rose to importance under Dupleix, its Governor from 1731 to 1741. Before his time, we are told, the hearing of mass was the chief business of the French in Bengal. Before he left they had a fleet of 72 vessels trading not only to France, but also to Arabia, Persia and China. It was captured by the English in 1757, 1783, 1793 and 1802, and was restored to the French for the fourth and last time in 1816. It is now a quiet little riverside town of no commercial importance.

Chapra (42,373). Headquarters of Sāran district, and once an important river mart, at the confluence of the Ganges and Gogra, with Dutch and English factories.

Chinsura. Headquarters of the Hooghly district and Burdwān division, situated on the river Hooghly. With the town of Hooghly, it forms a municipality having a population of 28,916. It was a Dutch settlement from

1656 till 1825, when it was ceded to the English. The only memorials of Dutch rule are part of their barracks, a cemetery with tombs dating back to 1743, an octagonal church with old hatchments, which was built in 1767, and the Commissioner's house on the river bank, which was the Dutch Governor's residence. The Armenian church is the oldest in Bengal next to that at Bandel, having been built in 1695–7.

Chitpur. See Cossipur.

Chittagong (28,766). Headquarters of the Chittagong district and division, situated on the river Karnaphuli, 10 miles from its mouth. It is a picturesque place with a number of hillocks, 150 to 200 feet high, on which bungalows are built.

A famous port as early as the fourteenth century, when it was visited by Ibn Batuta, the Portuguese traders and pirates of the sixteenth century called it Porto Grande or the great port. The Mughal forces took it from the Arakanese in 1666, and in 1760 it was ceded to the English. It was a favourite health resort in the days of Warren Hastings and Sir William Jones, the latter of whom had a house there. It is the terminus of the Assam-Bengal Railway and has a considerable foreign and coasting trade.

Comilla (22,692). Headquarters of Tippera district.

Cooch Behar (10,841). Capital of Cooch Behar State, containing the palace of the Maharaja.

Cossimbazar. A town in Murshidābād district on the river Bhāgirathi, which was formerly an important emporium and centre of the silk trade, with Dutch, French and English factories. As late as 1759 Rennell described it as "the general market of Bengal silk." The English and Dutch cemeteries contain interesting monuments; in the former is the tomb of Warren Hastings' first wife and infant daughter. At Saidābād, where the

French and Armenians had settlements, is an Armenian church erected in 1758.

Cossipur-Chitpur (48,176). A municipality comprising Cossipur and Chitpur in the suburbs of Calcutta.

Cuttack (52,528). Headquarters of the Cuttack district and division. The capital of the independent kings of Orissa, and later of its Mughal Governors, it was occupied by the Marāthas from the middle of the eighteenth century until 1803, when it was taken by a British force. The fort, which recalled to the mind of Motte, an English traveller in 1767, the west side of Windsor castle, has been demolished and most of its buildings converted into road-metal or utilized for other buildings. The Commissioner's house, called Lālbāgh, occupies the site of the Governor's palace, which was large enough for a zenana of 300 women. The town lies between the Mahānadi and Kātjuri, and is protected from their floods by embankments. It contains a college and the headworks of the Orissa Canals, and is noted for delicate silver filigree work. The name is a transliteration of Katak, meaning a fort. The civil station was a cantonment till a few years ago.

Dacca (108,551). Headquarters of the Dacca district and division. It was the capital of the Governors of Bengal for nearly a century (from 1608 to 1639 and again from 1660 to 1704), but few buildings of particular merit were erected by them. From Tavernier's account it appears that even in 1666 they regarded Dacca as a camping ground rather than as a capital to be beautified. "The Governor's palace," he said, "is a place enclosed with high walls, in the midst whereof is a pitiful house built only of wood. He generally lodges in tents which he causes to be set up in the great court of that enclosure." The principal memorials of their rule are the remains of the Lālbāgh fort commenced in 1678 but never completed, two dilapidated buildings of Shaista Khān, called the Bara Khatra (1664) and Chota Khatra (1663), the Husaini Dalān (1642) and some mosques. No traces remain of the old English, French and Dutch factories. Dacca was the capital of the province of Eastern Bengal from 1905 to 1912, when a Government House was built for the Lieutenant-Governor and fine buildings for the Secretariat. The latter are to be utilized for a University, which is shortly to be inaugurated. Other buildings are the Dacca College, Mitford Hospital, the Dhākeswari temple (whence the town probably derives its name) and Ahsun Manzil, the palace of the Nawāb of Dacca; the latter traces his descent to a Governor of Cashmere, who retired to Bengal after the sack of Delhi by Nādir Shāh. Waterworks were established in 1878. There is a large river frontage which has led to Dacca being described in the language of hyperbole as the Venice of the East—a very poor compliment to Venice. It has long been famous for delicate hand-woven muslins; fabrics called *jhappans* and *kasīdas* are still exported to Turkey and Arabia.

Daltonganj (7179). Headquarters of Palāmau district. It is named after Colonel Dalton, Commissioner of Chota Nagpur and author of *A Descriptive Ethnology of Bengal*, who founded it in 1862. Waterworks were installed in 1904.

Darbhanga (62,628). Headquarters of Darbhanga district. It contains the palace of the Maharaja of Darbhanga, the wealthiest landowner in the province of Bihar and Orissa and a member of its first Executive Council. The family is descended from a Brahman priest, who acquired land and power in the sixteenth century. The civil station is situated in the suburb of Laheriasarai.

Darjeeling (19,005). A Himalayan hill-station, which is the headquarters of the Darjeeling district, and, in the hot weather, of the Government of Bengal. It includes not only Darjeeling proper but also the military cantonments of Jalapahār, Katapahār and Lebong. Its area is nearly 5 square miles, and the difference between its highest and lowest points is close on 2000 feet, Katapahār being 7886 and Lebong 5970 feet above sea level: Observatory Hill in the centre has a height of 7163 feet. In

Fig. 95. Darjeeling

shape it resembles the letter Y, the upright portion being a ridge stretching from Katapahār through Jalapahār to Observatory Hill, while the two arms to right and left are represented by spurs on which stand Lebong and Birch Hill Park. In the hot weather, when there is an influx of visitors, the population rises to 25,000, as compared with 38,000 in Simla, 18,000 in Naini Tāl and 17,000 in Mussoorie.

Its situation is singularly beautiful, for it forms a kind of stage in an amphitheatre of mountains. The eye sees at a glance "the shadowy valleys from which shining mist-columns rise at noon against a luminous sky, the forest ridges stretching fold behind fold in softly undulating lines, dotted by the white specks which mark the situation of Buddhist monasteries, to the glacier-draped pinnacles and precipices of the snowy range." Kinchinjunga (28,146 feet) is only 45 miles distant as the crow flies, and on either side of it is a line of peaks clothed in eternal snow. The climate is temperate, the average temperature of the year being only two degrees above that of London, but it is subject to very heavy rainfall—there is a fall of 105 inches from June to October—and it is often shrouded in mist.

The place was discovered in 1829 by General Lloyd and ceded by the Raja of Sikkim in 1835, because, as stated in the deed of grant, the Governor-General had "expressed a desire for the possession of the hill of Darjeeling on account of its cool climate, for the purpose of enabling the servants of his Government, suffering from sickness, to avail themselves of its advantages." Government House, the summer residence of the Governor of Bengal was built in 1879, and the construction of the railway in 1881 brought the place within a day's journey of Calcutta. It contains several schools for the education of European and Eurasian boys and girls (of which the principal are St Paul's School and St Joseph's College), a sanitarium for Europeans and Eurasians and another for Indians, a Botanic Garden, a Roman Catholic convent, a Church of Scotland Mission and a Buddhist monastery.

Deoghar (11,394). A subdivisional headquarters in the Santāl Parganas and a much frequented place of pilgrimage, containing the temples of Baidyanāth. It is popularly known as Baidyanāth, but that name having been adopted for the railway junction close by and the town that sprung up round it, the residents changed the designation to Deoghar, meaning the home of the gods, in order to distinguish the two.

Dinājpur (15,945). Headquarters of Dinājpur district. It has a fine maidān or public park nearly two miles in circumference.

Dinapore (31,025). A subdivisional headquarters and cantonment in Patna district. There was an outbreak of the troops here in the Mutiny of 1857.

Dum-Dum (21,739). A town and cantonment in the 24-Parganas. The name means a raised mound or battery, an artificial acropolis, and was first applied to a fortified building standing on such a mound, which is said to have been a country house of Lord Clive. The place has been a cantonment since 1783 and was the headquarters of the Bengal Artillery until 1853. It was here that the seeds of the Mutiny were sown, when musketry classes were held to instruct the sepoys in the use of the new Enfield rifle with its obnoxious cartridges. It contains the ammunition factory of the Ordnance Department, which manufactures arms, shells, etc., and has given its name to the "Dum-Dum bullet," which was first made here.

Dumka (5629). Headquarters of the Santāl Parganas. One of the most picturesque stations in Bihar and Orissa.

English Bazar (14,322). Headquarters of Mālda district, so called from having been the seat of an English factory started in 1676. The cutcherry or court-house is the old Commercial Residency, a fortified building dating back to 1770. There were also Dutch and French settlements here; the house of the Civil Surgeon was a Dutch convent.

Farīdpur (13,131). Headquarters of Farīdpur district.

Gangtok. Capital of Sikkim containing the palace of the Maharaja and the Residency of the Political Agent. It is set in the midst of the Himalayas, at a height of 5000 feet, and commands a fine view of the snowy range.

Garden Reach (45,295). A municipality in the suburbs of Calcutta and a thriving industrial place. The king of Oudh resided here after his deposition in 1856.

Gaya (70,423). Headquarters of Gaya district. With

Fig. 96. Old Gaya from the South-West

its temple-crowned hills overlooking the river Phalgu, it is perhaps the most picturesque town, and it is certainly one of the hottest stations, in Bihar and Orissa. The situation of the old town on the high rocky ground and its medley of temple spires, lofty houses and *ghāts* leading down to the river form a combination that is unique in this part of India.

Gaya is one of the great places of pilgrimage in India for Hindus, who visit it and make offerings for the salvation of their ancestors, to deliver their souls from hell and ensure their translation to the paradise of Vishnu. There are many sacred sites in the town and its neighbourhood, but the chief is an indentation in the rock, which is supposed to be the impress of Vishnu's feet. This is enshrined in a granite temple erected in the eighteenth century by Ahalya Bai, a celebrated Marātha princess. A bell presented to the temple by a European Collector in 1790 is a testimony to a kindly catholic spirit. The Brahmajuni Hill above the civil station has been identified

Fig. 97. Gaya from the East

with Gayasirsa, from which Buddha delivered one of his most famous sermons. It is now a sacred Hindu site, as are also the other hills in and about the town, viz. Rām Gaya, Rāmsila and Pretsila.

Bodh Gaya, 6 miles to the south, is the most holy place in the world to many millions of Buddhists, for it was the scene of Buddha's great enlightenment. Eloquent witness of the veneration in which it has been held for over 2000 years is borne by the great Mahābodhi temple and by numerous Buddhist memorials, from the ancient railing of Asoka and the *stūpas* of different centuries to the humble votive offerings of the present day. This Buddhist Holy of Holies is now in the hands of Hindus.

Hāzāribāgh (17,009). Headquarters of Hāzāribāgh district, 1997 feet above sea level. It was a cantonment until 1874; some of the barrack buildings have been utilized for a reformatory school. It also contains a mission station and college of the Dublin University Mission.

Hooghly. Headquarters of the Hooghly district on the Hooghly river. With Chinsura it forms a municipality having 28,916 inhabitants. The Portuguese made a settlement here in the sixteenth century, before the end of which it became the royal port of Bengal. The Portuguese fort was taken by the Mughal forces in 1632 and the survivors of the siege were carried off into slavery. Soon after 1650, the English established a factory, which was their head Agency in Bengal. A Portuguese church (1660) at Bandel is the oldest church in Bengal; the monastery adjoining it was formerly occupied by Augustinian friars. The Hooghly Imāmbāra is an imposing building and the largest institution of its kind in the province.

Howrah (179,006). Headquarters of Howrah district. An industrial city of modern growth, with large manufactures, which stretches along the Hooghly for seven miles. It is the terminus of the East Indian and Bengal-Nagpur Railways and is connected with Calcutta by the Howrah bridge.

Jalpaiguri (11,469). Headquarters of the Jalpaiguri district and the Rājshāhi division, and a centre of the tea-planting industry of the Duārs.

Jamālpur (21,109). A subdivisional headquarters in Mymensingh.

Jamālpur (20,526). A town in Monghyr containing large works of the East Indian Railway.

Jessore (8911). Headquarters of Jessore district.

Kharagpur (18,957). Town and railway junction in Midnapore district, containing the engineering works of the Bengal-Nagpur Railway.

Khulna (12,996). Headquarters of Khulna district, on the fringe of the Sundarbans.

Krishnagar (23,475). Headquarters of Nadia district and of a diocese of the Roman Catholic Church. It contains a College and a mission station of the Church Missionary Society.

Kurseong (5574). A subdivisional headquarters of Darjeeling district. It is a hill station, situated on a ridge of the Himalayas, with an elevation varying from 7000 to 5000 feet. There are several educational institutions for Europeans and Eurasians.

Māniktala (58,767). A municipality in the suburbs of Calcutta.

Midnapore (32,740). Headquarters of Midnapore district.

Monghyr (46,913). Headquarters of Monghyr district situated on the Ganges. It is an old town, the history of which can be traced back to very early times. Its position made it of strategic importance throughout the period of Muhammadan rule, and it was the capital of Mīr Kāsim from 1761 to 1763, when it was captured by the English under Major Adams. The amenities of a British cantonment are preserved in the fort, of which the gates, battlemented walls and some bastions are still standing. Its picturesque position on the Ganges led Sir Joseph Hooker to describe it as "by far the prettiest town" he had seen on the river, and it has been justly admired by many other travellers. A house on Pīr Pahār Hill, three miles to the east, was the residence of Gurghin (Gregory) Khān, the Armenian general of Mīr

Kāsim. About two miles further on are the sacred hot springs of Sītakund.

Motihāri (14,876). Headquarters of Champāran district, situated on the bank of a lake, which at one time formed a reach of the river Gandak.

Murshidābād. A town on the Bhāgirathi in Murshidābād district, containing the palace of the Nawāb Bahādur of Murshidābād, a lineal descendant of Mīr Jafar Khān. It was the capital of Bengal from 1704

Fig. 98. Corner of the Fort, Monghyr

to 1772, during which time the Nawābs built themselves palaces and adorned the city with other fine buildings. After the battle of Plassey, Clive wrote—"This city is as extensive, populous and rich as the city of London, with this difference, that there are individuals in the first possessing infinitely greater property than in the last city." Murshidābād has now suffered from a century of decay and the earthquake of 1897. Some of the buildings have been swept away by the Bhāgirathi, others are dilapidated or ruinous; and the town, with its suburb of Azīmganj, has a population of only 25,096. The most imposing buildings are modern, viz., the palace of the Nawāb Bahādur, completed in 1837, and the Imāmbāra (1847). The place of greatest natural beauty is Motijhil (the pearl lake), on which stood a palace that was afterwards the Residency of the British Agent. Opposite Motijhil, on the other side of the river, is Khushbāgh or garden of happiness, the name given to the cemetery of Ali Vardi Khān, his grandson Sirāj-ud-daula and other members of the family. Higher up the river was the palace of Sirāj-ud-daula, in which Clive installed Mīr Jafar Khān after the battle of Plassey. Here were the famous treasure vaults, of which Clive said—"I walked through vaults which were thrown open to me alone, piled on either hand with gold and jewels. At this moment I stand astonished at my own moderation." At Jafarganj there are some remains of the palace of Mīr Jafar Khān, in which Sirāj-ud-daula was put to death. Murshid Kuli Khān, after whom the town was named, was buried under the stairs leading to a mosque that he built, humbly desiring that his dust might be trodden on by all who passed up and down.

Muzaffarpur (43,668). Headquarters of the Muzaffarpur district and the Tirhut division; it is also the headquarters of the Bihar Light Horse (a mounted volunteer corps) and a centre of the indigo planting industry. The town is built on the banks of two lakes that originally formed the bed of the Little Gandak river.

Mymensingh (19,853). Headquarters of Mymensingh district on the Old Brahmaputra.

Narayanganj (27,876). A subdivisional headquarters of Dacca district, and an important river mart and centre of the jute trade. It contains a number of jute presses, salt warehouses, an oil depot, a branch of the Bank of

Bengal and the agencies of several large jute firms. During the jute season "the river is packed with shipping and the mills with coolies."

Nawābganj (23,322). A town and river mart in Mālda district.

Noākhāli (7009). Headquarters of Noākhāli district.

Pābna (19,274). Headquarters of Pābna district.

Patna (136,153). Capital of Bihar and Orissa, extending along the Ganges for about nine miles; it includes Bankipore, a suburb in which are the headquarters of the Patna district and division. The modern city is built over Pātaliputra, the capital of India under the Mauryan emperors. Remains of this ancient city, including a great pillared hall of Asoka, have been found 20 feet below the surface. The present city has had an eventful history. It became the capital of Bihar in the sixteenth century, and, after its capture by Akbar in 1574, was made the seat of the Mughal Viceroys, more than one of whom was a prince of the imperial family. It has been taken and retaken, has suffered siege and sack, and has witnessed the proclamation of two Emperors. Its final capture by the English took place after the "Massacre of Patna," when 198 European prisoners were murdered, under Mīr Kāsim's orders, by the vile Somru, a German renegade whose original name was Reinhardt. An obelisk marks the grave of the victims of this tragedy, which surpassed the Black Hole of Calcutta in horror, for it claimed more victims, it was planned deliberately and it was carried out in cold blood by a European.

In spite of its historic past, the city has few buildings of archaeological or artistic interest. Scarcely any are constructed of stone; mud and brick predominate. The oldest is a mosque of Sher Shāh (1540–5); another mosque erected in 1626 is the handsomest; and perhaps the most interesting is a temple erected by Ranjit Singh, "the lion of the Punjab," on the site where Govind Singh, the great Sikh Guru and creator of the Sikh military brotherhood, was born. Certainly the most curious is the Gola (granary) at Bankipore, a beehive-shaped structure of brick, 96 feet high, which was built in 1786 for the storage of grain as an insurance against famine. Some of the buildings in the Opium Factory formed part of the old Dutch Factory, and there is a Roman Catholic

Fig. 99. Puri during the Car Festival

church built in 1772–9. The principal educational institutions are the Patna College and the Bihar School of Engineering. Close to the latter is the Patna Oriental Library with a fine collection of Arabic and Persian manuscripts, some of which are exquisite specimens of caligraphy originally belonging to the Mughal Emperors. The city is to be the seat of a High Court and University, and buildings are being erected for the residence of the Lieutenant-Governor and the accommodation of the provincial Secretariat. It has been declining for many years past owing to loss of trade and continued epidemics of plague; but it is hoped that the establishment of the capital will restore its waning prosperity.

Puri (39,686). Headquarters of Puri district situated on the Bay of Bengal. It contains the temple of Jagannāth, a splendid fane eight centuries old. The tower is 190 feet high; outside the Lion Gate or main entrance is a beautiful pillar of the sun-god, 15 feet high, which was brought here from Konārak. Puri is a world-famous place of pilgrimage, at which is celebrated every year the Car Festival that has made "Jagannāth's Car" a familiar expression in the English language. The car itself is sometimes erroneously called Jagannāth, but this is the designation of the god, an incarnation of Vishnu, and means "Lord of the World." Owing to its situation on the sea, Puri has of late years acquired some popularity as a health resort.

Purnea (14,784). Headquarters of Purnea district. It was the capital of Muhammadan Governors, who could put an army of 15,000 men into the field; one of the line unsuccessfully disputed the throne of Bengal with Sirāj-ud-daula.

Purulia (20,886). Headquarters of Mānbhum district and a junction for the railway line to Ranchi.

Rājmahāl (5357). A subdivisional headquarters of the Santāl Parganas on the Ganges. It was the capital of Bengal from 1592 to 1608 and again from 1639 to 1660. The remains of the capital extend for four miles on the west of the modern town, but most of the buildings have been destroyed or are in ruins.

Rāmpur Boālia (23,406). Headquarters of Rājshāhi district, situated on the Ganges. It contains an old Dutch factory and a large College.

Rānchi (32,994). Headquarters of Rānchi district and of Chota Nagpur. It is also the hot weather capital of Bihar and Orissa. Situated 2169 feet above sea level, it enjoys a more temperate climate than the towns of the plains. It is the headquarters of the Chota Nagpur diocese of the Church of England and a centre of missionary enterprise.

Rangpur (16,429). Headquarters of Rangpur district.

Rāniganj (15,497). A town in Burdwān district, with large pottery works and a paper mill. It was formerly the centre of the coal-mining industry in the Rāniganj coal-field, but of late years has been eclipsed by Asansol.

Sakchi (5672). A town in Singhbhūm district, containing the works of the Tata Iron and Steel Co., to which it owes its existence as a town.

Sambalpur (12,981). Headquarters of Sambalpur district and of the Political Agent of the Orissa Feudatory States.

Sāntipur (26,703). Town in Nadia district on the river Hooghly. It was once the centre of a flourishing weaving industry, and its muslins had a European reputation.

Sasarām (23,097). A subdivisional headquarters of Shāhābād, situated two miles from the northern escarpment of the Kaimur Hills. An interesting old town, containing the mausoleum of Sher Shāh, Emperor of India (1540–5), and that of his father, both fine specimens of the Pathān style of architecture. In a large tank half a mile away from the mausoleum of Sher Shāh is the tomb of his son, the Emperor Salīm Shāh; his body was brought from Gwalior (1553), and the building of a mausoleum over the tomb was commenced but never completed. An edict of Asoka of the year 231 or 232 B.C. is inscribed in a cave on the Chandan Pīr Hill to the east of the town. The repulse by the citizens of a band of 2000 rebels in the Mutiny of 1857 was rewarded by the Government declaring officially that the town was to be known as Sasarām Nāsir-ul-Hukkām, i.e., the loyal town.

Serampore (49,594). A subdivisional headquarters of Hooghly district, on the river Hooghly. It was a Danish settlement for a century and a half, and was ceded to the British in 1845. The principal memorials of the Danes are their cemetery with tombs dating back to 1781, their church erected in 1805 and dedicated to St Olaf, the jail built in the same year, and the Governor's house, which is now the court-house. In the Mission Cemetery are the graves of Carey, Marshman and Ward, who established the well-known Serampore Mission in 1799. Interesting buildings connected with them are the Serampore College which they founded, the Mission Chapel, the Pagoda, an abandoned Hindu temple which Henry Martyn fitted up as an oratory, and Aldeen House, the residence of their friend, the Rev. David Brown. The town also contains large jute mills, a Roman Catholic church of 1776, and a temple of Jagannāth; the Car Festival celebrated here every year is the largest of its kind outside Puri. The name is a corruption of Srīrāmpur.

Sirājganj (24,777). A subdivisional headquarters of Pabna district on the river Jamuna. An important centre of the jute trade.

Suri (9131). Headquarters of Bīrbhūm district. The cemetery contains the tomb of John Cheap, the first Commercial Resident in Bīrbhūm, who was styled "Cheap the Magnificent" and has been immortalized in Sir William Hunter's *Annals of Rural Bengal*. Suri is also the *mise-en-scène* of the same writer's delightful work *The Old Missionary*.

Titagarh (45,171). A town in the 24-Parganas on the river Hooghly with a paper mill and large jute mills employing over 30,000 hands.

Vishnupur. See Bishnupur.

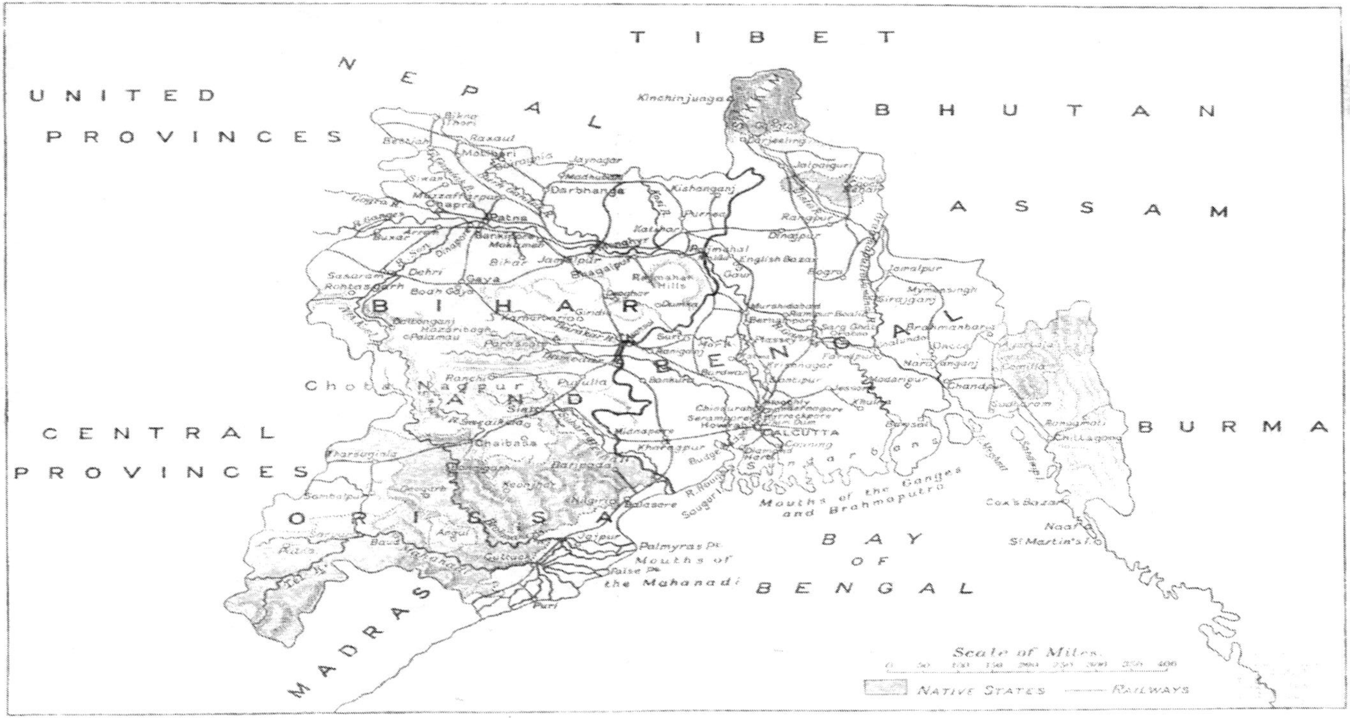

Fig. 100. Bengal—Bihar and Orissa and Sikkim

LIST OF BOOKS, ETC., PLACED UNDER CONTRIBUTION

Administration Report of Bengal for 1911–12.
Administration Report of Bihar and Orissa for 1911–12.
BALL, V. Economic Geology of India, 1881.
—— Tavernier's Travels in India, 1889.
BEAL, S. Buddhist Records of the Western World, 1884.
BERNIER, F. Travels in the Mogul Empire, 1891.
BUCKLAND, C. E. Dictionary of Indian Biography, 1906.
CROOKE, W. Things Indian, 1906.
District Gazetteers of Bengal and Eastern Bengal.
DUTT, R. C. Literature of Bengal, 1895.
GAIT, Sir E. A. Census Report of Bengal, 1901.
Geological Survey of India, Records and Memoirs of.
GRIERSON, Sir G. A. Linguistic Survey of India, 1904–8.
HOLDERNESS, Sir T. W. Peoples and Problems of India, 1912.
HOLDICH, Sir T. H. India (Regions of the World Series), 1904
HUNTER, Sir W. W. History of British India, 1899–1900.
—— The Indian Empire, 1892.
Imperial Gazetteer of India, 1907–09.
LANE-POOLE, S. Mediaeval India (Story of the Nations Series), 1903.
LYALL, Sir A. C. British Dominion in India, 1907.
OATEN, E. F. Travels in India, 1909.
OLDHAM, R. D. Manual of the Geology of India, 1893.
O'MALLEY, L. S. S. Census Report of Bengal, Bihar and Orissa and Sikkim, 1911.
PRAIN, Sir D. Bengal Plants, 1903.
SMITH, V. A. Early History of India, 1904.
Statement of the Moral and Material Progress of India from 1901–2 to 1911–12.
STRACHEY, Sir J. C. India, its Administration and Progress. 1911.

INDEX